Common Care Counseling

HANDBOOK

Common Care Counseling

First Edition, First Printing
in the United States of America

Christian Equippers International
2941 Lake Tahoe Blvd.
South Lake Tahoe, CA 96150
1-800-662-0909   916-542-1509

Common Care Counseling HANDBOOK

By

Terry D. Edwards

And

William R. Kimball

Common Care Counseling Handbook

Contents

Introduction

BY TERRY D. EDWARDS
AND WILLIAM R. KIMBALL

Introduction

THE BODY OF CHRIST IS MADE UP of many different kinds of people at varying levels of maturity, all of whom experience a variety of personal needs. Most of these needs are not viewed as serious enough to take to the Pastor or the counseling staff of the church. Instead, the individual often chooses to work through the situation himself or attempts to get help from another Christian that he or she feels close to. The vast majority of what we term "common counseling problems" are handled by the regular members of the church. Whether the person in need receives appropriate help or ministry depends upon the maturity and experience of the one who ministers to him. The problem is that many Christians are not properly equipped to handle these counseling problems and therefore, even with the best of intentions, offer inadequate advice or counsel.

The purpose of this book is to better equip the believer in his ability to effectively minister to other Christians in those problem areas that are "common to man" (I Cor. 10:13). Hence we have called it the "Common Care Counselor's Handbook". It is a reference book for lay counselors that will help prepare them for the kind of counseling included in what the Bible refers to as the "ministry of reconciliation" (II. Cor. 5:18). The word "reconciliation" is derived from the Greek work "katallage" which means "exchange or restoration". It refers to the distinctive ministry each Christian is called to in order to assist others in the process of restoration into the image and likeness of Jesus Christ. We are all called to minister to one another in this area. By doing so, we "bear one another's burdens, and so fulfill the law of Christ" (Gal. 6:2). At the same time, we are helping to bring the Body of Christ to a place of health and strength.

This book is a collection of 24 booklets produced by Christian Equippers International and used in a local church training course entitled "Common Care Counseling". Each of these booklets are presented in this book in chapter form. This book can be used as a replacement for the 24 booklets that typically go with the course.

This book also stands completely on its own as a valuable reference source for the Christian who desires to be further equipped in the area of lay counseling. The first two chapters are the Counseling Guide I and Counseling Guide II booklets. The Counseling Guide I booklet describes the role of the believer in regards to counseling, and briefly examines some of the methods that should be employed in helping another person. The Counseling Guide II booklet reveals the role that sin has in creating the many common problems that people have to deal with.

The other 22 booklets contained within this book cover a large variety of different counseling need areas. Each subject is handled in a brief but comprehensive way. The lay counselor can minister to another person by reading the appropriate subject area with them, and by adding their own insights along the way. This method has proven to be very effective in bringing insights, understanding and spiritual breakthrough to those in need.

Finally, the material in this book also offers a wealth of teaching information for pastors and those who teach others. Every Christian needs to understand his or her role in how to help others and how to be more effective in doing so. Each of us struggle with some or all of the areas addressed in this book. Sermons or discussion groups that examine these areas can bring understanding, enlightenment and health to the people of God.

 *Chapter 1*

Counseling Guide I

By Terry D. Edwards

◀ INTRODUCTION ▶

The Counseling Guide I and Counseling Guide II are complimentary booklets designed to be read by all who want to be effective in helping others in times of need.

This booklet describes the role of the believer in regards to counseling, and briefly examines some of the methods that should be employed. Incorporating these into your counseling situations can mean the difference between success and failure. Every Christian has a lifetime of involvement with other people. Understanding these principles will allow for these relationships to be more productive.

We suggest that both Counseling Guides be studied thoroughly. Further questions should be addressed to your pastor.

-1-

◀ TABLE OF CONTENTS ▶

-2-

EVERY CHRISTIAN CAN COUNSEL

Every Christian is involved in some kind of counseling. In one sense, whenever we voice our opinion to another we are giving a form of counsel. From our observation, **the vast majority of what we call "common counseling problems" are handled by the regular members of the church.** Many of the less serious counseling needs never arrive at the office of the pastor. Rather, they are helped through a Christian brother or sister that the one in need feels they can trust. Often, a person feels his need is not significant enough to involve the church leadership.

We would like to term this form of counseling "COMMON CARE COUN-SELING". This kind of counseling is born out of a genuine concern for another's need.

-3-

It involves the kind of struggle, difficulties, or temptations that are *"common to man"* (I Cor. 10.13). These kind of problems can be adequately handled by those who have either found the victory themselves, or know clearly what the Bible says about achieving it.

There is a distinction between the trained ministerial counselor and the "common care counselor". Due to calling and training, the pastor or the counseling staff is responsible for and should handle the more complicated problems. However, the Bible clearly supports the idea of the saints being involved in "common care counseling". Concern and involvement in the lives of other Christians is commended in the scriptures.

-4-

For example, Galatians 6:2 tells us to *"bear one another's burdens, and so fulfill the law of Christ."* We are also to **watch the spiritual condition of our brethren** and where it is necessary, *"exhort one another daily . . . lest any of you be hardened through the deceitfulness of sin"* (Heb. 3:13).

We see how broad our responsibility and involvement in the lives of others is to be with the admonition: *"Now we exhort you, brethren, **warn those who are unruly, comfort the fainthearted, uphold the weak,** be patient with all"* (I Thess. 5:14).

Finally, the **Apostle Paul expresses his confidence in the saints** in this area by saying, *"I am satisfied about you, my brethren, that you yourselves are rich in goodness, amply filled with all knowledge, and **competent to admonish and counsel** and instruct one another also"* (Rom. 15:14, AMP.).

-5-

This booklet is designed to help the "COMMON CARE COUNSELOR" to understand some of the basic methods of counseling. Effective counseling requires more than good intentions. There are definite scriptural principles that must be employed in the counseling situation to achieve the success we desire. These principles and methods are briefly discussed in the following pages.

The terms "COUNSELOR" and "COUNSELEE" will be used frequently in this booklet. By the term "counselor" we merely refer to the individual who is helping another through instruction and counsel. We are not applying the professional term of counselor to this person. By "counselee" we are referring to the person who is in need and is receiving the counsel. Furthermore, the principles of counseling discussed in this booklet are in reference to Christians counseling other Christians.

-6-

KNOWING YOUR LIMITS

There are limits to the areas that the common care counselor should become involved in. Some problems strictly require the insights and abilities of the pastor or trained counselor. These would include marriage conflicts, severe mental and emotional problems, sexual problems, major business decisions, choices involving changes in someone's life direction, and others that the pastor may stipulate. **To offer wrong counsel in these areas could cause very serious consequences** and result in complicating the problem. If you have questions about the wisdom of getting involved with a situation, contact your pastor and ask his advice.

-7-

There are **two other guidelines** to use in limiting your involvement with a person:

1. **Counsel within the guidelines of God's Word**—If you do not know what the Bible clearly teaches concerning a solution to a problem, refrain from giving advice. Do not speculate. Instead, get counsel from someone who knows, or direct them to the church leadership.

2. **Counsel within the guidelines of your church oversight**—The leadership of the church is primarily responsible for the lives of those placed under their charge. Hebrews 13:17 says they must *"watch out for your souls, as those who must give account."* Your counsel should not conflict with the positions, counsel, and teachings of the church oversight.

-8-

A CONCERNED PERSON

The counselor must be an individual who is concerned about the needs of others. In the gospel of Luke, we have an incident that demonstrates why people were so drawn to Jesus as a leader and a counselor.

A distraught woman interrupts the dinner of Christ and a Pharisee by anointing the feet of Jesus. The Pharisee becomes angry and judgmental towards the woman and Jesus. The Lord, on the other hand, sees the deep need in her life which is causing her behavior. **Her problem becomes His priority.**

People in need will open up to a person they feel is genuinely concerned for them. We can demonstrate this concern by spending time with them, voicing our concern, praying with them, etc. The real key, though, is to actually be concerned. This comes through sharing in the burden of Christ for others.

-9-

SOLUTIONS — NOT JUST SYMPATHY

The goal of every counseling situation is to assist the counselee in understanding God's solution to the need or problem at hand.

Because life presents common difficulties to all of us, it is easy to sympathize with the needs of others. However, **our sympathy must not ignore the need for solutions,** nor reinforce attitudes or conduct in the other person that are contrary to the Word of God.

The aim of **our involvement is to offer guidelines that will bring positive changes** to the situation based upon God's Word. Explicit scriptural directions for change should be made regarding every area of the problem, including any sinful behavior in the life of the counselee.

-10-

UNDERSTANDING THE PROBLEM

It is important not to give counsel or direction to a person until there is a complete understanding of the problem. **An effective counselor takes the time to "listen" and to "ask questions" in order to understand the need of the counselee.**

"Be a Listener"

We must develop the art of being a good listener. Scripture tells us to *"be swift to hear, slow to speak"* (James 1:19). Before we speak, we want to feel confident that we have really "heard" what we need to hear. **Every problem requires a discernment** of where the sin and difficulty truly lies, and how to apply God's Word to it.

-11-

Often a concerned person that is willing to listen is all that is necessary for a troubled individual to sort out their own situation before God.

"Ask Questions"

Asking the appropriate questions is essential to arriving at a complete understanding of the counselee's situation. Probing through proper questioning can also assist the counselee to see and understand his own circumstances more objectively. All probing must be done in a sensitive and loving manner. People are often embarrassed about their circumstances and reluctant to reveal all of the details. Being sensitive in our approach can make it much easier for them to be open and honest.

We must also avoid asking overly personal questions that are embarrassing and not essential to understanding the real problem. At all times be considerate of how your question may affect the counselee.

-12-

Ask the kind of questions that will cause the person to elaborate on his situation. Avoid those that only require a "yes" or "no" answer. We must seek for specific details that will provide the entire picture. We should ask the counselee to explain general statements. For instance, if she says, "Diane was very unkind", we would ask, "How was she unkind?". Questions that answer what, why, how, how often, and when are good for providing specifics.

Allow your questions to emerge out of the information you are receiving. Their recent statements will usually provide the most natural questions pertinent to the situation.

• **Warning**—Situations involving other people always have two sides. Avoid forming rash conclusions or taking sides from only hearing one side of the problem.

-13-

BUILDING IDENTIFICATION

An effective means of helping a person open up to you is to **create a sense of identification with him.** A counselor errs in presenting himself as above the common trials and temptations of man. Scripture warns, *"let him who thinks he stands take heed lest he fall. No temptation has overtaken you except such as is common to man"* (I Cor. 10:12,13).

We all suffer the common struggles of life. **It is often helpful to identify with the person's problem by sharing that you have experienced a similar situation.** This can help create a feeling of trust and identification between you and the person you are counseling. It is not necessary to go into detail unless the keys of your previous victory can be directly applied to the counselee's present struggle.

-14-

CONFIDENTIAL INFORMATION

Personal information shared during a counseling situation must be held in confidence. Whether declared or not, in every counseling situation there is an assumed confidentiality. The Bible teaches *"A talebearer reveals secrets, but he who is of a faithful spirit conceals a matter"* (Prov. 11:13).

It is advisable to communicate this confidentiality to the counselee during your time together. This may facilitate a greater freedom in their openness.

Others should only be involved if they are part of the problem or part of the solution. Contacting them should be done with the consent of the counselee, unless the problem is serious enough to warrant otherwise.

-15-

INSTILLING HOPE

The counselor must be one who can inspire hope in the hearts of those who labor under the weight of their problem or dilemma. Hope is a confident expectation that we can have a personal victory either in or through the difficulty we are experiencing.

One of the first steps in inspiring hope is helping the person find meaning and purpose in his trial. Romans 8:28 says, *"all things work together for good to those who love God, to those who are the called according to His purpose."* There is always hope for the one who relates his life situations to God's purpose.

Once hope is inspired, it will provide the incentive to make changes, and the confident endurance to "press on" through to victory.

-16-

MOTIVATION FOR CHANGE

Almost every problem requires some kind of change on the part of the counselee. Often, sinful attitudes or behavior patterns in his life are contributing to or causing the difficulties.

People usually want things to change, but don't want to change themselves. **The task of the counselor is to motivate the person being counseled to change** in those areas that are necessary.

Change is often difficult because it involves new goals, new disciplines, time, and commitment. Our new life in Christ presents the proper motivations for change. The Christian counselor must use these incentives to challenge the counselee to change:

-17-

1. **God's Mercy**—Because of the mercies of God in regard to our sin and redemption, we are told to *"present your bodies a living sacrifice"* (Rom. 12:1). We are also told to be *"dead indeed to sin, but alive to God"* (Rom. 6:11).

2. **Our High Calling**—As Christians we are to *"walk worthy of the calling with which you were called"* (Eph. 4:1). This high calling is to express Christ's character and conduct in our lives.

3. **Our Future Inheritance**—Jesus has promised a future reward for every believer based upon our obedience during this life. In Revelation 22:12 He declares, *"And behold, I am coming quickly, and My reward is with Me, to give to everyone according to his work."*

-18-

JESUS MUST INCREASE

The goal of the counselor is to introduce Jesus Christ into the problem of the person being counseled. One of the titles given to the Lord in Isaiah 9:6 is that of "Counselor". Another person to share with during times of need is invaluable. However, the counselor must not allow himself to become a substitute for Jesus. As John the Baptist said, *"He must increase, but I must decrease"* (John 3:30).

Our failure to adequately cope with difficulty is usually related to a failure to relate to Jesus in it. We can introduce Christ into a person's problem by sharing what God's Word teaches, and how he can lean on Jesus in his particular situation. **Counseling times should be ended with a time of prayer for the specific areas of need which you have discussed.**

-19-

FOLLOW-UP

Many problem situations require an involvement beyond the initial counseling time. A wise counselor ends his first session by giving the counselee specific things he can do in order to bring about a change in the situation. This may require scripture memorization, more prayer time, changes in relationships, or other disciplines.

Once a counseling relationship develops, we have an obligation to remain involved until that person has been restored to a place of victory. **We should initiate another contact to indicate our concern, and to check up on their progress.**

• **Warning**—Some people want attention but will not institute change. If there is an unwillingness to change, you are free from the counseling obligation.

-20-

OTHER TIPS

1. **Avoid Successive Counseling with the Opposite Sex**—For the common care counselor, it is wise to avoid counseling a member of the opposite sex more than once. Ask a mature Christian who is of the opposite sex to contact them. We must avoid the emotional attachments that people in need are vulnerable to.

2. **Find an Appropriate Place to Counsel**—The general rule is to find a place where both of you are comfortable, and where there are a minimum of distractions or interruptions.

3. **Don't Get in Too Deep**—We want to be involved, but not overwhelmed. Once we become too attached we can lose our peace, objectivity, and effectiveness in helping others.

-21-

◄ CONCLUSION ►

This Counseling Guide is part of a package of "counseling booklets" designed to address some of the common counseling needs of people. These booklets cover a number of problem areas. They can assist the common care counselor by providing a concise yet comprehensive scriptural understanding of these areas of need.

They are designed to be read with the counselee, and then given to them for further reference. These booklets can be ordered by contacting the address on the back of this booklet.

For a brief summary of this booklet, please re-read the words in bold type on each page.

-22-

Chapter 2

Counseling
Guide II

BY TERRY D. EDWARDS

◀ INTRODUCTION ▶

Until a person comes to Christ, his attempts to cope with the problems of life are nothing more than shadowboxing. **It is only through a right relationship with God and His Word that we can understand the source and solution to our problems.**

The fall of man was devastating to the peace and harmony of both our personal and social life. The confusion that followed resulted in the error of pointing the finger at everything except the real problem.

Sin is the problem. To effectively counsel ourselves and others, we must understand how sin works and how it can be overcome. We will examine these areas in this booklet.

-1-

◀ TABLE OF CONTENTS ▶

-2-

SIN IS THE PROBLEM

The Bible points the finger at the true enemies of mankind: the world, the flesh, and the devil. All of these agents are the result of sin. Sin is acting independently of, and in rebellion against, God and His Word.

In Isaiah 14:12, 13 we are given the picture of Satan's rebellion against God. He attempted to exalt himself above God. God responded by casting him out of heaven.

In Genesis 3, Satan prompts Adam and Eve to sin by disobeying God's command concerning the Tree of Knowledge. By choosing to eat the forbidden fruit, they exalted themselves above the Word of God. The result was that **mankind received a sin nature,** and **Satan became the legal authority over this present world** (Eph. 2:2).

-3-

Through God's plan of redemption, mankind is offered forgiveness and freedom from the affects of sin. **At Calvary, Jesus broke the power of sin and Satan.** He that had never sinned became sin and died in our place to satisfy God's legal requirement which demands that sin be punished (II Cor. 5:21; Col. 2:14).

By this sacrifice, He broke Satan's power over our lives (I John 3:8). As we live under grace, as sons of God, **sin no longer has dominion over us** (John 1:12; Rom. 6:14).

In the following pages, we will examine sin and its effects and consequences. We will also explain how to apply Christ's victory to every area of our lives.

-4-

THE ROOT OF SIN

The root of sin is found in the choices we make. Sin entered both the universe and this world through choices that were made. We, likewise, face similar choices with our lives. **We either choose** to live according to **our feelings and desires,** or we choose **a life of obedience** to the Word of God.

One choice represents a sinful life style based upon self-centeredness. The other is a righteous life style based upon God-centeredness.

The first choice results in an immediate but temporary fulfillment of selfish desires which inevitably lead to spiritual and moral deterioration. The second leads to joy and freedom within God's order, and produces personal harmony and integration.

The one produces a conformance to the world, the flesh, and the devil. The other produces a conformance to the person and character of Jesus Christ.

-5-

Adam and Eve were given this kind of choice. They lived in a state of purity, harmony, and innocence with only one commandment to obey in order to maintain this condition.

Satan tempted Eve with the lust of the flesh, the lust of the eyes, and the pride of life (Gen. 3:6). **Both Adam and Eve chose to respond to their own selfish desires rather than God's commandment.**

Their eyes were *"opened"* (verse 7) to evil and independence, and they were brought under the dominion of sin.

The results of their sin typifies the consequences of all sin. We will examine these in the following pages.

-6-

THE RESULT OF SIN

I. SEPARATION FROM GOD

A. **A Break in Fellowship** — In Genesis 3:9 the Lord cries out to Adam saying, *"Where are you?"* Adam, because of his sin, was hiding, alienated from fellowship with God.

Sin always breaks our fellowship with the Lord. Any rejection of the Word of God is an enthronement of ourselves. By choosing to sin, we strengthen our self-trust and lessen our experience with the presence of God.

God cannot ignore sin. He spoke to Israel in Isaiah 59:2 saying *"your iniquities have separated you from God; and your sins have hidden His face from you."*

-7-

B. **Sin Brings Judgment** — Jesus said, *"He who rejects Me, and does not receive My words, has that which judges him"* (John 12:48). **Rejection of the Word of God is ultimately a rejection of God Himself.** By our choice we either judge the Word of God, or allow the Word of God to judge us.

When Satan and Adam and Eve rebelled against God, they did so by disobeying His command. Any deliberate rejection of His Word will result in judgment and chastening.

Adam and Eve's sin resulted in guilt (Gen. 3:8), child bearing problems (Gen. 3:16), a curse upon the entire creation (Rom. 8:22), the fallen sin nature (Eph. 2:3), and expulsion from the Garden (Gen. 3:23).

The judgment of God can only be appeased through the forgiveness offered in the righteous sacrifice of Jesus Christ at Calvary.

-8-

II. PERSONAL DISHARMONY

Sin also results in producing a disharmony in our personal lives. We see this immediately manifested in the reactions of Adam and Eve after the fall.

A. **Guilt** — *"And Adam and his wife hid themselves from the presence of the Lord"* (Gen. 3:8). **When we know we have sinned against God, we always experience guilt.** Our conscience has been given to us as an inner register of the "moral voice" of God. Guilt must be handled correctly or it will continue to fester within us, bringing disharmony to our personal experience.

B. **Fear** — *"I heard Your voice in the garden, and I was afraid"* (Gen. 3:10). **Guilt produces fear.** We are afraid because we know we have sinned against our Creator. Adam failed to act correctly toward his guilt and fear. Instead of repenting, he hid himself from God.

-9-

One of Satan's most deceptive tactics is to bring condemnation upon us during times of guilt, causing us to run away from God. In Hebrews 4:16 we are told instead to *"come boldly to the throne of grace . . . and find grace to help in time of need."*

C. **Confusion** — *"I was afraid because I was naked"* (Gen. 3:10). **Sin can even confuse us in regards to what sin is.** Adam wrongly blamed his guilt on his nakedness. We can fall victim to this same kind of confusion. Often, the real sin in our life lies concealed even from us underneath piles of rationalization and self-justification.

We may have to look under the surface excuses in order to discover the real areas of sin.

-10-

III. PROBLEMS WITH OTHERS

Besides destroying mankind's relationship with God, sin also created entirely new obstacles in our relationships with other human beings. On the following pages we have listed three common areas of problems in relationships which are caused by sin:

A. **Shifting the Blame** — *"The woman whom You gave to be with me, she gave me of the tree"* (Gen. 3:12). **To avoid personal responsibility for our sin, we quickly point the finger in another direction.** In this case, Adam blamed both God and Eve. God wants a confession, not an accusation. If we can't fully blame another, our tendency is to at least partially do so in order to lessen our responsibility.

B. **Bitterness and Resentment** — When Adam was confronted, his accusation against his wife revealed a degree of resentment for involving him in her transgression.

-11-

Sin often results in an underlying resentment towards others. These feelings must be dealt with promptly, or problems with others will only be complicated (Matt. 18:15; Eph. 4:32).

C. **Gossip and Slander** — *"Whoever hides hatred has lying lips, and whoever spreads slander is a fool"* (Prov. 10:18). One of the ways sin compounds its destructiveness is by camouflaging bitterness through true but harmful statements which we make about others. **If bitterness is not dealt with, gossip and slander are the results.**

We are also told that if a root of bitterness becomes established in our lives, *"many become defiled"* (Heb. 12:15). Both gossip and slander are a poison to the kinds of relationships we are to have in the body of Christ.

When sin manifests itself in one of these ways, we should identify the source and deal with it before God.

-12-

FINDING THE PROBLEM

We have examined the root and the results of sin. To effectively deal with sin, we must thoroughly understand how it works and what it produces.

The job of the counselor is to help the counselee identify the real source of his problem. By the time someone reaches out for help, there may be a number of outward symptoms which conceal the actual root sin. To further complicate the matter, the person may not want that area revealed. He may attempt to divert your attention in a different direction.

We must become wise to the dynamics of sin. Sin can have very sophisticated and deceptive ways of concealing and justifying itself.

-13-

Often the person you are counseling is blind to the real problem in his life — such as a bad attitude or motive. The counselor is like a surgeon that must first diagnose the cancer, and then use his skills in order to see it removed.

Genuine deliverance requires identification of the root sin. This demands a willingness on the part of the person being counseled to be honest and transparent. There must also be a willingness to take the scriptural approach to victory.

The counselor can help promote this willingness by confessing similar areas of difficulties that he has coped with. **Once the real problem is identified, the counselor must then be both sensitive and persistent in approaching this need.**

-14-

THE SOLUTION

I. ACKNOWLEDGEMENT OF SIN

Once sin is identified in our life, we must be willing to take personal responsibility for it. Though King David committed a terrible sin with Bathsheba, once it was challenged, he readily acknowledged it. Because of this repentance, we see that later God was able to call him *"a man after My own heart"* (Acts 13:22). It is not our sin that destroys us. Rather, it is our failure to acknowledge it and take responsibility for its correction that will cause our downfall.

Though our situation may also involve the faults of others, **we are only responsible for our own sin.** We should take responsibility for our wrong and let others do likewise. We must also be careful about excuses. There are always contributing factors to sin. None of these exempt us from our responsibility.

-15-

Acknowledgement of sin leads to repentance in two areas:

1. **Repentance to God**—*"If we confess our sins, He is faithful and just to forgive us our sins, and to cleanse us from all unrighteousness"* (I John 1:9). Our first responsibility is to repent before our Creator. David cried out, *"Against You, You only, have I sinned"* (Ps. 51:4). Though David hurt others, he recognized that **all sin is ultimately directed against God.**

2. **Repent to Others**—*"First be reconciled to your brother, and then come and offer your gift"* (Matt. 5:24). If our sin has affected the lives of others, we must go to them, apologize, and ask forgiveness. **We must be willing to do whatever is right in order to bring reconciliation with the person involved.**

-16-

II. COMMITMENT TO CHANGE

Sin produces sinful habits. A person develops the habit of bad language, rudeness, drug addition, or dishonesty. Our adult expressions of sin were not always as developed as they are now. They were gradually nurtured over many years. Our sin nature gave these bad habits incentive, and they grew into a life style.

But now in Christ we are new creations: *"old things have passed away; behold, all things have become new"* (II Cor. 5:17).

We must work within this truth to see a change in those areas where sin still dominates.

-17-

Change involves a two-fold process:

1. **Putting Off the Old**–*"That you put off, concerning your former conduct, the old man"* (Eph. 4:22). **All genuine change must begin in the heart.** We are new creations, so we want to act like it. We must identify that behavior that is not Christ-like and commit ourselves to positive change.

2. **Putting On the New**–*"Put on the new man which was created according to God, in righteousness and true holiness"* (Eph. 4:24). **We cannot put off old habits without putting on new ones.** Honesty must replace dishonesty. Personal responsibility for sin must replace blaming others. Through desire and discipline, new habits will become our life style.

-18-

THREE AGENTS OF CHANGE

I. THE POWER OF TRUTH

"For the word of God is living and powerful, and sharper than any two-edged sword" (Heb. 4:12).

The Word of God must be our source of counsel. If we are to effectively help others, we must know what the Bible teaches. A counselor without the Word of God is left to his own understanding and lacks both discernment and authority.

When we know what the Bible teaches, we can provide God's answers. **When His Word is spoken, it begins a deep work in the life of the hearer.**

-19-

The Word of God is not only *"living and powerful"* but is *"piercing even to the division of soul and spirit, and of the joints and marrow, and is a discerner of the thoughts and intents of the heart"* (Heb. 4:12).

We often feel like the counsel we have given has not had much of an impact. When we have spoken the Word of God, though, we can trust that **it will not return void** (see Isa. 55:11). A person may leave your presence, but the Word does not leave him. If his heart is right, it will eventually bring forth the fruit of enlightenment and change.

As he receives the Word, it begins the process of deliverance described in John 8:31,32: *"If you abide in My word . . . you shall know the truth, and the truth shall make you free."*

-20-

II. THE PERSON OF THE HOLY SPIRIT

"And I will pray the Father, and He will give you another Helper . . . even the Spirit of truth" (John 14:16,17).

God dwells within the life of every believer in the person of the Holy Spirit. One of the Spirit's functions, as described in John 16:13, is to *"guide you into all truth."* Jesus further states that *"He will take of what is Mine and declare it to you"* (John 16:14).

The counselor must depend upon the assistance of the Holy Spirit in ministering to the needs of others. He alone can give us a clear, scriptural discernment of the problem. He alone can empower the person in need to believe and apply God's solution to his life.

-21-

III. THE POWER OF PRAYER

"The effective, fervent prayer of a righteous man avails much" (James 5:16).

Prayer remains a mystery to the person who has not employed its power in his own life. The Bible is filled with examples of answered prayer. James 5:17 states that the fervent prayer of Elijah caused the heavens to withhold rain for 3½ years.

The person in need must be encouraged to pray for God's help in achieving a full victory. Words alone are not enough to secure deliverance. Victory comes through bringing God into the situation.

The person counseling must also pray for the one in need. Again, James 5:16 encourages us to *"pray for one another, that you may be healed."*

-22-

LOVE IN COUNSELING

I. THE ROLE OF LOVE

The Christian is admonished to *"by love serve one another"* (Gal. 5:13, KJV). **One of the greatest ways to serve your brother or sister is to be there to help in times of need.**

Contrary to the opinion of Cain in Genesis 4:9, we are our brother's keeper! We are to *"bear one another's burdens, and so fulfill the law of Christ"* (Gal. 6:2).

Genuine love is really determined by what it produces. Speaking kind words or being a shoulder to cry on may not always represent love. In counseling, love will often involve confrontation. **Genuine love is concerned with applying God's answer to the life of the person in need.**

-23-

Confronting an individual with their fault in the situation will require both tact and courage. The key of exercising tact is given in the phrase *"speaking the truth in love"* (Eph. 4:15). **How we say something is as important as what we say.** It often determines a person's ultimate reaction.

When confronting someone, we want to avoid any spirit of pride, accusation, or condemnation. We should seek to present the truth in such a way that he receives it from God and not from us.

Confronting someone requires courage. We must rise above our fears and relate to the real issues that are at stake. The goal of counseling is to see people freed from the binding effects of sin. When we speak to a person, we should do so with the goal of deliverance in mind.

-24-

II. THE GOAL OF LOVE

Earlier, we saw that the root of sin was choosing to live life on the basis of selfish feelings and desires rather than in obedience to the Word of God.

When counseling another toward obedience, we must show them that this is the path of love. Love is doing what's right before God. In fact, the goal of obedience is to produce genuine love in our life. Paul declares that *"the purpose of the commandment is love from a pure heart"* (I Tim. 1:5).

Likewise, **the power to live a commandment-centered life comes from our love for God.** Jesus said, *"If you love Me, keep My commandments"* (John 14:15). Love for God is both the motivation and goal for obedience.

-25-

◀ CONCLUSION ▶

This Counseling Guide is part of a package of "counseling booklets" designed to address some of the common counseling needs of people. These booklets cover a number of problem areas. They can assist the **"common care counselor"** by providing a concise, yet comprehensive scriptural understanding of these areas of difficulty.

We also encourage those helped by this booklet to continue their study on counseling by reading the many fine works on Christian counseling that are available. We especially recommend the writings of Gary Collins and Jay Adams which have been of great assistance to us.

For a brief summary of this booklet, please re-read the words in bold type on each page.

-26-

Chapter 3

The New
Life

By Terry D. Edwards

◄ INTRODUCTION ►

When we accept Jesus Christ as our Lord and Savior, we receive the gift of eternal life. This gift involves far more than a future reward. It means beginning a new life right now as a new person in the eyes of God.

We have been born again by the incorruptible seed of the Word of God (I Pet. 1:23). His Word is *"living and active"* (Heb. 4:12, NIV), and will produce a change in our beliefs, attitudes, motivation, goals, and desires. **Our new birth will affect every area of our life.**

On the following pages of this booklet, we will answer some important questions concerning our new life in Christ.

-1-

◄ TABLE OF CONTENTS ►

-2-

THE PROMISE OF A NEW LIFE

"Therefore, if anyone is in Christ, he is a new creation; OLD THINGS ARE PASSED AWAY; behold, ALL THINGS HAVE BECOME NEW." (II Cor. 5:17).

Most of us at one time in our life have thought, "I sure wish I could start over again!" God has made this a reality through your commitment to Jesus Christ. We still have the same name, address, and family, but we have begun a new life. The things concerning our old life have passed away. **Our present life in Christ has made all things new.**

-3-

WHAT HAPPENED TO THE OLD?

"Knowing this, that OUR OLD MAN WAS CRUCIFIED WITH HIM, that the body of sin might be done away with, that we should no longer be slaves of sin" (Rom. 6:6).

1. **It was condemned** - The penalty for sin is death (Rom. 6:23). God's justice requires that our life of sin and selfishness be condemned.

2. **It was crucified** - Jesus died for the sin of all humanity. Our "old man" was crucified with Him at Calvary.

3. **The power of sin was broken** - At the cross, Jesus Christ triumphed over sin and broke its power over all those who receive Him.

-4-

HOW DO WE BECOME NEW?

"I have been crucified with Christ; IT IS NO LONGER I WHO LIVE, BUT CHRIST LIVES IN ME; and the life which I now live in the flesh I live by faith in the Son of God, who loved me and gave Himself for me" (Gal. 2:20).

1. **By being forgiven** - When we repent before God for our old sinful life, He forgives us. *"If we confess our sins, He is faithful and just to forgive us our sins and to cleanse us from all unrighteousness"* (I John 1:9).

2. **By being born again** - God sends His Holy Spirit to live within us and to give us a new nature. *"Unless one is born of water and the Spirit, he cannot enter the kingdom of God"* (John 3:5).

3. **By living a life of faith** - The life we now live is one of faith in the promises and provision of God. *"And this is the victory that has overcome the word - our faith"* (I John 5:4).

-5-

WHAT BECOMES NEW?

In II Corinthians 5:17 we saw that *"ALL THINGS HAVE BECOME NEW."* It would require a thorough study of the New Testament to describe the complete renewal that is available to every believer. **God's plan is that each of us would be conformed to the image of Jesus Christ** (Rom. 8:29).

The Lord has sent His Spirit into our lives to accomplish this renewal. The Holy Spirit will convict us in those areas that need a change. As we yield ourselves to Him, He will begin the work of recreating us according to God's design.

In the following sections of this booklet, we will examine some of the more important areas that have been made new in our lives.

-6-

I. A NEW IDENTITY

*"For **YE ARE ALL THE CHILDREN OF GOD** by faith in Christ Jesus"* (Gal. 3:26, KJV).

Each of us have things related to our lives that give us our identity. Our job, family, and friends, along with our interests and hobbies, are some of these areas. They each contribute to our image of who we are.

Above everything else, **you are now a child of God!** You have been adopted into His eternal family. **This is a great privilege and responsibility.** It should affect every aspect of how we see ourselves and conduct our lives.

-7-

II. A NEW NATURE

*"And because you are sons, **God has sent forth the Spirit of His Son into your hearts,** crying out, 'Abba, Father!' "* (Gal. 4:6).

Along with our adoption into His family, **God has also given us a new nature.** II Peter 1:4 states that we are *"partakers of the divine nature."* His Spirit has been sent into our hearts, depositing within us the likeness and character of God. **He gives us new motives, new desires, and new attitudes.** We can no longer enjoy thinking, feeling, and behaving in a way that is displeasing to Him.

Instead, we have a deep sense of love and commitment to Him as our heavenly Father.

-8-

III. A NEW POWER

*"And what is the **exceeding greatness of His power toward us who believe,** according to the working of His mighty power"* (Eph. 1:19).

The sinful tendencies of the old man kept us in bondage all of our lives. Our best attempts to live righteously were frustrated.

Now there is a new power inside of us through the Holy Spirit. It is the same power that raised Christ from the dead. It is the power to live uprightly as a child of God, and to express His likeness. **It is the power to do whatever He has called us to do.**

Christians are not to consider what is possible by merely evaluating their own abilities. Instead, our faith should be like that of the Apostle Paul who said, *"I can do all things through Christ who strengthens me"* (Phil. 4:13).

-9-

IV. A NEW LORDSHIP

"For we do not preach ourselves, but Christ Jesus the Lord" (II Cor. 4:5).

The root of all sin is an independent nature. It is doing what is right in our own eyes apart from God. The old sin nature lives according to this rule. If we allow it to prevail in our lives, it will cause us to take this same course.

In Christ, we are no longer the lord of our lives. We have submitted ourselves to the authority of God. The Bible is a revelation of the mind and will of God. **We are to submit our thoughts and ways to Him, and seek to live by His Word.**

-10-

V. A NEW UNDERSTANDING

*"That the God of our Lord Jesus Christ, the **Father of glory, may give to you the spirit of wisdom and revelation** in the knowledge of Him"* (Ephesians 1:17).

With our acceptance of Jesus Christ comes an entirely new understanding of life and its purpose. We realize that other philosophies and religions are merely man-made attempts to explain what only God can.

He does so in the Bible, and He gives us the spirit of wisdom and revelation to understand it. Our entire perspective changes. We now understand life through God's plan, purpose, and present involvement.

-11-

VI. A NEW PEACE

*"**YOU WILL KEEP HIM IN PERFECT PEACE,** whose mind is stayed on You, because he trusts in You"* (Isaiah 26:3).

Life apart from Christ was filled with fears and concerns. The world seemed chaotic and unpredictable. Our own life lacked meaning and purpose. We seemed so alone.

Now we know there is an authority behind it all. Our trust is no longer in this life, but in God. We belong to Him. He is in control. **As we center our trust in Him, a new peace fills our life.**

-12-

VII. A NEW PURPOSE

*"Thou art worthy, O Lord, to receive glory and honour and power: for thou hast created all things, and **for thy pleasure they are and were created"** (Rev. 4:11, KJV).*

Part of our new understanding is that the universe does not revolve around us. Rather, it was created by and for a perfect, holy God whose nature is love.

As part of His creation, we are to live for His pleasure, and to bring Him glory. God receives pleasure and glory when we act in the way of truth, righteousness, and love. These qualities are consistent with both the nature of God and His kingdom.

-13-

VIII. A NEW DESTINY

*"Beloved, now we are children of God; and **it has not yet been revealed what we shall be,** but we know that when He is revealed, **WE SHALL BE LIKE HIM,** for we shall see Him as He is"* (I John 3:2).

We have a glorious destiny ahead of us. This life is only preparation for our place in God's eternal kingdom. Not everything about our future is revealed. What the Bible does show is exciting. We will judge the world (I Cor. 6:2). Our works will be rewarded (Rom. 2:6). We will receive a new body (I Cor. 15:54).

The most exciting thing of all is that **we shall see Jesus, and be made like Him.** We will enjoy eternity with a full experience of His life within us.

-14-

THERE IS STILL A STRUGGLE!

*"For the **sinful nature desires what is contrary to the Spirit, and the Spirit what is contrary to the sinful nature.** They are in conflict with each other, so that you do not do what you want"* (Gal. 5:17, NIV).

Though the old man has been crucified with Christ and the power of sin has been broken, **we still experience an inner struggle between the old nature and the Spirit of God.** This is common to every believer. We will have this struggle, to some degree, as long as we are in these mortal bodies.

In Christ, though, our victory is guaranteed. On the next two pages we will look at how we can achieve this victory.

-15-

DENY SINFUL DESIRES

*"Therefore **DO NOT LET SIN REIGN IN YOUR MORTAL BODY,** that you should obey it in its lusts"* (Romans 6:12).

In Galatians 5:19-21, we are given a list of the acts of our sinful nature. They include immorality, idolatry, witchcraft, hatred, discord, jealousy, rage, selfish ambition, dissensions, envy, drunkenness, and others.

The first step in our victory over these areas is a commitment to resist them. We must see this behavior as alien to the new life God has given us. We must line up our will with God's will. *"And those who are Christ's have crucified the flesh with its passions and desires"* (Gal. 5:24).

-16-

LIVE BY THE SPIRIT

*"So I say, **LIVE BY THE SPIRIT,** and you will not gratify the desires of the sinful nature"* (Gal. 5:16, NIV).

By building strong spiritual lives, we will lessen the intensity of sinful desires within us. We will also build our strength to resist the temptations we do encounter. Here are five ways to build strong spiritual lives:

1. **Read the Bible** - This enlightens our mind to God's will.

2. **Pray** - This builds our communion with God.

3. **Worship** - This increases our sense of His presence.

4. **Fellowship** - Christian friends help fortify our commitments.

5. **Witness** - Telling others about Christ will release His love within us.

-17-

◀ CONCLUSION ▶

You have a new life in Christ. It is a life filled with great potential. As you continue to follow the Lord, this potential will steadily unfold.

Remember that nothing grows without nourishment. We must develop a discipline of prayer, Bible reading, and church fellowship. Through these, our spiritual life will be nurtured and strengthened. A strong spiritual life will bring glory to God, and allow us to truly express the image of Jesus Christ (Rom. 8:29).

For a brief overview of the main points in this booklet, please re-read the boldly printed words on each page.

-18-

Chapter 4

*Breaking Bad
Habits*

<small>By William R. Kimball</small>

◀ INTRODUCTION ▶

Life is filled with habits — some good, some not so good. We are creatures of habit. We've all managed to acquire a host of habits in the course of our development.

Many habits are innocent, unnoticeable, and of little consequence. However, some habits are deadly, obvious, and of major consequence to our lives.

When we embraced Christ, we renounced a life of sinful habits and practices. But **many Christians find it difficult to break old habits and forsake well-established patterns.** In this booklet, we will examine the subject of breaking bad habits, and offer some liberating steps for accomplishing this.

-1-

◀ TABLE OF CONTENTS ▶

-2-

WHAT IS A HABIT?

A habit is "an established practice, tendency, or manner of behavior."**It is a behavioral pattern which is acquired through frequent repetition.**

A habit implies something which we have learned to do unconsciously and often compulsively. It is a life pattern which has been reinforced through repeated use.

A habit can be harmless, or life-threatening. It can range from a facial mannerism, to something as deeply ingrained as a character weakness. It can involve something as simple as putting the right shoe on first, to something as serious as drug addiction.

-3-

HOW IMPORTANT ARE HABITS?

Habits can be extremely important. They often have a tremendous impact upon the course of our lives. **They can even affect our eternal destiny.** The following saying captures this truth well:

> **Sow a thought, reap a deed;**
> **Sow a deed, reap a HABIT;**
> **Sow a HABIT, reap a personality;**
> **Sow a personality, reap a destiny.**

Since our habits can have such a significant impact upon our lives, we must not ignore them or take them lightly. Those habits which are beneficial need to be appreciated and reinforced. Those habits which are detrimental need to be carefully examined and eliminated.

-4-

THE CHALLENGE OF CONQUERING HABITS

The challenge of overcoming destructive habits can be a formidable obstacle. **Some habits are so firmly established in our lives that they seem like insurmountable barriers.**

Habits sometimes appear to be areas which are impossible to change. The prophet Jeremiah presented a question which appropriately characterizes the dilemma which we sometimes encounter when confronting the challenge of breaking bad habits:

> "Can the Ethiopian change his skin, or the leopard its spots? Neither can you do good who are accustomed to doing evil" (Jeremiah 13:23, NIV).

-5-

A SOURCE OF FRUSTRATION

The struggle of wrestling with habits can often produce a deep sense of frustration.

The difficulty of achieving a permanent victory over alcoholism, drug dependence, and smoking can become a grueling experience. **Our previous inabilities to defeat sinful habits can create an overwhelming sense of hopelessness and despair.**

Those who have sought to overcome such habits have soon discovered that they are not always easy to defeat. It is not a problem which can be solved with simplistic answers or quick-fix remedies. However, **it is a problem which can be successfully answered through Christ.**

-6-

IS THERE GENUINE HOPE?

★**Yes!** Before we can successuflly deal with sinful habits, we must understand that **there are no hopeless situations in Christ. Our habits are no exception.**

In I Corinthians 6:9-10, **Paul lists** the sinful practices which the Corinthians had been habitually involved in. He included such things as **drunkenness, homosexuality, and thievery.**

In verse eleven, he followed with this important statement: *"And such WERE SOME OF YOU."* This verse is a strong encouragement for all those seeking a lasting release from life-dominating habits. The wording is in the past tense — *"WERE"*. **Paul reveals that God has made it possible to overcome what seems to be impossible — our old ways.** Jesus didn't just provide a temporary, half-way solution. He gives a permanent victory over every conceivable practice. If He could do it for them, He can do the same for us!

-7-

IS THERE A SOLUTION?

★**Absolutely!** This is the guarantee of scripture: *"I CAN DO ALL THINGS THROUGH CHRIST who strengthens me"* (Phil. 4:13). However, some Christians have convinced themselves that this is not possible.

They have made so many unsuccessful attempts to overcome their habits that they have resigned themselves to failure. They have defeated themselves even before they begin.

We may have lost a few battles, but we have not lost the war. In spite of our previous failures, we must not settle for total defeat. **We must re-commit ourselves to follow God's divine instructions for victory.** On the following pages, we will examine the scriptural steps for achieving a complete and permanent victory over our sinful habits.

-8-

I. WE MUST SINCERELY REPENT

"IF WE CONFESS OUR SINS, He is faithful and just to forgive us our sins and to cleanse us from all unrighteousness" (I John 1:9). Sincere repentence is the first step.

Before any Christian can defeat sinful habits, he **must recognize them as a sinful practice.** If we fail to grasp this fundamental fact, we will not succeed in overcoming them.

We must not endeavor to conquer our sinful habits just to alleviate guilt or sooth a troubled conscience. Our motive must not be based upon the compulsion or coaxing of others only. It must be based upon a sincere, godly conviction to please God and appropriate His cleansing power and forgiveness.

-9-

II. WE MUST APPROPRIATE GOD'S POWER

Before we can bring God's power to bear upon the problem, we must recognize that we have a problem. If we ignore it, minimize it, or overlook it, our sinful habit will only reinforce itself.

We must identify the habit and give careful consideration to its nature, frequency, and occurrences. When we have given proper attention to the problem area, we can begin to wage successful warfare against it.

After isolating the problem, we should begin to attack it through persistent prayer. If we will begin to draw upon the power of Christ through prayer, He will impart the necessary strength. We must not rely upon our own might, but upon the divine resources of the Holy Spirit to combat our sinful habits.

-10-

III. WE MUST STRIVE FOR CHANGE

The scriptures teach us that change is a vital part of our development in Christ (II Cor. 3:18). The process of change is a fundamental requirement for overcoming sinful habits.

Without change, our habits will continue to persist. However, change must be more than just attempting to stop practicing a sinful habit. Many attempt this form of change without lasting success.

Change must involve more than saying "NO!" Change isn't just a matter of willpower, human resolve, or sheer determination. It isn't turning over a new leaf or making bold promises to quit. **Quitting is not change. This is only a half-way response which only provides half-way results.** If this is all we do to change, our change will only be temporary.

-11-

◆**Scriptural change involves a two-fold process: Real change isn't just stopping sinful habits, but replacing them with godly actions.** Only when we begin to change our practices and relearn positive habits can we really achieve lasting victory.

Paul points out this two-fold process in Colossians 3:8. He exhorts us to **"put off" our old practices.** He then encourages us to **"put on the new man"** (Col. 3:10).

This putting *"off"* is the negative side of change. This is important, but in itself, insufficient. We must also apply **the positive side of change** which **involves the putting *"on"* of biblical alternatives.** This is the key to successful change.

We must begin to restructure our lives according to the Word of God. We must change in the right directions.

-12-

IV. BE FILLED WITH THE SPIRIT

*"And **do not be drunk with wine,** in which is dissipation; **BUT BE FILLED WITH THE SPIRIT"** (Eph. 5:18). This verse illustrates both the positive and negative side of change.*

Instead of allowing ourselves to be dominated by old habits, we should strive for the Holy Spirit to be the prevailing influence in our lives on a daily basis. **When we are filled with His presence, we receive the necessary strength, support, and will power to successfully overcome the *"lust of the flesh"*** (Gal. 5:16, 17, KJV).

We must replace our old habits with constructive alternatives. Paul reveals some of the practical steps for accomplishing this in verses 19 and 20 of Ephesians, chapter 5.

-13-

V. APPLY THE CLEANSING POWER OF THE WORD

"How can a young man cleanse his way? BY TAKING HEED ACCORDING TO YOUR WORD" (Psalms 119:9). The Word provides an effective sourse of cleansing for our old ways.

In referring to God's desire for His church, Paul stated: *"That He might sanctify and CLEANSE IT WITH THE WASHING OF WATER BY THE WORD"* (Eph. 5:26). **The Word is a cleansing agent for our thoughts, desires, and inclinations.**

We should carefully consider those scriptural passages which have a specific bearing upon the need for godly change and His provision for help. If we will meditate upon God's Word and take heed to His counsel, it will gradually begin the process of cleansing our ways and purifying our habits. -14-

VI. WE MUST BRING OUR HABITS UNDER SUBJECTION

*"But **I DISCIPLINE MY BODY AND BRING IT INTO SUBJECTION,** lest, when I have preached to others, I myself should become disqualified"* (I Cor. 9:27).

We must exercise a firm hand in disciplining our sinful habits. The tendency to participate with our old ways must be confronted and supressed. **If we allow our minds to fantasize, flirt with, or entertain the possible justification of our sinful habits, we will suffer defeat.**

Victory depends upon decisive action. **When we are tempted to continue a sinful habit, we must challenge the desire with the Word of God.** The temptation should also serve as a warning signal to drive us to the Lord in prayer. Our determination to promptly confront our habits when they arise is an effective safeguard against failure.

-15-

VII. WE MUST FORM RIGHT RELATIONSHIPS

The scriptures reveal the destructive power of wrong relationships: *"**DO NOT BE MISLED: BAD COMPANY CORRUPTS GOOD CHARACTER"*** (I Cor. 15:33, NIV). Harmful relationships only reinforce sinful habits (Prov. 22:24, 25).

Old friendships and associates can be a destructive influence. Our old hangouts can also create compromising situations for those endeavoring to overcome sinful habits.

This fact demands a godly alternative. **We must terminate those associations which hinder us and surround ourselves with healthy relationships which reinforce godliness.** We must strengthen the ties of Christian fellowship and center our activities around the church (Heb. 10:24, 25).

-16

VIII. WE MUST NOT GIVE UP!

"A JUST MAN FALLETH SEVEN TIMES, AND RISETH UP AGAIN" (Prov. 24:16, KJV). In the process of striving for victory, **we may occasionally fall short; however, we must rise up and continue to press on.**

We must persevere in order to achieve victory. We must not allow our failures to discourage, frustrate, or disillusion us. They must not cause us to give up. **It takes time to re-establish godly alternatives. There is no such thing as instant success.** It takes about 30 days to relearn a godly habit. Therefore, persistence and determination are essential.

We must **never entertain a spirit of quitting or defeat.** We must press on in the confidence that we *"CAN DO ALL THINGS THROUGH CHRIST who strengthens"* us (Phil. 4:13).

-17-

◄ CONCLUSION ►

We must recognize that a lasting victory over sinful habits is guaranteed in Christ. We are not hopelessly bound to them. Change is possible if we will diligently apply the steps covered in this booklet:

1. We must sincerely **repent.**
2. We must **appropriate God's power.**
3. We must **strive for change.**
4. **"Be filled with the Spirit."**
5. **Apply** the cleansing power of **the Word.**
6. We must **bring** our **habits under subjection.**
7. We must **form right relationships.**
8. We **must not give up.**

For a quick overview of this booklet, we recommend that you re-read the boldly printed words. We also recommend that you read the counseling booklet on "Overcoming Temptation".

-18-

Chapter 5

Overcoming Temptation

By Terry D. Edwards

◄ INTRODUCTION ►

The Christian is in a unique position in this present life. We are members of the kingdom of God. We have been adopted into God's eternal family. We have a high calling in Christ.

Yet we are still living in a world that is hostile to the God we serve. It is ruled by Satan, the prince and power of the air.

Because of this, **we must face temptations** that work to destroy our Christian commitment. These temptations come in many different forms that the believer must identify if he is to have a victory over them.

In this booklet, **we will study this subject of temptation** and see how God has provided for our victory.

-1-

◄ TABLE OF CONTENTS ►

-2-

THE HIGH CALLING

In Philippians 3:14 the Apostle Paul proclaims, **"I PRESS TOWARD THE MARK** *for the prize of the high calling of God in Christ Jesus"* (KJV).

Just as an Olympic runner gives himself to those disciplines that are necessary to win the race, so **Paul was willing to do whatever was required to live up to the high calling of God in Christ Jesus.** He exhorts others to have this same determination in I Corinthians 9:24 when he says, *"Run in such a way that you may obtain it."*

Being a member of God's family is both a privilege and a responsibility. We have a new life and destiny. We are to live up to the calling of being sons and daughters of the living God.

-3-

WHAT DOES THIS CALLING INVOLVE?

★ It involves both **doing God's will,** and **expressing His likeness** in our character:

• *"As servants of Christ, **doing the will of God** from the heart"* (Eph. 6:6).

• *"For whom He foreknew, He also predestined to be **conformed to the image of His Son"*** (Rom. 8:29)

It is impossible for us to fulfill these two conditions in our own strength. God has given us the Holy Spirit to enable us to fulfill this calling. However, we still encounter many temptations along the way that can cause us to compromise this high calling in God. **We must identify these and know how to deal with them.**

-4-

WHAT IS TEMPTATION?

★**Temptation is being enticed to do wrong through the promise of pleasure or gain.** The Christian is tempted when he is enticed to do something that would hurt or hinder God's purpose in his life.

There are many things in this life that could offer us a temporary pleasure or gain that must be resisted since they are contrary to the will of God. **Giving in to these temptations will hurt or destroy us spiritually.**

We must **choose the spiritual gain and reward** that obedience to God's will brings us rather than the temporary pleasures of sin. Moses chose *"rather to suffer affliction with the people of God than to enjoy the **passing pleasures of sin"*** (Heb. 11:25). The scriptures further say that he did so because *"he looked to the reward"* (Heb. 11:26).

-5-

THE SOURCE OF TEMPTATION

The scriptures identify Satan as a major source of temptation. He deliberately works against the purposes of God. He is called *"the tempter"*, *"your adversary"*, and the father of lies (I Thess. 3:5; I Pet. 5:8; John 8:44). **He is a master deceiver** who initiated the first temptation in the garden of Eden.

Not all temptation, though, is a direct attack by Satan. The fall resulted in all of mankind receiving a sin nature. **This fallen nature is filled with lusts or evil and excessive desires.** The born-again Christian still contends with the desires of the old nature (see Gal. 5:17). **Most of our temptations are a result of these desires being enticed.**

-6-

IN WHAT AREAS ARE WE TEMPTED?

★*"For all that is in the world - **THE LUST OF THE FLESH, THE LUST OF THE EYES**, and **THE PRIDE OF LIFE** - is not of the Father but is of the world"* (I John 2:16).

There are many different forms of temptation. However, **all temptations will fall into one of these areas:** the lust of the flesh, the lust of the eyes, or the pride of life. These areas are of the world and not of the Father.

Satan is called *"the god of this world"* (II Cor. 4:4, KJV). He seeks to set man's fulfillment above the will of God. Human pride and fleshly desires are a normal part of the spirit of this world.

Temptation works upon these three areas of the old nature to bring us into sin and bondage.

Let's examine each of these areas more closely.

-7-

I. THE LUST OF THE FLESH

The lust of the flesh has to do with our bodily appetites. God gave us our appetites and the pleasure associated with them, but He has also made His will clear in regards to the use and control of these appetites.

Sin has perverted these into excessive and selfish desires. Sexual immorality, drunkenness, gluttony, and drug addiction are some of the sins of the flesh.

Most of us were given over to these areas of fleshly lusts before our conversion to Christ. **We must resist the temptation to give in** to these areas anymore. We are told in Galatians 5:24 that *"those that are Christ's have crucified the flesh with its passions and desires."*

-8-

II. THE LUST OF THE EYES

The lust of the eyes is an excessive desire for the things of this world. The world appeals to this area like a Christmas tree enchants a small child. It attempts to capture our attention, getting us to **put material things in the place of God.**

There is nothing wrong with money or possessions in themselves. It is our relationship to them that causes problems. Matthew 6:33 commands us to *"seek first the kingdom of God."* I John 2:15 warns us to *"not love the world or the things in the world."*

Failure to *"set your affection on things above"* (Col. 3:2, KJV) will make you vulnerable to many temptations. **Covetousness, greed, idolatry, love of money, and financial dishonesty are a result of the lust of the eyes.**

-9-

III. THE PRIDE OF LIFE

The pride of life is the desire for self-glory. It comes from the self-centered tendency of our old nature.

We have each been given gifts, talents, and abilities by God. **The pride of life would use these apart from God,** or fail to give Him the glory for them.

The pride of life is tempted by worldly honors, reputation, and position. To achieve these, the world usually requires a compromise in our standards.

The Christians should **use his gifts and abilities for the glory of God,** remembering that *"He who glories, let him glory in the Lord"* (I Cor. 1:31).

-10-

JESUS OVERCAME TEMPTATION

In Hebrews 4:15 we find that **Jesus *"was in all points tempted as we are, yet without sin."*** Because of this, He was able to say to His disciples, *"Be of good cheer, I have overcome the world"* (John 16:33).

At the beginning of His ministry, He was led by the Spirit of God into the wilderness. There He was tempted by the devil for forty days. **Satan enticed Him in all three areas:** the lust of the flesh, the lust of the eyes, and the pride of life.

In each case, **Jesus resisted him and countered with the Word of God.** On the following page, we see the temptations He faced and how He responded.

-11-

The Lust of the Flesh

- **Temptation:** Having not eaten for forty days, Satan tempted Christ to turn a stone into a loaf of bread.

- **Jesus Responded:** *"It is written, 'Man shall not live by bread alone, but by every word of God' "* (Luke 4:4).

The Lust of the Eyes

- **Temptation:** Satan offered Christ the kingdoms of this world if He would worship him.

- **Jesus Responded:** *"It is written, 'You shall worship the Lord your God, and Him only you shall serve' "* (Luke 4:8).

The Pride of Life

- **Temptation:** Satan tempted Christ to jump off the temple in Jerusalem to prove that the angels would protect Him.

- **Jesus Responded:** *"It has been said, 'You shall not tempt the Lord your God' "* (Luke 4:12).

-12-

IS TEMPTATION SIN?

*"But each one is tempted when he is drawn away by his own desires and enticed. Then, **WHEN DESIRE HAS CONCEIVED, IT GIVES BIRTH TO SIN**"* (James 1:14, 15).

We are tempted when the world entices us through the flesh to do something against the will of God. Temptation is common to every believer.

Temptation, itself, is not sin. Jesus, Himself, was tempted. **When lust conceives, it brings forth sin.** This happens when our will acts in agreement with the temptation.

Temptation endeavors to capture our will and bring us into sin. Once this occurs, we give ourselves over to sinful thoughts, words, or deeds.

-13-

CAN I LIVE WITHOUT SINNING?

I John 1:8 states that *"if we say that we have no sin, we deceive ourselves, and the truth is not in us."* The flesh is the seat of sin. Therefore, total freedom from sin will have to wait until we shed these mortal bodies and *"shall have put on immortality"* (I Cor. 15:54, KJV).

However, the scriptures teach us that *"sin shall not have dominion over you, for you are not under law but under grace"* (Rom. 6:14). A life lived *"under grace"* gives us the desire to live for God, and the power to resist sin. If we should sin, God's forgiveness is available so that we would not be overcome with condemnation (see Rom. 8:1).

Each Christian should be growing in his victory over temptation and sin. We are *"more than conquerors through Him who loved us"* (Rom. 8:37).

-14-

YOU CAN OVERCOME TEMPTATION

"And God is faithful; he will not let you be tempted beyond what you can bear. But when you are tempted, he will also provide a way out so that you can stand up under it" (I Cor. 10:13, NIV).

God's Word promises us a way to triumph over every temptation.

Temptation always begins in our thoughts. The key to victory is to resist it right there. **We must not give in to entertaining sinful thoughts.** If we do, we must repent and receive forgiveness (see I John 1:9).

However, as long as the battle is kept in our minds and we do not sin in our actions, we are on our way to victory. **As we continue to resist, the temptation will lose its power.**

On the following pages of this booklet, we will see how we can triumph over temptation.

-15-

I. BUILD A STRONG SPIRITUAL LIFE

"Finally, my brethren, BE STRONG IN THE LORD and in the power of His might" (Eph. 6:10).

Building a strong spiritual life is "preventative maintenance" when it comes to resisting temptation. Jesus could resist all temptation because of His vital relationship to the Father.

Temptation can be compared to rocks in a stream bed. The water is like our spiritual life. If the level of the water is low, the rocks stick out and are easy to bump into. When the water is raised, the rocks are submerged and the boat easily floats over them.

A strong spiritual life keeps us from being susceptible to many temptations. We build this strength through consistent prayer, worship, Bible reading, and fellowship.

-16

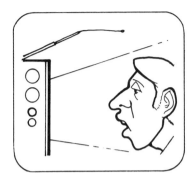

II. AVOID HARMFUL INFLUENCES

"Do not love the world or the things in the world" (I John 2:15).

Human beings can be subtly influenced by what they are exposed to. Knowing this, **we should protect ourselves from what would adversely affect us.**

Much of the music, literature, television, and movie programming in our society is polluted. We should control as much of this influence as is reasonably possible. We can do this by setting standards for the kind of entertainment we will participate in.

-17-

III. STAND ON THE WORD

*"For **THE WORD OF GOD IS LIVING AND POWERFUL,** and sharper than any two-edged sword"* (Heb. 4:12).

Jesus responded to every temptation in the wilderness by taking His stand on the Word of God. **Our commitment to God's Word allows us to rise above the influences of this world.**

I John 5:4 says *"and this is the victory that has overcome the world - our faith."* Where our faith is placed determines our response to temptations.

Therefore, we must be familiar with what the Bible teaches. We should **memorize scriptures** that apply to areas we are tempted in. As soon as temptation enters our thoughts, we should **counter with the Word of God.**

-18-

IV. FLEE FROM TEMPTATION

"FLEE ALSO YOUTHFUL LUSTS; but pursue righteousness" (II Tim. 2:22).

There are occasions when the **best way to handle temptation is to get away from it.** When Joseph was tempted by Potiphar's wife to commit adultery, it says that he *"fled and ran outside"* (Gen. 39:12).

Likewise, if our job, living situation, or other activities are causing us to stumble, we need to make a change.

God will always care for us if we are making choices in accordance with His will. We are told to *"seek first the kingdom of God and His righteousness, and all these things shall be added to you"* (Matt. 6:33).

-19-

V. RESIST THE DEVIL

*"Therefore submit to God. **RESIST THE DEVIL** and he will flee from you"* (James 4:7).

Satan will continue to press us until he is convinced that our commitment to God will not waver. **Once he sees that we will not give in, he will flee from us.**

He usually will not leave the first time you quote him a scripture. Instead, **he will test your commitment to the Word.**

Temptations often involve periods of time. We are told that *"blessed is the man who endures temptation"* (James 1:12), and that *"the trial of your faith, being much more precious than of gold that perisheth"* (I Pet. 1:7, KJV).

Through these temptations, our faith is enlarged and we learn how to draw from God's strength.

-20-

WHAT IF I FALL?

"IF WE CONFESS OUR SINS, HE IS FAITHFUL AND JUST TO FORGIVE US OUR SINS AND TO CLEANSE US FROM ALL UNRIGHTEOUSNESS" (I John 1:9).

The sincere Christian takes sin very seriously. We want to live for God. If we do fall into temptation, our hearts are grieved.

However, **God makes provision for the fall.** If we confess and repent of our sin, **He will forgive us and cleanse us** from all guilt.

We then must forgive ourselves and go forward. Proverbs 24:16 says, *"For a righteous man may fall seven times and rise again."*

We must not fall under the condemnation of the devil who is called *"the accuser of our brethren"* (Rev. 12:10). He will attempt to drown you in discouragement and a sense of failure.

-21-

◄ CONCLUSION ►

Christians are called to be overcomers. We are given a promise in Revelations 2:7: *"To him who overcomes I will give to eat from the tree of life, which is in the midst of the Paradise of God."*

Though we may experience occasional falls and temporary setbacks, as we yield ourselves to God, He will help us to become overcomers. **The future reward of our obedience will be great.**

For a brief summary of the main points of this booklet, read the words in bold print on each page.

◄ ASSIGNMENT ►

Memorize a scripture that declares God's will in the area you are being tempted in. Use it to counter any attacks on the enemy.

-22-

Chapter 6

Overcoming
Envy

BY TERRY D. EDWARDS

◀ INTRODUCTION ▶

All of us have had to cope with feelings of jealousy or envy. In fact, it is common to hear someone say, "Oh, I'm so jealous of her!" A statement like this usually indicates a harmless level of feeling.

Too often, though, **envy or jealousy is a serious matter,** and usually when it is, the person involved doesn't talk about it. They become consumed with intense feelings that seriously affect the way they think and feel about the person who they are jealous of.

In this booklet, we will see how serious this emotion is and examine the biblical steps for dealing with it.

-1-

◀ TABLE OF CONTENTS ▶

-2

WHAT IS ENVY?

Envy is a feeling of jealousy and resentment that arises when we become aware that another person is enjoying an advantage or blessing that we wish was ours.
Envy can be experienced in different degrees of intensity. It is usually felt more acutely toward people that are closer to us. We rarely feel intense envy when hearing of someone's good fortune that we don't know. There is great potential for envy in relation to those people we feel a competition with.

Once envy takes root in our heart, it becomes very destructive. Proverbs 27:4 says, *"Wrath is cruel, and anger is outrageous; but WHO IS ABLE TO STAND BEFORE ENVY?"*

-3-

WHAT IS IT'S SOURCE?

Galatians 5:21 identifies "envyings" as one of the works of the flesh. This emotion rises from our old sin nature.

The tendency of the old nature is to put "me first" ahead of both God and others. Romans 12:10 teaches that we should *"be kindly affectioned one to another with brotherly love; in honour preferring one another."*

Envy demonstrates the exact opposite of this. **We want the best for ourselves and actually begin desiring the worst for the one that we envy.**

Envious thoughts run contrary to the mind and will of God.

-4-

WHAT DOES ENVY DO?

I. ENVY HURTS YOU

"ENVY SLAYS THE SIMPLE" (Job 5:2, NIV).

Our jealousy of others works to destroy us in several ways:

1. **Envy produces self-centeredness** — Though the object of our envy is someone else, it produces a total absorption with ourselves. Self-centeredness always brings unhappiness and inner turmoil. Through it, we lose objectivity and our ability to reason fairly. The scriptures teach that *"A sound heart is the life of the flesh: but envy the rottenness of the bones"* (Prov. 14:30).

2. **Envy will progress to other stages** — Sin and self-preoccupation do not remain at the same level.

-5-

Left unchecked, they begin a downward spiral. **Envy easily progresses to self-pity, anger, bitterness, and even depression.** The psalmist writes, *"But as for me, my feet were almost gone; my steps had well nigh slipped. For I was envious at the foolish . . ."* (Psalms 73:2, 3). In this Psalm, this man had allowed envy and self-pity to bring him to the brink of rebellion against God.

3. **Envy will destroy our relationship with God** — We become angry that God has blessed someone else instead of ourself. We feel that He has passed over us and our desires. We begin to complain and murmur about our station in life. This attitude poisons our relationship with God.

-6-

ENVY HURTS OTHERS

The Bible teaches *"For where envying and strife is, there is confusion and every evil work"* (James 3:16). Envy is a dangerous passion that can cause us to strike out and hurt the person we are envious of. Let's examine some of the outworkings of envy.

1. ENVY LEADS TO STRIFE

"But if ye have BITTER ENVYING AND STRIFE in your hearts, glory not, and lie not against the truth" (James 3:14).

Envy and strife go hand in hand. We usually will not admit to others or even ourselves that we are envious. Instead, we *"lie . . . against the truth."* **We find other reasons that will justify our ill feelings toward the person. When this happens, the result is confusion and strife.**

-7-

2. ENVY LEADS TO SLANDER

*"To **SPEAK EVIL** of no man . . ."* (Titus 3:2).

The Bible teacher, **Bill Gothard, defines slander as "speaking the truth with a decision to hurt."**

Once envy gets hold of the tongue, it becomes a deadly little weapon. James 3:6 tells us that the tongue is *"set on fire of hell."* We will find ourselves saying just the right things about the person we envy in order to discredit their reputation. We can even make our motivation for sharing these negative statements appear spiritual. Underneath it all, we are striking out at that person. The "truths" that we share are designed to hurt them.

-8-

3. ENVY LEADS TO CRUELTY

*"And **his brethren envied him . . . and sold Joseph** to the Ishmeelites for twenty pieces of silver"* (Genesis 37: 11, 28).

Joseph was Jacob's favorite son. His brethren were jealous and developed a hatred for him. Joseph received a dream from God and recited it to his family. The implications were that they would be subservient to him. This infuriated his brethren all the more. They finally sold him into slavery to a band of Ishmeelites.

Envy may cause us to behave in a very cruel way. We may even devise plots whereby we can hurt the one we envy. Whatever the outworkings, envy will always put a "yoke of bondage" on the object of its cruelty.

-9-

4. ENVY LEADS TO REBELLION

*"**They envied Moses** also in the camp, and Aaron the saint of the Lord"* (Psalms 106:16).

Envy can lead us to rebellion against those in positions of spiritual oversight. This Psalm is speaking about an incident which occurred in the journeys of the children of Israel to the land of Canaan. **Korah led a revolt against Moses, claiming that he was assuming too much authority.**

After all attempts to change the mind of Korah had failed, the Lord had to respond with a severe judgment. **The earth opened and swallowed Korah and the others responsible for the revolt.**

We must guard our heart against a rebellious attitude that is based upon envy.

-10-

5. ENVY LEADS TO MURDER

"For he knew that FOR ENVY THEY HAD DE-LIVERED HIM" (Matt. 27:18).

The destructive nature of envy reached its peak when it motivated the religious leaders of Israel to seek Christ's death. Even Pilate, the Roman governor, knew that Jesus did not deserve this judgment. From the above verse, we see that he easily read the motivation behind their actions.

From what happened to Jesus, we can learn several more things about envy. First, we are likely to feel envy toward those who excel in our area of service. Secondly, **envy may cause us to strike out** at those who become popular and gain a following. Finally, **envy will prompt us to** eliminate those who threaten us.

-11-

WHAT DOES THE BIBLE SAY?

*"Therefore, **rid yourselves of all malice and all deceit, hyprocrisy, envy,** and slander of every kind"* (I Peter 2:1, NIV).

The Christian is commanded to get rid of all envy in his life. It is a work of the flesh, and will poison both the life of the individual and the life of the church.

We are told in Galatians 5:26 not to *"be desirous of vain glory, provoking one another, **envying** one another."* The believer is to be perfected in the love of God, and this love *"envieth not"* (I Cor. 13:4).

Victory over envy is your responsibility. You can rid yourself of this destructive passion. On the following pages, we will look at the five things that should be done in order to effectively deal with envy.

-12-

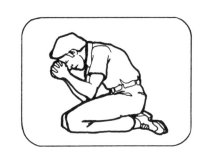

I. REPENT

*"**IF WE CONFESS OUR SINS,** he is faithful and just to forgive us our sins, and to cleanse us from all unrighteousness"* (I John 1:9).

Envy is sin. We have seen its destructive pattern and effects. We cannot treat this area of sin lightly in our lives. It will grow like a cancer.

As soon as you become conscious of envy in your heart, identify it and confess it to God. Be specific. Define exactly what it is and who it involves.

Ask God to forgive you and to cleanse your mind from those thoughts associated with it.

Determine to resist any further feelings of envy, should they come back.

-13-

II. REJOICE

*"**REJOICE** with them that do rejoice"* (Romans 12:15).

Victory over sin requires both a putting off of old attitudes, and a putting on of new ones. We must reject our sin and yield to truth and love.

In this case, our envy is based upon being jealous over another person's blessing. In our response, we are actually rejecting God. God chose to bless another person. We are refusing to rejoice in the will of God being done in that person's life.

We must now thank God for what He has done and wait before Him in prayer until we see our situation from God's perspective.

-14-

III. RECONCILE

*"Therefore, if you are offering your gift at the altar and there remember that your brother has something against you, leave your gift there in front of the altar. **FIRST GO AND BE RECONCILED TO YOUR BROTHER"** (Matt. 5:23, 24, NIV).*

As we have seen, we usually strike out at the person we are envious of. If this has been the case, **it is our responsibility to correct the harm that has been done.**

We need to go to those with whom we have shared slanderous information and apologize.

If we have openly hurt or mistreated the person we were envious of, then we must go to them and ask for forgiveness.

-15-

IV. ACCEPT YOUR CIRCUMSTANCES

"HUMBLE YOURSELVES therefore under the mighty hand of God, that he may exalt you in due time" (I Peter 5:6).

The Lord has infinite wisdom and understanding. He knows everything about you. We are told that *"the very hairs of your head are all numbered"* (Matt. 10:30). His mighty hand controls the destiny of the entire earth. **The circumstances of your life are also under His authority.**

Therefore, we should accept our circumstances and life situation without begrudging. We must give Him praise with faith in our hearts that *"**all things work together for good** to them that love God, to them who are the called according to his purpose"* (Rom. 8:28).

-16-

V. DEVELOP YOUR GIFTS

"His lord said unto him, Well done, good and faithful servant; **thou hast been faithful over a few things,** *I will make thee ruler over many things: enter thou into the joy of thy lord"* (Matt. 25:23).

The parable of the talents in Matthew 25 reveals some very important points. **The Lord gives each of us certain gifts, talents, and abilities.** We are only responsible for what He gives to us. If we are to be pleasing to God, we must develop and use our own gifts.

Often, we are envious of others for advancements or priviliges that they have earned. God has blessed them for their diligence and faithfulness with what He has given them. Likewise, **if we cultivate and use our abilities and gifts, we will also receive the blessing.**

-17-

◀ CONCLUSION ▶

The outworkings of envy are never good. If we will deal with envy with the harshness and honesty that it deserves, we will be delivered from it.

A victory over envy will increase our capacity to love others. We must turn envy into a genuine appreciation for the gifts and talents of others. We must also learn to respect God's right to bless whoever or wherever He choses.

All of this is part of the highest privilege of being conformed to the image of Christ.

For a brief overview of the main points in this booklet, please re-read the boldly printed words on each page.

-18-

Chapter 7

Victory In Affliction

By William R. Kimball

◀ INTRODUCTION ▶

Everyone experiences affliction. But it is a confusing subject for many, especially for Christians who soon discover that **it is a common occurence** in their lives.

This booklet offers a concise study of the reasons for affliction in the believer's life.

Before we start, let us pray that the Lord will give us understanding, and will quicken the scriptural keys for finding victory in all our afflictions.

-1-

◀ TABLE OF CONTENTS ▶

-2-

WHAT IS AFFLICTION?

Affliction is a broad term which includes many forms of adversity such as **trials, tribulations, persecution, mental and emotional stress, and even physical suffering.**

The Bible's word for affliction traces its original meaning back to an Assyrian form of torture. The Assyrians were a nation, during the Old Testament period, who were continual enemies with Israel. They were fond of torturing some of their prisoners by staking them to the ground and slowly piling rocks on them untill they were crushed to death under the weight of the stones.

-3-

The Greeks adopted the meaning of this form of torture into their language. The word **"affliction" came to mean, "the pressure and stress of unfavorable circumstances which befall a person's life."**

This same word is translated tribulation, persecution, troubled, burdened, and pressed in different passages. For example:

- *"We were **burdened** beyond measure . . ."* (II Cor. 1:8).
- *"We are **hard pressed** on every side . . ."* (II Cor. 4:8).
- *"I am exceedingly joyful in all our **tribulation"*** (II Cor. 7:4).

As we can see, affliction includes many forms of adversity.

-4-

THE PROBLEM WITH AFFLICTION

Many Christians do not understand why afflictions still exist in their new life. Some are deeply troubled and confused. Often, this is due to **the mistaken belief that Christianity somehow guarantees us immunity from pressures and problems, trials and tribulations.**

Some have been subtly misled by the false notion that our "abundant life" in Christ means freedom from troubles. Consequently, many are shaken in the faith when afflictions begin to arise (see Mark 4:17).

The problem with affliction is one which God's people have struggled with for centuries. The first step to understanding this difficult subject is to see what the scriptures say.

-5-

WHAT DO THE SCRIPTURES SAY?

- **PETER** cautioned us not to view the sudden appearance of trials as an unusual event in the believer's life: *"Beloved, DO NOT THINK IT STRANGE concerning the FIERY TRIAL which is to try you, as though some STRANGE THING happened to you"* (I Pet. 4:12).

- **PAUL** reminded us that, *"we MUST THROUGH MANY TRIBULATIONS enter the kingdom of God"* (Acts 14:22). He also told us *"That we would SUFFER TRIBULATION"*, and even went so far as to remind us that God had appointed us to go through them! (I Thess. 3:3, 4).

- **JESUS** even warned the church of coming tribulations: *"IN THE WORLD YOU WILL HAVE TRIBULATION; but be of good cheer, I have overcome the world!"* (John 16:33).

-6-

WHO SUFFERS FROM AFFLICTION?

★**Everyone!** Both the believer and the unbeliever experience the pressures of affliction.

Sometimes it is much easier to understand why the ungodly suffers from affliction, especially when we consider his sin and rebellion against God: *"Fools, because of their transgression, and because of their iniquities, are afflicted"* (Psalms 107:17, KJV).

However, it is not so easy to understand why the godly suffers from affliction, especially when he loves God and serves Him willingly. But the Bible is filled with examples of the righteous suffering affliction, and even declares that, *"MANY are the AFFLICTIONS OF THE RIGHTEOUS"* (Psalms 34:19). There is some comfort in knowing that even godly people suffer affliction.

-7-

WHAT ARE SOME GODLY EXAMPLES?

- **JOB** said, *"see thou MINE AFFLICTION"* (Job 10:15, KJV).
- **MOSES** chose *"to SUFFER AFFLICTION with the people of God"* (Heb. 11:25).
- **DAVID** said, *"I am AFFLICTED very much"* (Psalms 119:107).
- **THE PROPHETS** — *"Take, my brethren, the prophets . . . FOR AN EXAMPLE OF SUFFERING AFFLICTION"* (James 5:10, KJV).
- **JESUS** *". . . was oppressed and He was AFFLICTED"* (Isaiah 53:7).
- **PAUL** *". . . out of MUCH AFFLICTION and anguish of heart I wrote to you, with many tears"* (II Cor. 2:4).

-8-

WHY DOES GOD ALLOW AFFLICTION?

It's not enough to know that godly people suffer affliction. Many want to know why — even Moses cried, *"WHY have You afflicted Your servant?"* (Numbers 11:11).

— Afflictions Are For Our Own Good —

David stated that God *"IN FAITHFULNESS HAST AFFLICTED ME"* (Psalms 119:75, KJV).

Q. Why would David thank God for faithfully afflicting him?

A. Because he had discovered that there was a divine purpose in them, and that purpose was good. Before we can successfully deal with our own afflictions, **we must recognize that they have a divine purpose in our lives,** and that God is working that purpose for our good.

-9-

ARE AFFLICTIONS WORKING FOR OUR GOOD?

★**Yes!** The scriptures are very clear on this point.

"For our light affliction, which is but for a moment, is working for us a far more exceeding and eternal weight of glory" (II Cor. 4:17). This verse reveals that **our afflictions are working for us a *"FAR MORE EXCEEDING AND ETERNAL WEIGHT OF GLORY!"*** They are working for us, not against us.

"And we know that all things work together for good to those who love God, to those who are the called according to His purpose" (Rom. 8:28). Again, this scripture reveals that **all things are working for us** — not just the good things, or some things, or most things, but **all** things. **THIS INCLUDES ALL OF OUR AFFLICTIONS.**

-10-

WHAT GOOD DOES AFFLICTION ACCOMPLISH?

A. **It produces Christ-like character in our lives.** God wants to mold us into His image. One of the most effective ways of accomplishing this is through the pressures of affliction.

- Just as **a diamond is formed through intense pressure,** Christ's character is formed in our lives through the pressures of adversity.

- Just as **gold is purified through intense heat,** our character is refined and perfected through the flames of adversity: *"Behold, I have refined you . . . I have tested you in the furnace of affliction"* (Isaiah 48:10).

Christ's character is often forged in the blast furnace of affliction.

-11-

As we have seen, our light afflictions work for us *"a far more exceeding and eternal weight of glory"* (II Cor. 4:17).

Our afflictions are like employees who work for us. They are diligently working on our behalf to produce the eternal qualities of Christ-likeness in our lives. God often produces the *"fruit of the Spirit"* in us through the afflictions we experience.

- When God wants to produce **peace**, He doesn't bring peaceful situations but trials and stress.

- When God wants to produce **love,** He often brings disagreeable, insensitive people into our lives.

- When God wants to produce **longsuffering** — you've got it, He allows us to suffer long.

-12-

AFFLICTIONS BUILD OUR FAITH

Our natural tendency is to think that afflictions weaken us and undermine our faith. But just the opposite is true. The trials and tribulations of life actually build up our faith.

Just as an athlete exercises diligently to build up his muscles, the pressures which come into our lives work to increase our faith. They work to strengthen our trust and confidence in God.

Paul praised the Thessalonians because their faith increased greatly in the midst of their afflictions and persecutions (II Thess. 1:3, 4).

-13-

AFFLICTIONS BUILD SPIRITUAL ENDURANCE

". . . but we glory in tribulations also: KNOW-ING THAT TRIBULATION WORKETH PA-TIENCE" (Rom. 5:3, KJV).

The word **"patience" simply means endur-ance.**

Again, our natural tendency is to view tribulations as obstacles which hinder our spiritual progress and weary us.

But just the opposite is true. They produce endurance and fortitude. They build determination in us to keep pressing forward in God. Just as James reminds us: **"Knowing that the testing of your faith produces patience"** (James 1:3).

-14-

AFFLICTIONS HELP US COMFORT OTHERS

*"Blessed be the God . . . who comforts us in all our tribulation, that **WE MAY BE ABLE TO COMFORT THOSE WHO ARE IN ANY TROUBLE . . ."** (II Cor. 1:3, 4).*

Afflictions equip us to comfort others. The school of affliction trains us in the fine art of ministering the comfort of God. Often, those who have suffered adversity are better prepared to relate to others who are experiencing afflictions.

One of the great benefits of afflictions is that they help us to be sensitive to the hurts and pains of others. **The afflictions that we have experienced help us to feel the problems of others as our own,** and minister to them the tenderness, understanding, and love of God which they need.

-15-

HOW SHOULD WE RESPOND TO OUR AFFLICTIONS?

Many think that the only victory in affliction is in escaping from them or when they finally end. The Christian challenge is to find our victory **IN** our affliction and not **AFTER** our affliction. **God is glorified when we find victory in the midst of affliction.**

The foundation for victory is built upon a proper attitude towards afflictions. We must recognize that they have a divine purpose. We must see them as God does. We must correct our perspective, and line it up with what the Word of God declares. We must place our faith in the reality that *"ALL things work together for good . . ."*(Rom. 8:28). This is the first step to victory.

Often, we must examine our attitude and **clear our hearts of any bitterness or anger towards the afflictions we experience.**

-16-

I. WE SHOULD PRAISE THE LORD

"IN EVERYTHING GIVE THANKS . . ." (I Thess. 5:18).

When we see that afflictions aren't a curse but a blessing, we have good reason to rejoice in the Lord.

We can react negatively to our afflictions, or we can react positively. **We can resent them as unwelcomed intruders, or we can receive them as faithful friends.**

To those who respond with a negative spirit, *"all the days of the afflicted are evil"* (Prov. 15:15). Those who recognize a beneficial purpose in their afflictions can have the same confession as James who said: **"Consider it pure joy, my brothers, whenever you face trials of many kinds"** (James 1:2, NIV).

-17-

II. WE SHOULD PRAY

"Is any among you afflicted? LET HIM PRAY" (James 5:13, KJV).

Afflictions should bring us closer to the Lord in communion and prayer. When adversities, trials, and pressures come into our lives, we should turn to the Lord in prayer. Rather than trouble our lives needlessly by communing with our fears, natural understanding, and insecurities, we should look to Jesus.

Prayer is often the key to comfort, peace, confidence, and understanding in Christ. Often, we do not understand why an affliction has come into our life. But prayer unlocks the door to understanding and insight. Prayer focuses us upon the power of God, instead of our problems.

-18-

III. WE SHOULD LOOK TO GOD'S WORD

"Before I was afflicted I went astray, but now I keep **Your word**" (Psalms 119: 67).

Afflictions should direct us to the counsel of God's Word for answers.

As we have already seen in this booklet, the Bible has a great deal to say about affliction. The Bible has all the answers for every problem in life. God wants us to go to His Word because it is a source of comfort, encouragement, and understanding.

- *"This is my comfort in my affliction, for* **Your word** *has given me life"* (Psalms 119:50).

- *"Unless* **Your law** *had been my delight, I would then have perished in my affliction"* (Psalms 119:92).

-19-

IV. WE SHOULD EXERCISE FAITH AND PATIENCE

"Rejoicing in hope, **PATIENT IN TRIBULATION,** *continuing steadfastly in prayer"* (Romans 12:12).

Patience is an important ingredient in achieving victory. Without it we soon become impatient and frustrated in our afflictions.

Our natural tendency is to react impatiently and squirm out of our afflictions as soon as possible. When we do this, we fail to give God the time He needs to accomplish what He desires in our life.

If we look to Jesus and wait patiently upon Him, we give God room to perfect the good work He wants in us, that we may become all that He intends us to be.

"But let patience have its perfect work, that you may be perfect and complete, lacking nothing" (James 1:4).

-20-

WHAT ARE GOD'S PROMISES TO THE AFFLICTED?

- **DELIVERANCE:** *"Many are the afflictions of the righteous, but the Lord delivers him out of them all"* (Psalms 34:19).

- **MERCY:** *" . . . the Lord has comforted His people, and will have mercy on His afflicted"* (Isaiah 49:13).

- **HEARS HIS PRAYER:** *" . . . for He hears the cry of the afflicted"* (Job 34:28).

- **GOD FEELS OUR AFFLICTIONS:** *"In all their affliction He was afflicted . . . "* (Isaiah 63:9).

- **GOD DOESN'T DESPISE THE AFFLICTED:** *"For He has not despised . . . . the affliction of the afflicted"* (Psalms 22:24).

[Additional Scriptures: Romans 8:35; Hebrews 13:5; Jeremiah 16:19; Psalms 18:27.]

-21-

◄ CONCLUSION ►

The Christian life is not just a life of fun and relaxation. God has a destiny for His people, and a divine purpose to fulfill. He wants to conform us into *"the image of His Son"* (Rom. 8:29). One of the ways He accomplishes this is through afflictions. The Bible clearly states that *"all things work together for good to those who love God, to those who are the called according to His purpose"* (Rom. 8:28). They do so in order to conform us into His image. **It doesn't say that all things are good, but that all things are working for our good.** This is a liberating revelation. When we embrace this truth, we begin to see that **our afflictions are not a curse, but a blessing designed by God to truly benefit our lives.** When we receive this revelation, we can **join with the Apostle Paul in declaring, *"WE ALSO GLORY IN TRIBULATIONS"*** (Romans 5:3).

For a brief overview of the main points in this booklet, please re-read the boldly printed words on each page.

-22-

Chapter 8

Conquering Condemnation

By William R. Kimball

◀ INTRODUCTION ▶

Condemnation is a common condition which we all inevitably encounter. But **it is a particularly troublesome problem for many Christians.** It's easy to understand why a sinful and rebellious world experiences condemnation. But it is often quite difficult to comprehend why Christians experience it. This is especially true when we consider the fact that we have been cleansed, forgiven, and reconciled to God.

In this counseling booklet, we will present a concise study on the subject of condemnation. **We will offer some liberating keys for overcoming this problem area in our lives.**

-1-

◀ TABLE OF CONTENTS ▶

-2-

WHAT IS CONDEMNATION?

Condemnation is not easily defined. Capturing the essential meaning of this term can present us with a difficult challenge.

Simply stated, **condemnation carries the thought of a judgment against wrong-doing.** In a strict legal sense, it conveys the thought of a verdict executed against a transgressor. **It includes the thought of irreversible punishment.** It is a hard, judicial sentence which, by its very nature, demands punishment and wrath against the offender.

-3-

CONDEMNATION VERSUS CONVICTION

There are distinct differences between condemnation and conviction. **Condemnation carries an air of finality and doom. It offers absolutely no hope or help for the offender.** It is a harsh, irrevocable judgment which ignores the mercy and grace of God and focuses solely upon the aspects of punishment and reprisal. It is a futile, dead-end situation for the transgressor.

Conviction, on the other hand, is merciful. It leads the offender to repentance. While condemnation is harsh and destructive, conviction is compassionate and constructive. It leads the wrong-doer to recovery and restoration. Though God lovingly convicts us, He never condemns us when we are judged: *"The Lord will not . . . condemn him when he is judged'* (Psalms 37:33).

-4-

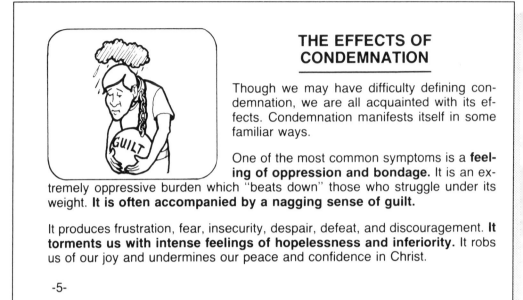

THE EFFECTS OF CONDEMNATION

Though we may have difficulty defining condemnation, we are all acquainted with its effects. Condemnation manifests itself in some familiar ways.

One of the most common symptoms is a **feeling of oppression and bondage.** It is an extremely oppressive burden which "beats down" those who struggle under its weight. **It is often accompanied by a nagging sense of guilt.**

It produces frustration, fear, insecurity, despair, defeat, and discouragement. **It torments us with intense feelings of hopelessness and inferiority.** It robs us of our joy and undermines our peace and confidence in Christ.

-5-

WHO IS UNDER CONDEMNATION?

". . . through one man's offense (Adam) judgment came to all men, resulting in condemnation" (Romans 5:18).

The entire human race has been subjected to the righteous condemnation of God. The sins of mankind have brought the world under the divine judgment of God (Romans 1:18). The only exceptions are those who have surrendered to Christ:

"He who believes in Him is NOT CONDEMNED; but he who does not believe is condemned already, because he has not believed in the name of the only begotten Son of God. And this is the CONDEMNATION, that light has come into the world, and men loved darkness rather than light, because their deeds were evil" (John 3:18, 19).

-6-

IS CONDEMNATION MEANT FOR CHRISTIANS?

★**Absolutely not!** *"There is therefore NOW NO CONDEMNATION to those who are in Christ Jesus, who do not walk according to the flesh, but according to the Spirit"* (Romans 8:1).

God is not the author of our condemnation. It is not His will that we suffer condemnation in any form. Christ has provided complete deliverance for the following reasons:

1. **We Are Not Under the Law but Grace** — We are no longer under the penalty and curse of the Law. We are no longer under the *"ministry of condemnation"* (II Cor. 3:9). **Christ fulfilled the demands of the Law** through His sacrificial death. He satisfied God's justice, **so we are no longer under condemnation but under God's loving grace.**

-7-

2. **We Are Justified** — We have been forgiven and made righteous in Christ. We are now justified and in right standing with God. *"It is God who justifies. Who is he who condemns?"* (Rom. 8:33, 34).

3. **We Are at Peace with God** — *"Therefore, having been justified by faith, we have peace with God through our Lord Jesus Christ"* (Rom. 5:1). **Since we are no longer hostile to God, we are no longer under His divine condemnation and wrath.** We are reconciled to God and at peace with Him.

4. **We Are Righteous in Christ** — *"For He made Him who knew no sin to be sin for us, that we might become the righteousness of God in Him"* (II Cor. 5:21). Since **we are no longer unrighteous transgressors,** we are not subject to the condemnation of God.

-8-

WHAT IS THE SOURCE OF CONDEMNATION?

There are two predominant sources of unrighteous condemnation which afflict us:

1. **SATAN:** He is the greatest source of condemnation. He is called ***"the accuser of our brethren"*** (Rev. 12:10, KJV). He constantly badgers Christians with accusations, criticism, and condemnation. He attacks our minds with the "fiery darts" of condemnation in order to wear us down and bring us into mental bondage.

   Since Satan abides under the constant condemnation of God, he seeks to share his condemnation with us. He tries to undermine our testimony of righteousness by destroying us with condemnation. He knows that as long as our witness remains, it stands as an open judgment against him.

-9-

2. **SELF:** *"For if our heart condemn us . . ."* (I John 3:20). Though we may not realize it, we are often guilty of compounding the condemnation of Satan by inflicting incredible amounts of self-condemnation upon ourselves.

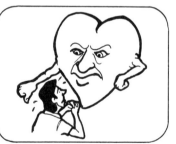

We often give Satan the day off and work overtime condemning ourselves. **Some people are very hard on themselves.** They possess little patience or tolerance for their shortcomings and imperfections. Consequently, when they don't "measure up" to their own expectations or standards, they retaliate by tormenting themselves with condemnation. **Though God no longer condemns us, many spend their lives in a perpetual state of self-condemnation.**

-10-

WHY DO WE EXPERIENCE CONDEMNATION?

On the following pages, we will review the reasons why Christians needlessly allow themselves to fall under the condemnation of Satan and self:

I. POOR SELF-ESTEEM

Many people possess little or no self-esteem. They often feel "good-for-nothing", and suffer from a deep sense of inferiority and worthlessness. Low self-esteem is particularly susceptible to condemnation.

Our present self-image is often the result of past conditioning. **If we grew up in an overbearing, critical, or judgmental environment, we may lack a genuine sense of approval, acceptance, or self-worth.** This condition can often contribute to poor self-esteem and an attitude which is self-depreciating and self-condeming.

-11-

II. AN IMPROPER VIEW OF GOD

Many Christians possess a distorted concept of the way God relates to us. They don't see Him as a loving Father, but as a stern, exacting judge.

It's hard for some to accept the reality that God truly loves us and accepts us. **Many Christians have a deep-seated notion that God disapproves of them.** They secretly feel that He is a critical Father with impossible demands, who is impossible to please.

This negative perspective only reinforces the potential for condemnation, and allows Satan to beat us down with the feeling that God doesn't really like us or accept us.

-12-

III. WHEN WE FAIL

*"For **a righteous man may fall seven times** ..."* (Prov. 24:16). In the process of growing unto perfection, we may occasionally fall short. If we react improperly, we can fall into self-condemnation.

We often respond to our weaknesses, shortcomings, and inadequacies by condemning ourselves. **Our past mistakes can create a sense of failure and frustration which leads to self-criticism and condemnation.**

Not only do we have a tendency to beat ourselves down when we fall short, but Satan is only too willing to take advantage of our failures. He loves to ridicule, criticize, and belittle us in order to produce a spirit of defeat and condemnation.

-13-

IV. SELF-PUNISHMENT

Christians can sometimes fall into the deceitful trap of self-punishment. **When we make mistakes or commit sins, we may attempt to make atonement in our own strength.** We can try to alleviate the guilt by paying for our errors through the self-inflicted pain of condemnation.

Rather than accepting the cleansing forgiveness which Christ alone can provide, we foolishly afflict ourselves with penance. We torment ourselves mentally and emotionally until we feel that we have suffered sufficiently.

This kind of condemnation is a subtle form of self-works. It is a destructive and sinful tendency toward self-justification which ignores God's grace, and overlooks His cleansing power. It is a common source of self-condemnation.

-14-

V. THE CONDEMNATION OF OTHERS

We occasionally encounter relationships which produce a subtle feeling of condemnation in our life. These relationships can involve casual associations, friends, and even loved ones.

People sometimes relate to us in a legalistic manner. Some individuals are extremely judgmental. They carry a critical, intolerant attitude towards others. They are excessively demanding, and impose unreasonable expectations upon those around them.

Their relationships with others is based on performance. They cannot tolerate those who fail to "measure up" to their strict standards. When people fall short, they retaliate by inflicting a judgmental spirit of condemnation upon them.

-15-

VI. UNRESOLVED GUILTS FROM THE PAST

Many people suffer from longstanding guilt feelings from the past. These unresolved feelings are often an underlying cause of condemnation.

Some individuals are haunted with memories of the sins they committed before they were saved. They have not fully accepted God's cleansing and forgiveness, so they find it difficult to forgive themselves, or forget the mistakes of yesterday. The consequence is often self-condemnation.

Satan also capitalizes upon these deep-seated memories by tormenting us with guilt and condemnation. He delights in reminding us of our past failures. Some of the more common areas of unresolved guillt are: **divorces, broken relationships, abortions, sexual sins, harmful acts against others, and past backslidings.**

-16-

IS THERE A SOLUTION TO CONDEMNATION?

★**Yes!** Since God is not willing that we suffer from condemnation, He provides the necessary counsel and direction through His Word to combat this problem.

The scriptures declare that, "*. . . if our heart condemns us, GOD IS GREATER THAN OUR HEART, and knows all things*" (I John 3:20).

We have assurances through the Word that God is greater than any problem we may encounter. He is able to supply the necessary guidance and insight, in spite of the condemnation we are experiencing. If we will give proper attention to His counsel, rather than the faulty counsel of our own hearts, we will find a release from condemnation.

-17

HOW SHOULD WE RESPOND TO CONDEMNATION?

There are several vital keys for overcoming condemnation. We will examine them on the following pages. However, the most important step is to challenge the "lie of condemnation."

I. CHALLENGE THE LIE

The first step is to take immediate, decisive action. We must strike at the root of the problem. **We must forcefully reject the deceitful lie that condemnation is acceptable for God's people.**

We must recognize that this is a lie from the father of lies (John 8:44). As long as we accept this falsehood and entertain this deception, we will subject ourselves to further condemnation.

-18-

II. WE MUST STAND ON GOD'S WORD

"If our heart does not condemn us, we have confidence toward God" (I John 3:21). We must **set our confidence and trust upon the reality of God's Word** in order to gain deliverance from condemnation.

We must challenge the spirit of condemnation with truth. We must wash our minds with the cleansing power of scripture. The scriptures clearly state that, *"He who believes in Him IS NOT CONDEMNED"* (John 3:18). This statement is emphatic.

We must discipline our thought life with the absolute reality of God's Word. *"There is THEREFORE NOW NO CONDEMNATION . . ."* (Romans 8:1). If we will stand firmly upon this truth, we will be liberated from the spirit of condemnation.

-19-

III. WE MUST CORRECT A WRONG SELF-IMAGE

As we have stated, a poor self-image can be a significant contributing factor to condemnation. Our past experiences can adversely affect our present attitudes.

We must recognize that *"in Christ"* our past has been washed away. We are now *"new creations"* in Christ (II Cor. 5:17). Therefore, **we must reject the corrupt feelings of inadequacy, worthlessness, and inferiority which result in self-condemnation.**

We must embrace the reality of who we now are in Christ. We are no longer unacceptable, but *"accepted in the Beloved"* (Eph. 1:6). We are *"sons and daughters"* of God (II Cor. 6:18). We possess dignity, honor and destiny (Rom. 8:29). We've been made useful, profitable, and valuable to God (I Cor. 12:15-27). **Godly self-esteem is a powerful remedy for self-condemnation.**

-20-

IV. RENEW OUR CONCEPT OF GOD

As we have stated, much of our condemnation can be traced back to a distorted and inaccurate view of how God relates to us.

The picture which the scriptures paint is vastly different than the one we often discolor. He is not a harsh judge just waiting for us to make the slightest mistake so He can punish us with condemnation. **He is not a religious tyrant, an exacting ruler, or a disapproving Father.**

He is the loving Father who so loves us that He *"gave His only begotten son"* for us (John 3:16). **He accepts us, approves of us, and embraces us** with the same heartfelt love as the father in the parable of the prodigal son (Luke 15:11-24).

-21-

V. WE MUST PROPERLY ACCEPT OUR IMPERFECTIONS

The familiar bumper sticker reads, "Christians aren't perfect — just forgiven." However, many Christians have a hard time accepting this truth. Instead of graciously accepting the reality that we will inevitably make mistakes, they punish themselves with self-criticism and condemnation.

As we grow unto perfection, we are going to occasionally fall short. Even Paul stated that he had not yet reached perfection (Phil. 3:12-15). The Bible states that *"A righteous man may fall seven times and rise again"* (Prov. 24:16). Though a righteous man sometimes falls, he gets up.

If we do occasionally "slip-up", we must not allow ourselves to wallow in self-pity or dwell upon defeat and self-condemnation. We must rise up in faith, brush ourselves off, and continue on to perfection in God's forgiveness and grace.

-22-

VI. WE MUST PROPERLY RESPOND TO THOSE WHO CONDEMN US

We can do this in the following ways:

1. **We must recognize that there is no justified condemnation for Christians** who are walking after the Spirit and not after the flesh (Rom. 8:1). The scriptures challenge any source of condemnation against our life: *"Who is he who condemns?"* (Rom. 8:34).

2. **We must respond to those who condemn us in a Christ-like way.** Jesus endured the ultimate condemnation of all: *"And THEY ALL CONDEMNED HIM to be worthy of death"* (Mark 14:64). But He did not retaliate with hatred or vengence. He responded in love and forgiveness. He set the example that we might not be *"overcome by evil, but overcome evil with good"* (Rom. 12:21).

-23-

VII. WE MUST BURY THE PAST

*"... but ONE thing I do, **forgetting those things which are behind** and reaching forward to those things which are ahead, I press toward the goal ..."* (Phil. 3:13, 14).

We must bury the negative thoughts and guilts of the past. God no longer remembers our former sins, so we must not dwell upon them either. *"Their sins and iniquities will I REMEMBER NO MORE"* (Heb. 10:17, KJV).

We must *"**lay aside every weight,** and the sin which so easily ensnares us ..."* (Heb. 12:1). **This includes the burden of guilt and the haunting memories of yesterday.** We must accept the reality that *"old things have passed away; behold, all things have become new"* (II Cor. 5:17).

-24-

VIII. DEAL WITH UNRESOLVED SIN(S)

If we fail to deal with our sins, whether publicly or privately, we may gradually pay the price in condemnation.

A reluctance to co-operate with the convicting power of the Holy Ghost can create inner tensions and guilt which produces increasing condemnation.

The Scriptures teach us that *"There is . . . now no condemnation to those . . . who do not walk according to the flesh, but according to the Spirit"* (Rom. 8:1). **If we are walking after the flesh and failing to confess our sins and seek Christ's cleansing, the sense of conviction will eventually turn into a feeling of condemnation.**

-25-

◄ CONCLUSION ►

We have briefly examined the causes and cures for condemnation. We should carefully review the scriptural responses which apply to our personal situation, and make a determined commitment to follow them:

1. **Challenge the lie of condemnation.**
2. We must **stand on God's Word.**
3. We must **correct a wrong self-image.**
4. We must **renew our personal concept of God.**
5. We must **properly accept our imperfections.**
6. We must **properly respond to those who condemn us.**
7. We must **bury the past.**
8. We must **deal with an unresolved sin(s).**

For a brief overview of the main points covered in this booklet, please re-read the boldly printed words on each page.

-26-

94

Chapter 9

Overcoming
Loneliness

BY WILLIAM R. KIMBALL

◄ INTRODUCTION ►

Loneliness has troubled mankind since the beginning of time. Adam's relationship with God was disrupted, and humanity has suffered from the pain of loneliness ever since.

It may be easy to understand why an unbeliever who lives in a self-centered world with no meaningful fellowship with God can suffer loneliness, but it is not so easy to understand why Christians occasionally suffer also. This is a difficult subject for many.

In this booklet we will examine this subject and offer some helpful guidelines for achieving victory over our loneliness.

-1-

◄ TABLE OF CONTENTS ►

-2-

WHAT IS LONELINESS?

Loneliness is "an emotional feeling of sadness and dejection because of a lack of companionship or separation from others."

Loneliness is a sickening feeling of being "left out", rejected, and unwanted. It is a feeling of being removed and "cut off" from others, whether real or imagined. It is a painful awareness that we lack meaningful contact with other people.

It is a sense of inner emptiness accompanied by an intense longing to be needed and wanted by someone else.

-3-

HOW DOES LONELINESS AFFECT PEOPLE?

Whether loneliness lasts for a few moments or persists for a lifetime, it affects us in some common ways. Feelings of rejection, isolation, hopelessness, despair, and anxiety often characterize loneliness. Loneliness commonly manifests itself in a sad countenance or dejected look.

One of the predominant characteristics is a tendency to withdraw from others. **Lonely people often retreat into a state of self-centeredness, discouragement, and self-pity.** They often carry a "poor me" attitude which fosters a feeling that no one really cares or understands.

Occasionally, lonely people attempt to conceal their loneliness by escaping into drugs, alcohol, and other diversions.

-4-

HOW COMMON IS LONELINESS?

Loneliness is such a common problem that it periodically afflicts everyone. It has been called one of the most universal causes of human suffering.

Loneliness has no favorites. It strikes both young and old, men and women, rich and poor, educated and uneducated, healthy and unhealthy, godly and ungodly.

It is so widespread that it has reached epidemic proportions. It is estimated that **75 to 95% of all Americans suffer from chronic loneliness.** It is a major source of unhappiness and pain in today's world.

-5-

WHAT DOES THE BIBLE SAY?

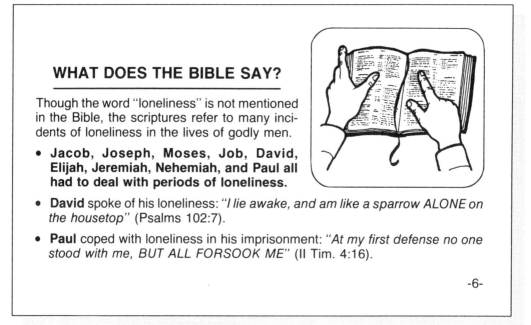

Though the word "loneliness" is not mentioned in the Bible, the scriptures refer to many incidents of loneliness in the lives of godly men.

- **Jacob, Joseph, Moses, Job, David, Elijah, Jeremiah, Nehemiah, and Paul all had to deal with periods of loneliness.**

- **David** spoke of his loneliness: *"I lie awake, and am like a sparrow ALONE on the housetop"* (Psalms 102:7).

- **Paul** coped with loneliness in his imprisonment: *"At my first defense no one stood with me, BUT ALL FORSOOK ME"* (II Tim. 4:16).

-6-

COMMON CAUSES OF LONELINESS

One of the most significant, underlying causes of loneliness is the present condition of the world.

Our fast-paced, ever-changing, materialistic world tends to breed loneliness. **The de-humanizing spirit of this age actually isolates people from close, meaningful contact.** It disrupts relationships, severs friendships, breaks up families, destroys a neighborhood and community spirit, and causes people to avoid close relationships which could eventually end in painful separation.

The characteristics of this age tend to force relationships into shallow, short-lived experiences which often result in inevitable loneliness.

-7-

LOW SELF-ESTEEM

Lonely people often have a negative opinion of themselves. Poor self-esteem or feelings of worthlessness can be both a symptom and a cause of loneliness.

Poor self-esteem produces a destructive feeling of uselessness and inadequacy. These individuals have little self-confidence.

They conclude that since they are unwanted and unloved, they are not worth anything.

When we embrace these feelings, it makes it difficult to build relationships. Low self-esteem makes people feel intimidated, weak, and shy. **These attitudes only alienate us further by causing us to withdraw from people, thus reinforcing our sense of isolation and loneliness.**

-8-

NEGATIVE ATTITUDES

Some people harbor self-defeating attitudes which create loneliness. Attitudes of self-pity, self-centeredness, anger, or fear actually drive people away and deepen the feelings of being isolated and unloved.

1. **Self-pity** — Self-pity contributes to loneliness. Some people nurse a "poor-little-me" attitude which ministers constant self-doubt and criticism. They frequently remind themselves that no one really cares or understands them. This negative confession only deepens the "cycle of loneliness", and creates a negative attitude in a person's life which others are reluctant to fellowship with.

-9-

2. **Self-centeredness** — Some people are so ambitious, pushy, competitive, egotistical, or critical and intolerant of others that they repel people. This conceited pride is only concerned with self. It is a quick "turn-off" to others. It soon destroys any potential relationships.

3. **Anger** — Some individuals cannot build relationships because of their underlying attitude of antagonism and hostility. This "uptight" characteristic intimidates others and quickly drives them away.

4. **Fear** — Many people are insecure, intimidated, and fearful. Fear of intimacy, rejection, or being hurt can erect barriers which prevent a person from reaching out to others and breaking the deadlock of loneliness.

-10-

SITUATIONAL CAUSES

There are certain circumstances which tend to contribute to a state of isolation and loneliness. **We all face situations which increase the potential for loneliness.**

When we are single, living alone, widowed, elderly, or grieving, we are particularly susceptible to loneliness. For example, we've all experienced homesickness and loneliness when separated from loved ones by time and distance.

Those who are in leadership positions, wealthy, exceptionally talented, newcomers to an area, foreigners, handicapped, or suffering from deformities and disease are especially subject to lonelines.

-11-

SPIRITUAL CAUSES

One of the underlying factors in loneliness is an individual's lack of vital relationship with God. Often, a deficiency in this area of the human experience will be a significant contributing factor to loneliness.

Man was created to have a meaningful realtionship with God. We were destined to find our ultimate fulfillment through an intimate fellowship with our Creator. Because of man's rebellion and sin, that relationship was severed. When this divine purpose is disrupted or unrealized, men experience a spiritual emptiness which often results in loneliness.

People in the world experience a great deal of inner frustration and loneliness because of a non-existent or inadequate relationship with God.

-12-

IS THERE HOPE?

★**Yes!** Loneliness is not a dead end. It is not a hopeless situation. **God understands the problem intimately and offers the keys to victory.**

Even Jesus endured loneliness. He tasted the ultimate agony of loneliness when He cried out on the cross, *"My God, My God, why have You forsaken Me?"* (Matthew 27:46).

There is genuine comfort in knowing that Christ is truly *"touched with the feeling of our infirmities"* (Heb. 4:15, KJV).

The reality that He, too, suffered the pains of loneliness assures us that He understands our hurt and can minister the divine healing and compassion which we long for.

-13-

HOW SHOULD WE RESPOND?

★We must respond according to God's prescription. **There are many "quick fix" remedies which cannot adequately cure the problem.** Many suggestions have been given to help people deal with loneliness, but they usually fall short: change a job, travel, take up a hobby, read a book, go to the movies, join a club, watch television, listen to the radio, renew goals, have fun, get married, become aggressive, never be alone, etc.

These all may offer temporary relief for the pain of loneliness, but they do not deal with the problem at its deepest level, or produce the desired results.

On the following pages we will examine some important keys for successfully treating the problem of loneliness.

-14-

I. CORRECT NEGATIVE ATTITUDES

Before loneliness can be alleviated, we must go the the root. **We must challenge those destructive, self-defeating attitudes which are hindering relationships with others.**

If we have erected barriers instead of bridges, we need to make some adjustments. **We may be unconsciously manifesting negative character traits which are driving people away and reinforcing our sense of alienation and loneliness.**

We must openly deal with a self-centered, angry, or self-pitying spirit by confessing our sins to the Lord and sincerely asking Him to cleanse our hearts and help us to correct these destructive tendencies.

-15-

II. DEVELOP A GODLY SELF-IMAGE

We must forcefully challenge the sin of self-pity and self-criticism, and **correct any false perspective which tends to view ourselves as worthless, inferior, and useless.**

The Word teaches us that we have worth and dignity in Christ (I Cor. 12:14-27). **One of Satan's greatest lies is that we have no value.** He seeks to promote this deception in order to destroy godly self-esteem and cause us to withdraw from life and drown in loneliness. If he can instill a sense of worthlessness and inferiority, he can suppress our participation in the kingdom, and hinder the work of God in our lives. **We must reject this falsehood by standing on the reality of who we really are as new creatures in Christ.**

-16-

III. WE MUST CHALLENGE OUR FEARS

We often contribute to our own loneliness by failing to bridge the self-imposed barriers of fear. **Fear only reinforces loneliness.**

Fear comes in many forms: the fear of rejection, of being hurt, of intimidation, of intimacy, and of faces and people. **If we dwell upon our fears, we will avoid forming relationships and withdraw further into a barren life of loneliness.**

We must challenge our fears by seeking a release through Christ and His Word: *"For God has not given us a spirit of fear, but of power and of love and of a sound mind"* (II Tim. 1:7).

-17-

IV. WE MUST REACH OUT TO OTHERS

The popular jingle, "Reach out, reach out and touch someone" contains an important key for overcoming loneliness. **We must take the initiative to reach out to others.**

In order to build relationships, we must work towards this end. **Relationships don't happen spontaneously. They take time and effort to develop them.** Meaningful relationships are never a one way road. We must cooperate with others to build them.

Loneliness is often the result of simply failing to cultivate relationships. Even the scriptures admonish us that *"a man that hath friends MUST SHEW HIMSELF FRIENDLY"* (Prov. 18:24, KJV).

-18-

V. FELLOWSHIP WITH GOD

People need people to help avoid loneliness, but ultimately, **without a meaningful relationship with Christ, loneliness will never completely disappear.**

This is no less true for Christians! It is sad to say, but many Christians still suffer loneliness simply because they have based their ultimate happiness and fulfillment in people, rather than in Christ.

We cannot ignore or minimize the God-given need for meaningful human contact, but without a fulfilling relationship with Jesus Christ, we can never be really healed of loneliness.

-19-

God earnestly desires a deeper communion with us. In Revelation 3:20 Jesus says: *"Behold, I stand at the door and knock. If anyone hears My voice and opens the door, I will come in to him and dine with him, and he with Me."*

We need not suffer loneliness if we will allow Him into our hearts and actively cultivate a vital relationship with Him. Here are some simple keys for accomplishing this:

1. **By reading and meditating upon His word,** we are brought into closer communion with Jesus (Psalms 1:2).

2. **Through prayer,** we learn to talk with Jesus and share every area of our life with Him (Psalms 61:1-4).

3. **Through worship and praise,** we are ushered into intimate fellowship with the very presence of God (Psalms 22:3).

-20-

VI. CHRISTIAN INVOLVEMENT

"So continuing daily with one accord in the temple, and breaking bread from house to house, they ate their food with gladness and simplicity of heart" (Acts 2:46).

As Christians, God has provided the best possible environment for overcoming loneliness. He has birthed us into a spiritual family called the church.

If we draw back and live a passive, non-committed Christian life, we can remain lonely strangers even in the body of Christ. However, **if we will avail ourselves of the fellowship of the saints and actively participate in the many areas of Christian service and involvement, we will begin to build vital relationships and a sense of belonging.**

-21-

◄ CONCLUSION ►

We have briefly examined the subject of loneliness. We have reviewed the significant causes and cures for loneliness. We have seen that a growing relationship with God and man forms the basis for overcoming this painful area in our life.

We need to thoughtfully consider each of the points of response covered in this booklet, and commit ourselves to making the necessary adjustments in our life. **Without an active response, the problem of loneliness will only deepen and linger.**

We would recommend that you review the counseling booklets on "Building Self-Esteem" and "Overcoming Condemnation" for further insight into this problem area.

For a brief overview of the main points in this booklet, please re-read the words in bold print on each page.

-22-

 *Chapter 10*

*Building
Self Esteem*

BY WILLIAM R. KIMBALL

◄ INTRODUCTION ►

Feelings of inferiority and worthlessness are widespread in today's world. Many peopole possess little or no sense of personal worth. Countless individuals are plagued with poor self-esteem. It is one of the fundamental problems affecting mankind.

This destructive condition is so common that it even affects Christians. **Many Christians quietly struggle under the oppressive burden of poor self-esteem.** They are weighted down with deep feelings of inadequacy and uselessness. However, this is not a condition which Christians should be troubled with.

In this booklet, we will examine the cause of poor self-esteem, and will offer some helpful steps for overcoming this problem in our lives.

-1-

◄ TABLE OF CONTENTS ►

-2-

WHAT IS SELF-ESTEEM?

Self-esteem refers to our personal evaluation or opinion of our worth, competence, and importance. Though it includes our thoughts, feelings, and attitudes towards ourselves, it may have nothing to do with reality.

Self-esteem can be negative or positive. However, the vast majority of people possess a poor self-image. Many perceive themselves to be ugly when they are beautiful, unlovable when they are loved, unsuccessful when they have succeeded, useless when they are talented, worthless when they possess great value.

Proper self-esteem is a healthy condition which produces godly contentment and self-worth. **Poor self-esteem is an unhealthy condition** which hinders godly contentment and produces an underlying sense of frustration, inferiority, and inadequacy.

-3-

WHAT ARE THE EFFECTS OF POOR SELF-ESTEEM?

Poor self-esteem is a cancerous condition which corrupts our emotions, actions, attitudes, thoughts, and values. A poor self-perspective is the root of many destructive symptoms.

Poor self-esteem produces a deep sense of self-criticism, self-hatred, and self-rejection. It creates a nagging feeling of being unwanted, unneeded, and unloved. It destroys self-acceptance.

It undermines our sense of self-worth and self-confidence. **It causes us to gradually withdraw from people and isolate ourselves.** It stifles initiative, quenches motivation, and reinforces the feelings of inadequacy, hopelessness, and weakness.

It is sometimes camouflaged by a negative, complaining, and argumentative spirit. It makes us jealous, unforgiving, resentful, intolerant, and suspicious toward others. It causes us to be overly sensitive, moody, depressed, and introverted.

-4-

WHAT ARE THE CAUSES OF POOR SELF-ESTEEM?

Many factors contribute to a poor self-image. On the following pages, we will review some of the more common causes.

I. FAULTY THEOLOGY

One of the underlying causes of poor self-esteem among Christians is a distorted theological perspective. **Some Christians tend to focus upon the scriptural revelation of man's fallen state.** They tend to stress the utter worthlessness of man. They mistakenly assume that our previous sinful condition has forever rendered us insignificant and worthless before a holy, sovereign God.

They attack any attitude of self-love or self-esteem as being a subtle form of pride. They often embrace a false humility which is nothing more than self-inflicted condemnation. **This distorted theology overlooks our present standing in Christ, and emphasizes our feelings of inferiority and inadequacy.**

-5-

II. THE DECEPTION OF THE ENEMY

Satan is a constant source of agitation. He is referred to as *"the accuser of our brethren"* (Rev. 12:10). He strives to destroy our godly self-esteem through accusation, criticism, and discouragement.

One of his greatest lies is that we are useless, inadequate, and of little value to God.
He will even twist scriptures in his clever attempts to sow this falsehood. He works to promote this deception in order to undermine our godly self-esteem, and cause us to withdraw from life and drown in despair.

He tries to instill a sense of worthlessness and inferiority in order to quench our enthusiasm, suppress our participation in the kingdom, and hinder the work of God in our lives.

-6-

III. UNRESOLVED GUILTS

Poor self-esteem can often be the consequence of longstanding guilts. Unresolved guilts from the past can torture us with an overwhelming sense of failure, inadequacy, and wretchedness.

Many Christians cannot seem to forget the sins of yesterday. They are haunted with memories of past mistakes. They have not fully accepted Christ's cleansing power and forgiveness, so they find it hard to forgive themselves or forget their former transgressions.

The nagging feeling of guilt creates remorse, self-condemnation, and a deep-seated disappointment in ourselves which only reinforces our sense of inferiority and failure.

-7-

IV. PAST EXPERIENCES

Our present self-esteem is often the result of past conditioning. **If we grew up in a household of criticism, rejection, and disapproval, we may have quietly acquired a negative self-image.**

This kind of environment only creates a sense of insecurity, inadequacy, and inferiority. A continual lack of emotional support or encouragement results in an attitude of self-contempt and rejection. When parents withhold love, acceptance, and forgiveness, a child grows up with a sense of poor self-esteem.

When people, in any relationship, are subjected to a spirit of condemnation, belittling, and disapproval, a gradual feeling of self-hatred and dislike can begin to develop in our opinion and evaluation of ourselves.

-8-

V. SOCIAL FACTORS

Social influences can have a tremendous impact upon our self-esteem. **Social pressures can work to diminish or even destroy a healthy self-image.**

Society imposes certain values and standards which can cause an individual to feel second-rate, inferior, or even abnormal. The cruel injustices, prejudices, and "value systems" of society can inflict deep wounds upon a person's sense of personal worth.

A person can be rejected and held in contempt because of his race, ethnic background, social standing, lack of schooling, or religious upbringing. **Many people grow up in a society which slowly robs them of their human dignity and worth.** The tragic result is often a sense of poor self-esteem.

-9-

VI. UNFULFILLED EXPECTATIONS

Everyone grows up with idealistic expectations for their future. We all have our goals and dreams we would like to see fulfilled. However, many people fail to realize their great expectations. They find that life has dealt them a cruel hand.

Life is filled with setbacks, disappointments, and delays. Many people find that the saying, "The best laid plans of mice and men often go astray" is an appropriate characterization of their lives.

When we fail to achieve our goals, measure up to our expectations, or fulfill our dreams, we can gradually fall into a "failure syndrome." This only works to undermine self-confidence and reinforce a growing sense of inadequacy, incompetence, and inferiority.

-10-

VII. FAULTY THINKING

A poor self-image is often the consequence of prolonged negative thinking. Negative thinking is so deeply rooted in the thought lives of many people that it corrupts every area of their lives.

Our thinking patterns have a tremendous impact upon our emotions, attitudes, and will. **Many who suffer from poor self-esteem have an overly pessimistic view of themselves.**

They constantly reinforce their feelings of worthlessness and inferiority by ministering self-doubt and self-criticism. They only see themselves as deficient, useless, and inadequate.

This mental rut is extremely destructive. It only encourages the feelings of failure, despondency, and poor self-esteem.

-11-

HOW DO WE CORRECT A POOR SELF-IMAGE?

I. EMBRACE A PROPER BIBLICAL PERSPECTIVE

In order to establish a sound self-image, we must confront poor self-esteem with sound theology. Though the Bible doesn't ignore man's sinful state, it doesn't demean our God-given value either.

Those who doctrinally stress our utter wretchedness are unconsciously delivering a "slap-in-the-face" to the gracious work of Christ on our behalf. This negative, one-sided theology is an open affront to God.

The Word declares that *"we are His workmanship, created in Christ Jesus for good works"* (Eph. 2:10). Any theology which downgrades or minimizes God's glorious workmanship should be rejected. God has not created us to wallow in dejection, self-pity, or feelings of worthlessness.

-12-

II. WE MUST RESPOND TO THE CLARITY OF GOD'S WORD

We must confront the deceptive lie that we are worthless rejects with the absolute reality of God's Word. **We must set our confidence and trust upon the clear teachings of scripture concerning our self-worth.**

The scriptures declare that *"we are His workmanship, created in Christ Jesus for good works"* (Eph. 2:10). We are sons and daughters of God (II Cor. 6:18). We are *"the salt of the earth"* (Matt. 5:13). We are *"joint heirs with Christ"* (Rom. 8:17). We are *"crowned . . . with glory and honor"* (Psalms 8:5). We are people of dignity and destiny (Rom. 8:29, 30).

Our previous state has been forever changed in Christ. We are now **"a new creation"** in Christ (II Cor. 5:17). Therefore, we must reject the feelings of inferiority, uselessness, and inadequacy, and realize that we are valuable in Christ.

-13-

III. WE MUST DISCIPLINE OUR THOUGHTS

". . . BRINGING EVERY THOUGHT INTO CAPTIVITY TO THE OBEDIENCE OF CHRIST" (II Cor. 10:5). **We must discipline our negative thoughts by submitting them to the positive reality of God's Word.**

The scriptures remind us to set our mind on those things which are true, honest, just, pure, lovely, and of good report (Phil. 4:8).

We must guard our thought life. Our mind can be our worst enemy, or a good friend. Our thoughts can either build godly self-esteem or undermine our sense of self-worth. If we continually yield to corrupt thinking or indulge in negative confessions about ourself, we will inevitably destroy our self-esteem.   -14-

IV. WE MUST HAVE A GODLY SELF-LOVE

The Bible assumes that we should possess a healthy self-love (Eph. 5:28, 29). Without a godly self-love, we have no basis for proper self-esteem.

Some Christians find it difficult to accept the reality that God desires us to love ourselves. They view self-love as a subtle form of self-pride or self-adoration. But when we speak of self-love, we are not referring to a self-centered, egotistical love. This form of self-love is selfish love.

Godly self-love simply means that we see ourselves as worthwhile creatures in Christ. We see ourselves as valued and loved by God. We see ourselves as creatures bearing the divine image of dignity and honor. Our self-love is based upon a realistic self-appraisal of our present standing as gifted and useful members of the body of Christ (I Cor. 12:12-24).

-15-

V. WE MUST ACCEPT GOD'S FOR-GIVENESS

"IF WE CONFESS OUR SINS, HE IS FAITHFUL AND JUST TO FORGIVE US OUR SINS AND TO CLEANSE US FROM ALL UNRIGHTEOUSNESS" (I John 1:9). **A failure to embrace Christ's forgiveness can often result in poor self-esteem.**

Many individuals quietly suffer from longstanding guilts and feelings of deep remorse over their past mistakes. When we dwell upon our former shortcomings, we unconsciously contribute to destroying our present self-image and self-acceptance.

Poor self-esteem is often the result of failing to alleviate the burden of guilt. Feelings of unresolved guilt can gradually create a sense of failure, frustration, inadequacy, self-condemnation, and self-disappointment. If this is the case, we must appropriate the cleansing power of forgiveness which Christ offers.

-16-

VI. WE MUST ACCEPT OUR LIFE SITUATIONS

"AND WE KNOW THAT ALL THINGS WORK TOGETHER FOR GOOD TO THOSE WHO LOVE GOD, TO THOSE WHO ARE THE CALLED ACCORDING TO HIS PURPOSE" (Rom. 8:28).

Many circumstances are beyond our control. We cannot choose our birthplace, our physical features, who our parents will be, the color of our skin, our ethnic origin, whether we will be born rich or poor, or whether we will have physical handicaps. However, if we fail to view our life situations from a biblical perspective, we will inevitably fail in accepting ourselves.

We must recognize that God created us the way we are for a divine purpose. God doesn't see our life situations as liabilities. **He often uses the very things we consider to be hindrances for our eternal benefit.** When we accept our circumstances, we can begin to accept ourselves and gradually build godly self-esteem.

-17-

◄ CONCLUSION ►

We have briefly examined the causes of poor self-esteem. In order to correct an imbalanced self-appraisal, we must respond to the biblical steps we have presented in this booklet:

1. **Embrace a proper biblical perspective.**
2. We must **respond to the clarity of God's Word.**
3. We must **discipline our thoughts.**
4. We must **have a godly self-love.**
5. We must **accept God's forgiveness.**
6. We must **accept our life situations.**

We would also recommend that you read the counseling booklets on "Condemnation" and "Depression" in order to overcome these two common results of poor self-esteem. **For a brief overview of the main points in this booklet, please re-read the boldly printed words on each page.**

-18-

Chapter 11

Defeating
Depression

BY WILLIAM R. KIMBALL

◀ INTRODUCTION ▶

We've all wrestled with depression. Everyone experiences their "dark days" and "blue moods". Each of us have felt "down" at various points in our lives.

But **depression is not inevitable. It can be avoided,** and it can be overcome. Depression is a difficult problem, but God can provide the necessary answers. In this booklet, we will examine this subject and consider some scriptural keys for finding victory over our depression.

-1-

◀ TABLE OF CONTENTS ▶

-2-

WHAT IS DEPRESSION?

Though all of us have a vague understanding of what depression is, most of us would have some difficulty in defining it.

Depression comes from the word "depressed". Simply stated, it is a feeling of having been pressed low in our spirits. It is a condition of feeling dejection and heaviness in our heart. **It has been described as feeling down, feeling blue, or feeling disheartened.** It is often a state of desperation which gives a person the feeling of hopelessness. It is a close relative of despair, despondency, and discouragement.

-3-

WHO SUFFERS FROM DEPRESSION?

Depression is so common and widespread that **everyone experiences it in some form** at some point in their life. It cuts across every conceivable boundary.

No one is exempt — no one is immune. Depression afflicts the young and old, men and women, rich and poor, learned and unlearned, healthy and unhealthy, godly and ungody.

It is considered to be the most common mental and emotional problem affecting mankind. In fact, it is claimed that more human suffering has resulted from depression than from any other single disease!

-4-

WHAT DOES THE BIBLE SAY?

Though the word "depression" is not mentioned in the Bible, the scriptures contain many references to this common problem.

The Bible points to many incidents of depression in the lives of godly men. As we have stated, it is not a problem which just affects the ungodly.

It appears that **Job, Moses, David, Elijah, Jonah, Peter, Paul, and the entire nation of Israel suffered from depression.** Jeremiah even expressed his deep depression in a book entitled, Lamentations.

[See Job 3; Numbers 11:10-15; Psalms 42, 43; I Kings 19:4; Jonah 4:1-3; Matthew 26:75; II Corinthians 1:8; and Exodus 6:9]

-5-

WHAT ARE SOME GODLY EXAMPLES?

- **MOSES was overwhelmed** with depression in the wilderness (Numbers 11:10-15).

- **JOB was consumed with a sense of despondency** because of his problems (Job 3).

- **DAVID cried out** *"Why are you cast down, O my soul?"* (Psalms 43:5).

- **PETER experienced deep depression** after denying the Lord (Matthew 26:75).

- **PAUL stated that he *"despaired even of life"*** because of the intense pressures he experienced (II Cor. 1:8).

-6-

WHAT CAUSES DEPRESSION?

Many factors contribute to depression. We will consider some of the most important causes on the following pages.

The most common cause of depression is stress. Life is filled with pressing difficulties, delays, disappointments, setbacks, and tragedies. **If we do not deal with the problems of life properly, they can gradually wear us down, weaken us, and create a growing sense of depression.**

Often, these pressures are beyond our control. The loss of a job, health, an opportunity, possessions, or a loved one can all contribute to a state of depression.

-7-

When it appears that we have no real control over the problems we experience, depression and discouragement are often the result. Sometimes it seems we have no say concerning the events which crowd into our lives. Occasionally, we feel like we've lost control and become a helpless victim of circumstances. At times like this, we may feel like we've reached a dead-end with no way out.

When we feel like we are unable to do anything to change our situation, a sense of hopelessness and frustration sets in.

When we encounter circumstances over which we have no control, we may assume that our actions are useless, no matter how hard we try. When it seems that we've run out of answers for our problems, we begin to sink beneath the waves of depression.

-8-

NEGATIVE THINKING

Depression can usually be traced to negative thinking. Negativity is so strongly rooted in the thought life of some people that it adversely affects every area of their life.

Our thinking patterns have a great influence upon our emotions, our attitudes, and our will. Depression and discouragement are often a result of wrong thinking. Depressed people see only the dark side of life. They usually have a pessimistic outlook. Life to them is an endless succession of burdens, obstacles, and disappointments. They have convinced themselves that life is hopeless. Having painted a picture of despair in their own minds, they reinforce their feelings of despondency.

-9-

Many who suffer from depression also have a negative view of themselves. They have little or no self-esteem. They often feel deficient, inadequate, and useless. They constantly minister self-doubt and criticism to themselves. This negative feeling of failure inevitably breeds self-pity and a deep sense of depression.

Negative thinking not only affects the way we think about ourselves, but it also causes us to view the future pessimistically. All the future holds is continuing failure, hardship, and frustration.

This common tendency to think negatively is an extremely destructive pattern. **Negative thinking only encourages despair and self-pity.** It is a mental rut which many people have fallen into. **It is a habit which must be broken.**

-10-

SIN AND GUILT

A person can experience depression because of unresolved sin in his life. He may become despondent because of guilt from a particular sin which has not been properly dealt with.

Depression is often the result of ignoring sin or failing to deal with it promptly. Occasionally, we may try to conceal sin rather than face up to it honestly. When we try to cover up sin, it inevitably takes its toll. A spirit of heaviness and condemnation can develop as a consequence of sin which has been allowed to stubbornly remain in our life.

Often the sin of self-pity is a common cause of depression. Pent up resentment, lingering anger, unforgiveness, a critical spirit, or a tendency to murmur and complain can all be contributing factors to depression.

-11-

PRESSURES OF RESPONSIBILITY

Sometimes the trials, deadlines, and responsibilities that we face can create pressures which contribute to depression.

Occasionally, we all fall short. At times, we don't quite measure up. We fail to meet deadlines, achieve goals, or fulfill expectations. **The many demands of life can overwhelm us and produce depression and discouragement.**

When facing the responsibilities of entering Canaan land, the Israelites were overwhelmed by the challenge and sank into discouragement (Numbers 13, 14). When we sometimes face our own formidable giants of responsibility, we can also sink into depression.

-12-

PHYSICAL FACTORS

Physical factors can, and often do, contribute to depression. No matter how good our philosophy, no matter how well adjusted we are, and no matter how ideal our environment may be, **if we don't take care of ourselves properly we can pay the price in depression.** When we allow our physical health to "run down", we begin to prepare ourselves for possible depression.

Sometimes we suffer depression not because of sin, stress, or negative thinking, but simply because we have neglected our bodies. **Physical health contributes to mental and emotional well-being.** A healthy body is less susceptible to mental and physical illness. A lack of sleep, improper diet, or a lack of exercise can all contribute to depression.

-13-

WHAT ARE THE SIGNS OF DEPRESSION

There are not only many causes of depression, but **depression produces many symptoms and manifests itself in a variety of ways,** as well.

These can include sadness, pessimism, fear, apathy, weariness, fatigue, a loss of energy, a lack of enthusiasm, an inability to make decisions, a desire to withdraw from life, self-criticism, a sense of worthlessness, helplessness, a loss of interest in work, sex, and normal activities, a difficulty in concentrating, insomnia, and a loss of appetite.

As we can see, **depression has many side effects, all of which can be very destructive.**

-14-

WHAT IS THE ROOT PROBLEM?

The root problem is sin. Depression is not always sin, but our failure to deal with the problem is. *"To him who knows to do good and does not do it, to him it is sin"* (James 4:17).

Though we may not always be responsible for the circumstances which contribute to depression and discouragement, we are responsible for handling the problem in God's way. We must recognize that we are not helpless, but responsible and accountable to God.

When we don't seek God for answers, we assume the burden ourselves and inevitably fail. Depression is often the result. **The first step to victory is in focusing upon Christ, rather than ourselves.** This requires confessing our faults to God, and asking Him for grace and guidance.

-15-

IS THERE A SOLUTION?

★**Yes!** One of the greatest lies of Satan is that there is no hope for those suffering depression. This is a lie because God has the answers.

Even though our circumstances may look dreary, we don't have to give in to depression. Many times a depressed person is overcome by a sense of hopelessness, but **God understands our pain and offers compassion.** He is here to help if we will not shut Him out of our lives.

Christians must recognize that there are no hopeless situations in Christ. **People allow themselves to become hopeless because they haven't looked to Jesus.** Our situation doesn't have to look bleak if we will bring Christ into the picture.

-16-

125

HOW SHOULD WE RESPOND TO DEPRESSION?

★**In God's way — not ours.** Many Christians sink into a pit of despondency simply because they have not responded to their problems scripturally.

King David probably suffered from depression more than any other Bible character. He experienced great depths of prolonged depression, yet he learned some vital lessons for dealing with this problem. The Psalms are filled with examples of his suffering:

"Why are you cast down, O my soul? And why are you disquieted within me?" (Psalms 42:5; see also Psalms 42, 43, 69, 88, and 102).

Though he had many bouts with depression, he discovered some important keys for finding victory. We will examine the seven keys to overcoming depression on the following pages.

-17

I. TAKE IMMEDIATE ACTION

One of the most important things we can do is to deal with the problem of depression immediately.

Depression must be challenged promptly. If you allow it to remain, it will spread like a cancer and corrupt every area of your life. A common tendency is to brood over our problems and quietly nurse our depression, rather than taking decisive steps against it. Many sink into depression simply because they do nothing about it — instead they dwell upon self-pity and reinforce their despondency.

David recognized this important first step and responded by forcefully challenging himself and his depression: *"Why are you cast down, O my soul? . . . Hope in God!"* (Psalms 43:5). Take action now!

-18-

II. WE MUST DISCIPLINE OUR THOUGHTS

" . . . *bringing every thought into captivity to the obedience of Christ"* (II Cor. 10:5). **Christians must discipline their negative thoughts by submitting them to the Lordship of Christ.** If we don't, they can become very destructive.

This involves submitting our thoughts to the reality of God's Word. **Christians must guard their thought life.** We must not yield to corrupt thinking or indulge in negative confessions. **The Word exhorts us to** *"meditate on" whatsoever things are true, honest, just, pure, lovely, and of a good report* (Phil.4:8).

We must look at our life, our situations, and our future from God's point of view. We need to fix our thoughts obediently upon the reality of God's Word, meditate upon the scriptures, and cleanse our minds with the cleansing water of God's Word.

-19-

III. HOPE IN THE LORD

David challenged his soul to *"HOPE IN GOD!"* (Psalms 42:5). We must likewise place our hope firmly in Christ.

In I Peter 1:3 we see that God has called us to a "living hope." Our hope is not dead but alive because it is fixed upon a living God. It is a hope that is never disappointed because of God's loving commitment to us. **When we get our attention off of our problems and upon the power of God, we have access to confidence, courage, and strength.** David affirmed this in Psalms 31:24: *"Be of good courage, and He shall strengthen your heart, all you who hope in the Lord."*

-20-

IV. STAND ON THE PROMISES OF GOD

Christians must stand upon the reality of God's Word. We must recognize that *"ALL THINGS"* are working together for our good. When we receive this truth, we can accept our circumstances realizing that God has not forsaken us in them. There are no hopeless situations in Christ because God is in the midst of our circumstances. This is the absolute guarantee of God's Word!

When we trust in the reality of God's Word, we have great hope. **The scriptures contain all of the answers to life's problems.** They sustain us and encourage us in every way. The counsel of scripture can minister genuine hope in spite of our circumstances. David confirmed this when he wrote:

*"**My soul faints** for Your salvation, **but I hope in Your word"** (Psalms 119:81).

-21-

V. REJOICE IN THE LORD

One of the most liberating keys to victory is found in Philippians 4:4: *"**REJOICE IN THE LORD ALWAYS. AGAIN I WILL SAY, RE-JOICE!"***

This is the Christian's way to escape depression. **The answer is not in running from our circumstances or withdrawing from life, but in rising above them through praise.** We don't rejoice just when everything is going smoothly. **Paul said we are to rejoice always.** He also said *"Rejoice evermore . . . in everything give thanks"* (I Thess. 5:16, 18, KJV). We don't rejoice because we feel like it, but as an act of obedient faith, realizing that "in the Lord" we have grounds for confidence and rejoicing. **We know that the Lord is bigger than our problems,** and is working everything for our eventual good!

-22-

VI. CONFESS OUR FAULTS TO THE LORD

"IF WE CONFESS OUR SINS, HE IS FAITHFUL AND JUST TO FOR-GIVE US OUR SINS AND TO CLEANSE US FROM ALL UNRIGH-TEOUSNESS."

— I John 1:9

Sin can be both a cause of depression and a product of depression. **Often, when we have unresolved sin in our life, it produces guilt and self-condemnation which lead to despair.** When we harbor bitterness, resentment, anger, ill-will, jealousy, or any other sin in our hearts, it affects us negatively. Often, we fall into the pit of despair because of the sin of self-pity, murmuring, and complaining. Sin defiles our conscience and perverts our walk. If we have been concealing our sin or failing to deal with it promptly, we need to confess our sin to the Lord and seek His cleansing power. Often, when the weight of sin is removed from our shoulders, we are released from the burden of depression.

-23-

VII. WE MUST WATCH OUR HEALTH

As we have seen, **physical factors can play an important role in depression.** Poor health habits contribute to depression.

We not only have a responsibility to care for ourselves spiritually, but physically as well, because our bodies belong to the Lord (I Cor. 6:19). **When we abuse or neglect the temple of God, depression is often the consequence.**

We can help prevent depression if we will give proper consideration to the simple rules of good health.

-24-

SUMMARY

"And David was greatly distressed . . . BUT DAVID ENCOURAGED HIMSELF IN THE LORD HIS GOD" (I Samuel 30:6, KJV).

It is very helpful to have others encourage us during our times of depression. But David encouraged himself. Often our circumstances give us little encouragement, but in Christ we have access to great encouragement. David learned this through much experience. **The important thing to realize is that he didn't encourage himself in his circumstances, but *"IN THE LORD."*** In doing so, he set an example for us. We've already reviewed the keys for doing this:

1. Take immediate action
2. Discipline our thoughts
3. Hope in the Lord
4. Trust in His Word

5. Rejoice in the Lord
6. Confess our sins
7. Take care of our health

-25-

◄ CONCLUSION ►

We have briefly examined this difficult subject, and have offered some scriptural guidelines for dealing with it. Depression is a problem, but it is not an impossible barrier in our lives. It is not a permanent condition. It is one which will pass away with God's assistance. **We can usually overcome depression if we will simply follow God's prescription for the problem.**

However, we recognize that depression can be a complicated condition, difficult to define, and hard to treat. If this counseling booklet has not adequately answered this problem, **we encourage you to seek further counsel from your pastor.**

For a brief overview of the main points of this booklet, please re-read the boldly printed words on each page.

-26-

Chapter 12

Overcoming
Stress

By William R. Kimball

◀ INTRODUCTION ▶

Stress is one of the prevailing characteristics of the twentieth century. We live in a tension-charged, fast-paced, "pressure cooker" world. The complexities of modern life have caused stress to reach epidemic proportions.

Feelings of stress affect everyone. Even Christians are subject to its effects. The ever-increasing frequency of stress-related problems presents a serious challenge to the church to offer scriptural guidelines for overcoming this problem.

In this booklet we will examine the subject of stress and will present some constructive steps for successfully confronting this common dilemma.

-1-

◀ TABLE OF CONTENTS ▶

-2-

WHAT IS STRESS?

Stress is simply defined as "a factor that creates a mental, emotional, or physical strain." It is **"a state of unresolved tension arising from the pressures, irritations, and demands of life."**

In biblical terms, the word **"affliction" is the closest equivalent.** Affliction can also be defined as "the pressure which affects a person's life." It is a broad term which includes many factors which contribute to stress.

Though we may have difficulty defining stress, we are all familiar with its effects. It is a universal problem which periodically troubles Christian and unbeliever alike. Even Paul referred to the stress he experienced when he wrote: ***"We were PRESSED out of measure"*** (II Cor. 1:8, KJV).

-3-

WHAT ARE THE EFFECTS OF STRESS?

Stress can breed a host of destructive symptoms which affect us mentally, emotionally, physically, and spiritually.

These can include:
- mental and emotional fatigue
- drug and alcohol dependency
- loss of appetite
- high blood pressure
- physical weariness
- frequent headaches
- stomach problems
- heart problems
- hypertension
- migrains
- ulcers
- insomnia

Stress often produces a sense of anxiety, irritability, frustration, restlessness, and depression. It creates a feeling of hopelessness and disillusionment which undermines a person's sense of purpose, direction, and meaning in life.

As we can see, stress is a potentially deadly condition. It has many detrimental side effects which can gradually undermine our well-being if not handled properly.

-4-

COMMON SOURCES OF STRESS

A multitude of factors contribute to stress. These can include positive and negative circumstances, unexpected adversities, or stressful situations and encounters. **The unrelenting pressures of contemporary life, the constant challenges and deadlines of our fast-paced society, the everchanging state of our unstable world, and the pressures of fear and uncertainties concerning the future also create stress.**

The tempo of life, the strain of demands and responsibilities, a failure to seek adequate rest and relaxation, a poor use of time, wrong priorities, spiritual conflicts, a tendency to overextend ourselves, a poor diet, vitamin deficiencies, lack of exercise, insufficient communion with God, inter-personal conflicts, emotional problems, and unresolved sins are significant ingredients in stress.

-5-

THE POTENTIAL DANGER OF UNRESOLVED STRESS

Unresolved stress, regardless of the source, can become an extremely destructive condition. The accumulated effect of longstanding stress can eventually lead to a condition which is commonly referred to as "BURN-OUT SYNDROME."

Burn-out syndrome strikes people in all walks of life. **Burn-out syndrome is a "state of disillusionment arising from a sense of utter mental, emotional, physical, or even spiritual exhaustion."** But it is not a condition which is inevitable or incurable. **Stress, in any form, can be overcome** through the scriptural guidelines which God provides.

On the following pages we will examine ten steps for successfully combating stress in our lives.

-6-

I. VIEW CIRCUMSTANCES FROM A GODLY PERSPECTIVE

Life is filled with a wide variety of circumstances. Some situations are positive, some are negative. However, the circumstances we encounter, regardless of the nature, often produce feelings of stress. This is especially true of the adverse situations which suddenly affect or alter the course of our lives.

A great deal of stress can be alleviated or minimized by viewing our circumstances from a godly perspective. If we fail to perceive our life situations, at any point, as God perceives them, then we become susceptible to stress.

One of the greatest truths a Christian can embrace is the scriptural revelation that *"ALL THINGS WORK TOGETHER FOR GOOD TO THOSE WHO LOVE GOD"* (Rom. 8:28). This is a liberating revelation which can free us from much of the self-imposed stress we experience by seeing our circumstances in a negative light.

-7-

II. PACE YOURSELF

". . . and let us RUN WITH PATIENCE the race that is set before us" (Heb. 12:1, KJV). A wise athlete learns to set a proper pace for his life if he, or she, expects to finish the race.

Too many believers have not learned to regulate the tempo of their life. They have fallen in step with the "rush hour" spirit of this age. They sprint through life, racing from one stoplight, deadline, and appointment to the next without taking their time.

This "get there yesterday" mentality is a significant contributing factor to stress. It exerts internal pressure upon our nervous system and produces a tension-charged environment for us. Christians must respond to the warning, "Slow down, you move too fast", or they will suffer the conquences of stress.

-8-

III. REDEEM THE TIME

"See then that you walk circumspectly, not as fools but as wise, REDEEMING THE TIME . . ." (Eph. 5:15, 16). A wise use of our time is an important ingredient in relieving potential stress.

The daily schedule of some people is so chronically cluttered, cramped, and conjested that they suffer stress. **Many people waste time and manage it poorly.** The inevitable result is a stress-filled consciousness.

Each of us must periodically examine our use of time and carefully consider our priorities, commitments, and timetables. Our time must be structured wisely. **We must budget our time and spend it in the most beneficial manner.** This may require eliminating activities, re-evaluating priorities, saying "no", and restructuring our time.

-9-

IV. REST AND RELAXATION

" . . . for in six days the Lord made the heavens and the earth, and on the seventh day HE RESTED AND WAS REFRESHED" (Ex. 31:17). God set an excellent example by creating a day for rest and refreshing.

Rest and relaxation are strong antidotes for stress. But the problem with many stress-prone people is that they have never learned the value of rest and relaxation. **Some Christians seldom rest or cannot enjoy relaxation because of a false spirituality which mistakenly assumes that rest is somehow worldly or a sign of slothfulness.** They embrace an "I'll burn out for Jesus" mentality. However, without an occasional break from our busy schedules, we subject ourselves to increasing stress. We burn the candle at both ends and eventually burn out.

-10-

V. REST IN GOD

Not only do our bodies and minds require regular periods of rest and relaxation, but **our spirits need to be regularly refreshed in the presence of God.**

Many Christians have become so involved in the business of serving God and fulfilling spiritual responsibilities that they overlook a vital dimension in their relationship and experience in Christ. A lack of spiritual communion is a common cause of tension and stress in the Christian life.

Christians cannot function well without a vital communion with God. God has provided some helpful means for finding rest in Him. **An important way to achieve this is through regular times of worship, devotion, and prayer.** This is an essential source of spiritual refreshing and renewal through meaningful contact with the person and presence of God.

-11-

◆**Martha versus Mary** (Read Luke 10:38-42)

Many Christians have fallen into the "Martha syndrome." They scurry frantically about the kingdom doing this and doing that without ever taking quality time to sit at Christ's feet and commune with Him.

It is good to be actively involved in serving Christ, but we must give attention to what Jesus referred to as *"that good part"* (Luke 10:42). **If we fail to seek rest and refreshing through a vital and intimate communion with God, we will eventually become "worried and troubled about many things" like Martha** (Luke 10:41).

When our lives become cluttered, overtaxed, and overburdened, we become subject to stress. **Quality time spent with God is never wasted time.** It is a powerful ingredient for alleviating stress.

-12-

VI. PRAYER

"BE ANXIOUS FOR NOTHING, but in everything by PRAYER and supplication, with thanksgiving, let your requests be made known to God; and the peace of God, which surpasses all understanding, will guard your hearts and minds through Christ Jesus" (Phil. 4:6, 7).

A great deal of stress is the direct result of shouldering the burdens of life without turning to the Lord in prayer. We have access to *"the peace of God"* when we release our burdens to the Lord.

The scriptures speak of *"casting all your care upon Him; for He cares for you"* (I Pet. 5:7). When we fail to release our problems and cares to Christ, we begin to experience increasing tension, anxiety, and fear. Prayer is one of the most powerful remedies for stress.

-13-

VII. TRUST IN GOD'S WORD

*"For whatever things were written before were written for our learning, **that we THROUGH THE PATIENCE AND COMFORT OF THE SCRIPTURES might have hope"*** (Rom. 15:4).

The promises and counsel of scripture provides us with a rich storehouse of stress-relieving comfort and peace. Stress often results from failing to **stand upon the absolute reality of God's Word, in spite of our circumstances.**

When we confront life's problems, dilemmas, and uncertainties with the reality of God's Word, we can effectively overcome a great deal of the stress we suffer. When we firmly fix our confidence and faith on God's answers to life's problems, we have an effective safeguard against stress.

-14-

VIII. FELLOWSHIP

*"And let us consider one another in order to stir up love and good works, **NOT FORSAKING THE ASSEMBLING OF OURSELVES TOGETHER,** as is the manner of some . . ."* (Heb. 10:24, 25).

Fellowship can often provide a potent remedy for stress. Studies have proven that interaction with loved ones and friends helps relieve the pressures of stress. Those who isolate themselves and withdraw from people and relationships suffer a greater degree of stress-related problems.

Companionship with others provides access to warmth, love, understanding, comfort, counsel, and encouragement. Therefore, we should endeavor to spend regular times with friends and loved ones, doing things together, sharing with each other, having fun, and enjoying rest and relaxation.

-15-

IX. DEAL WITH ANY UNRESOLVED SINS

If we ignore sin or fail to deal with it promptly, we can gradually pay the price in increasing feelings of stress. **Sin generates inner tensions and conflicts.**

Occasionally, sin is the root problem of a person's stress. If we have any unresolved sin(s) in our life, whether public or private, we must sincerely seek Christ's cleansing power and forgiveness.

This may involve a healing of some inter-personal conflict with another person. **Conflicts with others create incredible amounts of stress.** If we are harboring hostility, hatred, resentments, or offense, we should seek genuine reconciliation, healing, and forgiveness through the scriptural steps God provides.

-16-

X. WE MUST WATCH OUR HEALTH

Physical factors often play an important role in stress. Stress can often be attributed to a failure to execute sound principles of good health in an individual's life.

If we neglect or unconsciously abuse our bodies, we can suffer the consequences of stress. We can help prevent stress if we will follow the basic rules of good health.

We must exercise regularly, get a proper amount of sleep, and maintain a balanced diet. We should minimize the intake of caffein drinks, sugar products, salt, and "junk foods". We should also take vitamin supplements which help relieve stress, such as "C" and "B" complex. If we will take heed to this area, a great deal of stress will be prevented.

-17-

◄ CONCLUSION ►

We have briefly reviewed the subject of stress and have offered some helpful steps for overcoming this problem:

1. **View Circumstances from a godly perspective.**
2. **Pace yourself.**
3. **Redeem the time.**
4. **Rest and relaxation.**
5. **Rest in God.**
6. **Prayer.**
7. **Trust in God's Word.**
8. **Fellowship.**
9. **Deal with unresolved sins.**
10. **Watch your health.**

We would also suggest a review of the Christian Equipper's counseling booklets on "Affliction", "Depression", and "Offense". **For a brief overview of the main points of this booklet, please re-read the boldly printed words on each page.**

-18-

Chapter 13

Single and Serving God

By Terry D. Edwards

◄ INTRODUCTION ►

The Christian single stands in a place of vulnerability and potential frustration. Our society often characterizes the single as a carefree swinger, moving from one adventure to another. The media also provides a constant blitz encouraging the single to go for the gusto and to live a life of experimentation, free from sexual restraint. On the other hand, Christianity rightfully exalts sexual morality and responsibility but frequently pressures the single with the idea that marriage is the only state where an individual can really be complete and fulfilled.

This can place the single Christian in a "no win" situation in terms of contentment and self-acceptance. Societal pressures and peers often ridicule their conservative values and life style, while well-meaning Christians pressure them to get married.

It is time for Christian singles to come to terms with their singleness in the light of the scriptures. **The purpose of this booklet is to help singles understand their station in life from a biblical perspective, and to establish proper guidelines for building a proper relationship with a potential mate.**

-1-

◄ TABLE OF CONTENTS ►

-2-

GOD HAS YOU SINGLE

There are over forty million people, one out of every three adults in the United States, that are unmarried. This figure includes roughly twenty-two million who have never been married and those who have lost a spouse through death or divorce. This does not include the vast number of single people throughout the world.

You are single, but you are not alone. There is an enormous number of people in this same station in life. As a Christian, you have a distinct advantage. You are not alone in another unique way - you have a personal relationship with Jesus Christ! You do not need to be tossed to and fro, blown about as a leaf in the wind through the influence of social pressures, others' opinions, insecurities, or identity struggles. You have a source of understanding, stability, and strength in God.

The Christian single must relate to their singleness from a biblical perspective. By so doing, you will be like the wise man who built his house upon

-3-

the rock and was able to resist the onslaught of the rains, the floods, and the winds (Matt. 7:24, 25).

The enemy has some special fiery darts that he uses quite effectively against the single Christian. Once they find their mark, they can have devastating results, either destroying your relationship with God, or crippling your potential for contentment and service. The following are three main areas he works on:

1. _Conformance to the World_ - Singles experience special temptations regarding companionship and sexual needs. Satan works doubly hard on these areas, hoping to bring you to a place which compromises God's standards.

2. _Failure to Accept Your Singleness Before God_ - Satan loves to promote insecurity and agitation in single Christians concerning their condition. Peace comes when we accept our station in life before God. Our Father knows the hairs on our head and every sparrow that falls to the ground, and can be trusted to guide and care for every detail of our lives.

3. _Marriage Obsession_ - It is not wrong to desire marriage. However, if this desire dominates our thoughts to the point where we lose our joy and strips us of spiritual productivity, we are giving Satan an unnecessary advantage.   -4-

GOD'S GOAL FOR SINGLES

"For I have learned in whatever state I am, to be content" (Phil. 4:11).

God's goal for every single is that they would enjoy a contentment, fulfillment, and acceptance of their single status and, from this experience, live a life of fruitful and productive service to Him and others.

Attainment of this goal is only possible by coming to a place of genuine trust and submission to God, and through resisting those ideas and attitudes that obstruct this from taking place.

Accepting your singleness requires seeing that your life does, in truth, belong to God (I Cor. 6:19). He controls every part of your destiny as you release yourself to Him. It also demands resisting the erroneous idea that you can never be truly complete or happy apart from marriage, or that your life will always be in a state of limbo until that time. **Genuine acceptance of your singleness will bring about a personal contentment, along with a release of your own creativity as an individual.**

-5-

SPECIAL NEEDS OF SINGLES

The following section provides an examination of some of the special areas of need which Christian singles encounter:

I. IDENTITY IN CHRIST

"For in Him dwells all the fulness of the Godhead bodily; and you are complete in Him" (Col. 2:9, 10).

We live in a time where identity problems are commonplace. Our computerized, fast-paced society, which is filled with changing values and broken homes leaves many struggling with the question, "Who am I?".

A prevalent error among singles is to think that love and marriage is the only solution to this type of problem. This is not true! **We are made for God and will never find security in our true identity apart from Him.**

The single Christian is not waiting to be completed. You are already a whole person in Christ and need only to ground yourself in a relationship with Him to experience stability and completion. **Whether God brings you a marriage partner or not, you are married to Him and must foundationally discover your personal identity in this union** (II Cor. 11:2).

-6-

II. COMPANIONSHIP

"A new commandment I give to you, that you love one another; as I have loved you, that you also love one another" (Jn. 13:34).

One of the major problems faced by singles is that of loneliness. God created each of us with a need for close personal companionship. He made the observation, *"It is not good that man should be alone"* (Gen. 2:18). With Adam, He fulfilled that need through a mate. However, this need for close personal interaction does not necessarily have to be fulfilled through marriage.

Jesus Christ never married but instead demonstrated that, within the purposes of God, singles could enjoy a covenant commitment and a rewarding friendship with each other. A significant fulfillment of this companionship need can be met apart from intimate relationship with the opposite sex.

Singles should receive the admonition to *"love one another"* in a special sense, learning to open their lives to each other. Avoid the tendency to isolate yourself, waiting for the perfect partner to show up. **Meet this companionship need through building close and committed friendships with other brethren.**

-7-

III. SEXUAL NEEDS

When God created us male and female, He created us with drives which give us a sexual appetite. **Next to loneliness, the problem of coping with sexual energy is perhaps the most prevailing concern among singles.** This problem is heightened by the sexually stimulating spirit of our age.

In order to maintain a life of purity before God, the single must exercise restraint in the following areas:

1. **Fornication** - God requires us to abstain from any sexual relationship outside of marriage. We are told to *"flee sexual immorality"* (I Cor. 6:18), and to *"glorify God in your body"* (I Cor. 6:20).

2. **Masturbation** - The Bible is silent on this area and we should not place it on the same level of sexual offense as fornication. However, the single should avoid this practice because of its emphasis on self-stimulation, sexual fantasy and lust, and the resulting outcome of guilt and self-condemnation.

3. **Impure Thoughts** - We must refuse to entertain impure and immoral thoughts and fantasies. Avoiding literature, influences, and movies which are sexually arousing is a must.

-8-

IV. RELATING TO THE OPPOSITE SEX

Friendship with members of the opposite sex can be both healthy and rewarding. **Christian singles should work on their capacity to relate to both brothers and sisters in Christ.** There are some definite restrictions, though, that should be exercised:

1. _Avoid the "Potential Mate" Obsession_ - Eliminate the tendency to look at every brother or sister attractive to you as possibly "the one for you". Trust God to bring the right person in His time.

2. _Don't Flirt_ - Flirting involves toying with another's feelings and can be a form of defrauding. Our behavior as Christians must always be based on sincerity and purity.

3. _Don't Stumble_ - Avoid wearing provocative clothing that is revealing or may be sexually stimulating to your brother or sister. Dress modestly with others in mind (I Tim. 2:9).

4. _Don't Get Too Close_ - Close relationships with members of the opposite sex can cause problems. Singles can be especially vulnerable to the desire for emotional or sexual intimacy. Avoid compromising occasions or situations that may lead to temptation.

-9-

V. OVERCOMING TEMPTATION

"God is faithful, who will not allow you to be tempted beyond what you are able, but with the temptation will also make the way of escape, that you may be able to bear it" (I Cor. 10:13).

Even the most committed singles go through seasons of struggle and temptation, wrestling with the enticements of the world and the flesh. Things can be smooth for a period of time, and then it seems like the very forces of hell are unleashed against you. Those who have lived loose and sexually permissive lifestyles prior to their salvation are the most vulnerable.

The key to victory in these seasons is given in James 4:8: _"Draw near to God and He will draw near to you."_ The more intense the battle becomes, the more fervent must be our seeking of Him and our resolve not to give in. During these times, increased prayer, fellowship, and even fasting can give us the breakthrough that we need. God will make a way of escape as we stand firm, strengthened in His Spirit. The promise to us is to *"Resist the devil and he will flee from you"* (James 4:7).

-10-

VI. INVOLVEMENT IN SERVICE

"Therefore, my beloved brethren, be steadfast, immovable, always abounding in the work of the Lord" (I Cor. 15:58).
Singles have a distinct advantage over marrieds in regard to service to the lord. Because you are free from the commitments of family life, you have much more time to invest in working for the kingdom of God.

Getting involved in service is a key to fulfillment for the single Christian. Don't waste your time waiting for your mate to show up. He or she will find you far easier if you're active and involved than if you're sitting alone at home. Realize that you are called with a purpose. God has given you gifts and abilities and the time to use them. Ask God to direct you to a place of service, or approach your pastor for counsel.

Involvement in an area of service brings with it a sense of fruitfulness, creativity, and fulfillment. It also contains the blessing of relationships with others who share the same interest or burden as you.

-11-

VII. WHAT IF I NEVER MARRY?

This is a fear that runs through the mind of almost every single person. **The thoughts of being alone for the rest of your life and the social stigma of never marrying can be very frightening.** Though chances are that you will marry, there are some vital issues here that should be resolved.

Many singles, especially those who are older, deal with problems of self-esteem. They find themselves wondering, "Is there something wrong with me?" Sometimes there are obvious character or personality problems at fault, but in most cases, this is not the deciding factor. The single who is sincerely yielding to God and open for change can trust that their normal human quirks or idiosyncrasies are not the culprit.

As long as you are not married, your objective is to trust that God has a purpose in your singleness. **Our life in Christ (Col. 3:4), and our contentment and self-esteem must be primarily found in Him.** Remember, the Bible not only implies that we can be content as singles, it actually exalts singleness as a fulfilling and fruitful life situation for those who give themselves wholly to serving God (I Cor. 7:7,32,40).

-12-

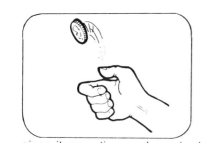

CHOOSING A MATE

Next to your commitment to Jesus Christ, your choice of a mate is the most important decision you will ever make. Many have made devastating mistakes in this decision. Their choice was made in the whirlwind of infatuation, based upon physical and emotional attraction alone. Their awakening comes too late and they realize that they should have given it more time and required other qualifications.

The person you marry will influence and affect every aspect of your life. The fires of love must change in time from blind infatuation to a deep and commited realism. The intensity of emotion gives way to a more mature and practical appreciation of what it takes to share life's responsibilities on a daily basis.

Because of this, considerations such as your partner's spiritual life, priorities, work habits, relationship with parents, and philosophy of child-rearing must be of paramount inportance. **Careful and realistic considerations in the early stages will prevent frustration and heartache later.**

-13-

CHOOSING A CHRISTIAN MATE

"Do not be unequally yoked together with unbelievers. For what fellowship has righteousness with lawlessness? And what communion has light with darkness?" (II Cor. 6:14).

The Bible is very forceful about the number one qualification for a marriage partner: he or she must be a Christian! We are to marry *"ONLY IN THE LORD"* (I Cor. 7:39). Those who ignore this mandate and marry an unbeliever face many stuggles, compromises, and frustrations later in life. They are unable to enjoy the spiritual unity and fellowship unique to the Christian marriage. Inevitably, differences also emerge concerning the moral and spiritual training of the children.

The following two guidelines are important in choosing a Christian mate:

1. *Set Your Standards Beforehand* - Christians should establish spiritual and character qualifications for a prospective partner. We should avoid emotional involvement or commitment with those not meeting these standards. We should likewise never date an unbeliever.

2. *Trust in God's Guidance* - As Rebekah was brought to Isaac through divine guidance (Genesis 24), so we can also trust the Lord to bring us the right person in His timing.

-14-

OTHER CONSIDERATIONS

Wise selection of a mate requires the consideration of other necessary conditions. Following are a list of some of the more important of these:

1. _Spiritual Compatibility_ - Both people being Christians does not guarantee compatibility. There are other questions to consider. Are you comfortable together in prayer? Do you agree on important areas of doctrine? Do you have complimentary goals in serving God? If both individuals can say "yes" to the above questions, there will likely be a strong spiritual dimension in the relationship.

2. _Similar Backgrounds_ - As a general rule, marriages have a greater chance for stability and success when both partners are similar in such variables as age, interests, values, socio-economic level, race, and education.

3. _Complimentary Needs_ - Two people have a greater opportunity for fulfillment when they share complimentary needs. For example, if both enjoy social contacts, even though one may be more shy than the other, they share complimentary needs. If, however, one loves mixing with people and the other is reclusive, their needs are not complimentary.

-15-

4. _Emotional Attraction_ - Choosing a mate on the basis of feelings alone is unwise, but ignoring the need for emotional attraction would also be a mistake. Someone can have all the right qualifications but without the spark of emotional magnetism, he or she is probably not for you.

5. _Physical Attraction_ - Physical attraction should never be the main qualification in a partner. However, it is important that your prospective mate at least be physically acceptable to you.

6. _Mental and Emotional Maturity_ - A successful relationship requires maturity. Maturity is witnessed by a number of factors such as a capacity to accept responsibility, self control, the ability to be objective with problems, acting your age, being sensitive to others, a responsible attitude toward money, a healthy attitude toward sex, an ability to make decisions, etc. The maturity factor of a prospective mate deserves careful consideration.

-16-

PRINCIPLES OF BUILDING A RELATIONSHIP

Most singles, by the time they are saved, have been fully indoctrinated into a worldly pattern of relating to the opposite sex. Many have spent years of practicing a lifestyle of loose morals and sexual permissiveness. Now as a Christian, you must be *"transformed by the renewing of your mind"* (Rom. 12:2). **The principles of building a relationship in the kingdom of God are different from that of the world.** The worldly pattern is built on the premise of receiving selfish pleasure and immediate gratification. **The kingdom pattern works toward building a lasting relationship that will bring glory to God and fulfillment to those involved in it.** It builds slowly and carefully, constantly testing the divine will, and allows God to give it shape and confirm its direction. **The Christian relationship must avoid being controlled by the elements of emotion, sexual desire, or premature commitment.** Instead, it should follow the guidelines given on the following pages.

-17-

I. AVOID THE DATING GAME

Christians must free themselves from the idea that frequent dating should be the normal lifestyle of a single person. It is safer and far more edifying to mix within groups of singles, than alone with the opposite sex. The Christian single is looking for God's choice in a mate, and trusting Him to bring the right one in His time. **Dating is not wrong if it is done God's way with the right person. The following are some guidelines:**

1. *Set Your Standards* - Don't get involved with anyone who is not fully committed to Christ.

2. *Relate Before You Date* - Really get to know a person through group fellowship and personal interaction before you do something alone together. Don't date without a sincere interest and attraction.

3. *Avoid Vulnerable Situations* - Stay in public places and away from situations that may lead to sexual temptation.

4. *Do Edifying Things* - Hiking, biking, picnics, dining out, etc. Give opportunity for fellowship and getting to know one another.

-18-

II. BUILD A STRONG FOUNDATION

Just as Jesus Christ is the chief cornerstone of the church (I Pet. 2:6), He must also be the foundation for every developing relationship. A soulish foundation is built merely on feelings. Though love is the power behind a growing relationship, the Christian must insure that the following stones are part of the initial foundation.

1. _Sense of God's Witness_ - There must be a "spiritual witness" about the relationship before any serious commitments are made.

2. _Spiritual Compatibility_ - A strong spiritual foundation is laid by fellowship around spiritual things (i.e., praying together and reading the Word). There should also emerge a similar spiritual perspective and a shared vision for service.

3. _Develop as Friends_ - Hot and heavy romances inevitably burn out! The ones that last have a strong friendship base where the two people share interests and enjoy the other's company in a variety of life's experiences.

-19-

III. COMING UNDER COUNSEL

"Obey those who rule over you, and be submissive, for they watch out for your souls, as those who must give account" (Heb. 13:17).

Once a relationship reaches a level of serious commitment, a couple should go to their spiritual oversight, i.e., pastors or elders, and communicate what is taking place with them. Leaders are set in the body to guide the church and to *"watch . . . for your souls"* (Heb. 13:17).

Seek their counsel regarding your relationship and any cautions or concerns that they may have. Because of their position and maturity, they may have some unique insights that can benefit the growth of your relationship. Marriage counsel is a vital part of preparation for marriage. As the date draws near, arrange for marriage counseling with your pastor or someone he may appoint.

A couple must avoid the impulse to get married as soon as they make a commitment to each other. **A sufficient amount of time must be given to the courtship stage in order to develop a realistic understanding and knowledge of each other.**

-20-

IV. WHAT ABOUT PETTING

"For I have betrothed you to one husband, that I may present you as a chaste virgin to Christ" (II Cor. 11:2).

As two people grow together in their commitment and begin to spend more time with each other, there is an ever present temptation for greater physical involvement. An affectionate kiss or holding each other's hand is no longer enough.

The above scripture gives us an important principle to honor in this aspect of a relationship. The word "chaste" means "clean or innocent". Paul desired to present the church to Christ free from all moral defilement. All sexual involvement including petting, apart from marriage, is inconsistent with this principle.

Courtship is a time for relating spiritually, mentally, and emotionally. The pleasures and privilege of sexual involvement come after marriage. Petting, apart from marriage, is a form of defrauding in that there is sexual arousal without the allowance of fulfillment. It is also toying with temptation.

Too often, the best intentioned couple goes too far and then must cope with guilt and condemnation. Though there is grace and forgiveness, keeping God's standards is the real goal.

-21-

◄ CONCLUSION ►

The Christian single is in a unique position to live a life of productive and fruitful service unto the Lord. The only obstacle to this is coming to a place of contentment and trust in God regarding your station in life.

The years of your singleness are a divinely ordained time meant to be used constructively and with purpose in God. Those should be years dedicated to spiritual growth, involvement in church life, and preparation toward career betterment.

The individual that uses this time in his or her life for these purposes becomes a wise steward and will look back with satisfaction upon their decisions. They will be like the profitable servant who invested the talents given to him, who later received the Lord's commendation, *"Well done, good and faithful servant . . . Enter into the joy of your Lord"* (Matt. 25:21).

For a brief summary of the main points of this booklet, read the boldly printed words on each page. We also recommend reading the C.E.I. counseling booklet entitled, "What the Bible Says About Sex".

-22-

Chapter 14

What The Bible
Says About Sex

By William R. Kimball

◀ INTRODUCTION ▶

The subject of sex is a sensitive and delicate issue to many people. Some individuals feel awkward, uncomfortable, and slightly embarrassed when discussing the subject. Yet, it is a crucial area of concern which we are repeatedly confronted with.

Furthermore, **the subject of sex is not a taboo topic as far as God is concerned. The Bible does not ignore this vital issue, but addresses it in a healthy, candid, and informative manner.** Since the scriptures are not silent regarding this issue, we should earnestly endeavor to determine what the Bible has to say.

This counseling booklet approaches the subject of sex in a comprehensive yet concise manner. It carefully examines this controversial subject in a sound and sensitive style. It strives to establish the biblical guidelines, perspectives, and understanding needed in order for God's people to be properly instructed and informed concerning this important area in the human experience.

-1-

◀ TABLE OF CONTENTS ▶

-2-

SEXUAL PRESSURES FROM SOCIETY

The sexually stimulating spirit of our age creates a constant climate of sensuality and sexual arousal which exerts tremendous influence upon our emotional, mental, physical, social, and spiritual well-being. **A great deal of pressure, confusion, and misinformation is often the direct by-product of society's extreme emphasis upon sexuality.** Western society is so obsessed with the subject of sex that it borders upon unofficially deifying it. Sex has become one of the major topics of concern in casual conversations, in business, politics, television, magazines, movies, theater, and the arts.

The emphasis upon sex and sensuality has become so commonplace and commercialized that the advertising media has used it to sell everything from toothpaste to soft drinks, bluejeans to cigarettes.

-3-

Its emphasis is so inescapable that one writer noted, "One would have to be a hermit to avoid the sexually arousing stimuli of our day."[1] **Our senses are literally bombarded by a constant glorification of sexual promiscuity, permissiveness, and outright perversion.**

The world often packages and promotes sexuality in a distorted and wreckless manner which encourages sexual gratification outside the boundaries ordained by God. **Society's attitude toward sex is often based upon a carnal system of amoral ethics which openly challenges and contradicts the clear teachings of God's Word.** Often, what society has deemed culturally acceptable is totally unacceptable to God's standard of righteousness.

The steady stream of sexual misinformation is responsible for misdirecting many. The popular emphasis upon permissiveness creates confusion for believer and unbeliever alike. **On the following pages we will examine the scriptural guidelines concerning sex to determine what the Christian response, perspective, and attitude should be.**

[1]Gary R. Collins, **Christian Counseling**, pg. 281.

-4-

WHO CREATED SEX?

God was the creator of sex. Man did not invent sex. Even though society and Satan have abused, perverted, and distorted the sexual experience, **God was the one responsible for originally instituting sex as a healthy, creative, and normal facet of the human experience.** Contrary to the misconceptions of some, sex is not a result of sin or the fall of man, but a divinely instituted dimension in the human experience which came into existence before sin and rebellion even entered the world.

In the beginning, God created male and female with the instruction to *"be fruitful and multiply"* (Gen. 1:27, 28). He also called them to be *"one flesh"* (Gen. 2:24). These facts clearly involve nakedness and intimate sexual union, and demonstrate that God was the original author of sexual intercourse.

-5-

WHY DID GOD CREATE SEX?

God ultimately created sex for the pleasure and fulfillment of man. Contrary to certain teachings, sexual contact was not primarily intended for procreation. Though the conception of children and the propagation of the race is an important outgrowth of sexual intimacy, this was not the sole purpose intended by God.

Sexual intimacy, within the framework structured by God, was intended to be a profoundly beautiful and gratifying activity to enrich the human experience between a man and a woman. The scriptures capture this fact well when they encourage the pleasures of physical sexuality between marriage partners:

". . . rejoice with the wife of your youth. As a loving deer and a graceful doe, let her breasts satisfy you at all times; and always be enraptured with her love" (Prov. 5:18, 19).

-6-

WHAT IS GOD'S ATTITUDE TOWARD SEX?

Within its godly context, sex is never scripturally characterized as something lewd, shameful, or unhealthy. Neither is it depicted as an act which God reluctantly tolerates as a necessary evil or obligation within the marriage contract. God clarifies this fact when He declares: *"Marriage is honorable among all, AND THE BED UNDEFILED"* (Heb. 13:4).

God's attitude towards sexual intimacy is never restrictive, prudish, or Victorian. The Bible portrays godly sexuality as a beautiful, rewarding, and wholesome experience. Neither is God ashamed to discuss the subject, for it is mentioned in almost every book of the Bible. In fact, the central theme of the Song of Solomon involves the sexual pleasures between married lovers.

God's attitude should not only challenge the corrupt concepts embraced outside the church, but should also check the unhealthy, negative, and scripturally unsound attitudes harbored within the church concerning the subject of godly sexuality.

-7-

GOD'S ORDAINED STRUCTURE FOR SEX

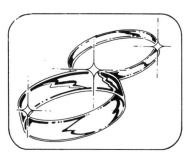

"Marriage is honorable among all, and the bed undefiled; but fornicators and adulterers God will judge" (Heb. 13:4). **God has ordained the marriage covenant as the proper sanctuary for sexual gratification and involvement.** God strongly condemns sexual permissiveness and experimentation outside the boundaries of marriage. God's sexual policy and program remains intact in spite of society's repeated challenges against it.

Even though society may condone sexual permissiveness and promote premarital sex, extramarital sex, and homosexuality, God has confined sexual involvement to the marriage structure. This is His divine framework for sexual pleasure and fulfillment. He also established it as an important safeguard against sexual sin: *"Nevertheless, because of sexual immorality, let each man have his own wife, and let each woman have her own husband"* (I Cor. 7:2).

-8-

SEXUAL SINS PROHIBITED BY THE BIBLE

The scriptures condemn a wide variety of immoral, sexual acts. We will examine the more predominant ones as follows:

I. FORNICATION

Fornication is simply defined as "sexual intercourse between unmarried individuals of the opposite sex". The word fornication is mentioned forty-seven times in the New Testament where it is strongly characterized as a sexual sin and denounced as a deviation from God's ordained pattern for sexual fulfillment.

The word fornication comes from the Greek word "PORNEIA". It is where we derive the English term "pornography". In a broader sense, the word fornication includes more than just illicit sexual intercourse. It covers a wide range of sexual sin and perversity such as incest, rape, prostitution, bisexuality, transvestism, sadomasochism, bestiality, exhibitionism, and voyeurism.

-9-

The following selected scriptures prohibit fornication:

- *"Do you not know that the unrighteous will not inherit the kingdom of God? Do not be deceived. Neither FORNICATORS, nor idolaters, nor adulterers, nor homosexuals . . ."* (I Cor. 6:9).
- *"Now the body is not for FORNICATION, but for the Lord . . ."* (I Cor. 6:13, K.J.V.).
- *"FLEE FORNICATION . . ."* (I Cor. 6:18, K.J.V.).
- *"Now the works of the flesh are evident, which are: adultery, FORNICATION, uncleanness, licentiousness . . ."* (Gal. 5:19).
- *"But FORNICATION . . . let it not even be named among you, as is fitting for saints"* (Eph. 5:3).
- *"For this is the will of God . . . that ye should abstain from FORNICATION"* (I Thess. 4:3, K.J.V.).

-10-

II. ADULTERY

Adultery is defined as "sexual intercourse between a married person and someone other than their mate." The Bible strongly condemns extramarital sex because it violates the sanctity of the marriage covenant. It is a sexual sin which is strictly forbidden by the Ten Commandments: *"You shall not commit ADULTERY"* (Ex. 20:14). The Bible repeatedly challenges the sin of adultery:

- *"Moreover you shall not lie carnally with your neighbor's wife, to defile yourself with her"* (Lev. 18:20).
- *"Do you not know that the unrighteous will not inherit the kingdom of God? Do not be deceived. Neither fornicators, nor idolaters, nor* **ADULTERERS,** nor homosexuals . . . (I Cor. 6:9).
- *"Marriage is honorable among all, and the bed undefiled;* **but fornicators and ADULTERERS God will judge"** (Heb. 13:4).

(See also Lev. 20:10; Deut. 22:22; Prov. 6:29; Rom. 13:9).

-11-

III. PORNOGRAPHY

Pornography is defined as "material (such as books or pictures) which depict erotic behavior intended to stimulate sexual arousal." Pornographic involvement is a sexual sin because it produces lustful thoughts which war against the soul (I Pet. 2:11). It is a deceitful sin because it arouses sexual desire without providing godly sexual fulfillment. **It is a potentially devastating sin because it is addictive and inevitably leads to further depths of sexual experimentation and perversion.** It pollutes our thought life with sensual fantasies and desires which often overwhelm a person with temptation and specific acts of sexual sin. **Pornographic lust has been proven to be a major contributing factor in other forms of sexual perversion such as rape, incest, prostitution, and child molesting.**

The Bible reveals the seriousness of sexually lusting with the eye when it places it on the same level as outright adultery (Matt. 5:28).

-12-

IV. HOMOSEXUALITY

Homosexuality is defined as "sexual activity between members of the same sex."

Throughout human history, homosexuality has experienced recurrent periods of popularity. Homosexuality has reached epidemic proportions in contemporary Western society. The so-called "gay movement" has been very vocal in its attempts to legalize homosexual acts between consenting adults and has exerted strong influence upon the public consciousness to condone homosexuality as a normal sexual alternative.

But in spite of the aggressive attempts to legitimize homosexuality and establish it as an acceptable sexual life-style, the Bible remains unwavering in its strong denunciation of homosexuality as a sexual perversion which is a blatant violation of God's ordained pattern for sexual fulfillment.

The Bible challenges the sin of homosexuality as follows:

-13-

- *"You shall not lie with a male as with a woman. It is an abomination"* (Lev. 18:22).
- *"Do you not know that the unrighteous will not inherit the kingdom of God? Do not be deceived. Neither fornicators, nor idolaters, nor adulterers, **NOR HOMOSEXUALS, NOR SODOMITES"** (I Cor. 6:9).*
- *"For this reason God gave them over and abandoned them to vile affections and degrading passions. For their women exchanged their natural function for an unnatural and abnormal one; men also turned from natural relations with women and were set ablaze with lust for one another, men committing shameful acts with men"* (Rom. 1:26, 27, Amp.).
- *"These laws are made to identify as sinners all who are immoral and impure: homosexuals . . . and all others who do things that contradict the . . . good news of our God"* (I Tim. 1:10, 11, L.N.T.).

-14-

V. MASTURBATION

A measure of confusion and conflicting opinion exists between Christian counselors concerning the subject of masturbation. A few view it as an acceptable means of releasing sexual tension and averting sexual abuse, while others strongly denounce it as a sexual sin. But one thing is clear: the scriptures are silent about this issue. Therefore, **we must be careful not to exaggerate the problem by placing masturbation on the same level of such sexual offenses as fornication, adultery, or homosexuality.**

However, there are factors each Christian should consider: 1.) Masturbation is a poor sexual substitute for marital fulfillment. 2.) Masturbation produces harmful results such as intense guilt, self-condemnation, fear, and anxiety, which can undermine our emotional, mental, and spiritual well-being. 3.) **The inescapable fact remains that masturbation involves sexual fantasies and lustful thoughts which are condemned by the scriptures** (Col. 3:5). These factors should strongly challenge us to seek God's help in achieving a higher standard of holiness which overcomes the sexual temptation and need for masturbation.

-15-

WHY HAS GOD PLACED RESTRICTIONS UPON SEX?

God has placed restrictions upon the sexual activities we have touched upon because they represent a perversion of God's perfect plan for mankind. **He has also imposed guidelines upon human sexuality because of the devastating consequences of sexual sin.**

Though sexual gratification outside the boundaries established by God may be intensely pleasurable, the scriptures state that the *"pleasures of sin"* are only for a season (Heb. 11:25). **Sexual permissiveness and perversion leads to inevitable disappointment.** Though the detrimental impact of sexual sin may not show up immediately, it will invariably exact a heavy toll upon our emotional, mental, spiritual, social, and physical well-being.

However, even if individuals manage to minimize the negative impact by justifying their sin or hardening their hearts against the effects of guilt, they cannot escape the inevitable consequences of violating God's sexual standards. The Bible makes this clear when it declares: *"Let no one deceive you with empty words, for because of these things the wrath of God comes upon the sons of disobedience"* (Eph. 5:6).

-16-

161

THE RESULTS OF REJECTING GOD'S SEXUAL STANDARDS

Sexual sins can produce many harmful results:

1. **MENTAL AND EMOTIONAL — The consequences of sexual sin often lead to emotional trauma and turmoil.** The results of rejecting God's Word often produces self-condemnation, guilt, anxiety, insecurity, and fear. Sexual sins often create deep emotional wounds which scar a person for life. The sexual hurts, offenses, and transgressions of the past can haunt a person for years. The so-called "sexual freedom" outside the scriptural boundaries established by God does not really produce liberty at all. People end up becoming emotionally and mentally enslaved to dehumanizing passions which progressively distort the God-given plan for genuine sexual fulfillment and pleasure.

2. **SPIRITUAL — Sexual sins have a devastating impact upon our spiritual well-being.** They are a common factor in the spiritual shipwreck of many. This is why the Bible so strongly warns us about the destructive consequences of unrepented sexual sins (I Cor. 6:9, 10).

-17-

3. **PHYSICALLY — Not only do sexual sins affect us mentally, emotionally, and spiritually, but they often have a destructive effect upon our physical well-being as well.** The scriptures clearly indicate this fact when they say:

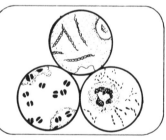

"Flee sexual immorality. Every sin that a man does is outside the body, but he who commits sexual immorality sins against his own body" (I Cor. 6:18).

The medical statistics substantiate this statement. The sexual revolution of the 60's and 70's has resulted in an unprecedented epidemic of sexually transmitted diseases such as Chlamydia, gonorrhea, syphilis, and genital herpes, as well as cervical cancer, pelvic inflammatory disease (PID), female sterility, illegitimate pregnancies, and abortions. Between 10 and 20 million Americans presently have genital herpes. The spread of homosexuality has also resulted in the outbreak of A.I.D.S., A.R.C. Syndrome, and certain strains of cancer. **History has consistently demonstrated a direct proporational link between sexual promiscuity and the physically related consequences.**

-18-

THE CHRISTIAN RESPONSE

Christians should not only have a healthy sexual perspective concerning the pleasures and fulfillment intended by God within the marriage covenant, but they must also recognize the devastating consequences of sexual sin.

We must recognize that sex is a powerful tool which Satan often uses to undermine our spiritual, emotional, and physical well-being. Satan knows that many are very vulnerable in this area of their life and will use sexual allurement as a weapon to attack us. For this reason, we should take heed to the following cautions and safeguards:

1. **"FLEE FORNICATION"** (I Cor. 6:18, K.J.V.). *"But now I have written to you not to keep company with anyone named a brother, who is a fornicator"* (I Cor. 5:11). **We must strive to avoid any situation, location, or individual which may have a detrimental influence upon us or may expose us to undue temptations and the danger of sexual compromise.**

-19-

We should flee fornication with the same prompt conviction and determination as Joseph who fled the sexual advances of Potipher's wife (Gen. 39).

2. **"So kill the evil desire lurking in your members — those animal impulses and all that is earthy in you that is employed in sin: sexual vice, impurity, sensual appetites"** (Col. 3:5, Amp.). We must *"make no provision for the flesh"* (Rom. 13:14) by yielding to the carnal impulses of the *"old man"* instead of to God. If we walk in the Spirit, we won't fulfill the lusts of the flesh (Gal. 5:16).

3. **"For this is the will of God, your sanctification: that you should abstain from sexual immorality;** *that each of you should know how to possess his own vessel in sanctification and honor, not in passion of lust"* (I Thess. 4:3-5). Instead of gratifying the carnal inclinations of the "old man", we should dedicate our lives to the pursuit of holiness, the advancement of God's kingdom, and the glorification of Christ in word and deed.

-20-

THE VIRTUE OF VIRGINITY

Virginity has lost much of its honor and sacredness in today's society. "Saving one's self" sexually for your husband or wife is frowned upon by many as being unrealistic, foolish, and old-fashioned. Yet **virginity is a virtue which is honorable before God.**

God is not only interested in the purity of our soul and spirit, but He is also concerned with the chastity and purity of our bodies. We must recognize that our bodies belong to the Lord and should be used to glorify Him (I Cor. 6:15-20). The Bible reminds us that, *"the body is not for sexual immorality but for the Lord . . . therefore glorify God in your body and in your spirit, which are God's"* (I Cor. 6:13, 20). **Keeping ourselves sexually undefiled before marriage is an act of glorifying God with our bodies.** Furthermore, the Lord considers a born-again Christian to be a virgin in spite of his or her past sexual involvements and sin. This is because, *"if any one is in Christ, he is a new creation; old things have passed away; behold, all things have become new"* (II Cor. 5:17).

-21-

◄ CONCLUSION ►

We have carefully examined the subject of sex in the light of the scriptures. Though it is a delicate and often controversial area, it is not a topic which God ignores or treats lightly. **Sex is a subject which all Christians have a responsibility to be informed about.**

We have seen that sex was intended to be a beautiful and immensely gratifying dimension in the human experience when fulfilled within the context of God's ordained structure for sexual expression. When men and women violate God's established guidelines, abuse the sexual role, or pervert the sexual act, they will experience the inevitable destructive consequences which affect our mental, emotional, social, physical, and spiritual well-being.

For further counsel concerning this sensitive subject, we recommend that you contact your pastor or church counseling staff. **For a brief overview of the main points in this booklet, please re-read the boldly printed words on each page.**

-22-

Chapter 15

Knowing
God's Will

BY TERRY D. EDWARDS

◄ INTRODUCTION ►

The scriptures reveal that **God is both omnipotent and omniscient,** i.e., all-powerful and all-knowing. In the book of Isaiah, we see that before Him *"the nations are as a drop in a bucket",* and *"its inhabitants are like grasshoppers"* (Isa. 40:15, 22). We are also told that *"there is no searching of His understanding"* (Isa. 40:28).

When we consider the greatness of God, we understand why David exclaimed, *"What is man that You are mindful of him?"* (Psalms 8:4). He is not only mindful of us, but actually has a purpose and plan for each of our lives.

In this booklet, we will see that **God desires for us to know His will.** We will also examine the different means He uses to reveal His will to us.

-1-

CAN WE KNOW GOD'S WILL?

★Yes! **Every Christian is given both the right and the responsibility of knowing the will of God.** We not only can know it, we are expected to know it. We are told in Ephesians 5:17, *"Therefore do not be unwise, but **understand what the will of the Lord is."***

We have received the privilege and ability to know God's will through our adoption into his eternal family (Gal. 4:5, 6). The sign of this adoption is the indwelling Holy Spirit who comes to *"guide you into all truth"* (John 16:13). **It is the Holy Spirit within us that enables us to know God's will** in every aspect of our life. Jesus spoke of Him in John 16:14 when He said, *"He will take of what is Mine and declare it to you."*

-3-

The Christian needs to know the will of God in these **two general areas:**

1. **How should I live?** — This question concerns our moral and spiritual conduct. We need to know how to behave ourselves in a fashion that will please God.

2. **What should I do?** — This area involves those decisions we must make concerning our life direction. Among these are choices concerning our employment, relationships, how to handle problems, whether to move, involvement in ministry, etc.

The answers to how we should live are clearly revealed in the Bible. Knowing God's will in decisions of direction can be more difficult. **In this booklet, we will see how to determine the will of God for these kind of choices.**

-4-

THE IMPORTANCE OF GOD'S WILL

At one point during the Sermon on the Mount, Jesus began to instruct His disciples on the proper way to pray. The second line in what we term the Lord's Prayer contains the phrase *"Your will be done on earth as it is in heaven"* (Matt. 6:10). In praying this, **Jesus reveals that God's desire is for those on earth to express His will just as it is done in heaven.**

This prayer will be fulfilled completely when Christ returns to subdue His enemies and to establish His rule on this earth (Rev. 19 and 20). Until then, His church is the place where His kingdom is to be manifested. **Every born-again believer is a member of His church, and is to live his life according to the will of God.**

-5-

We can see the importance of doing God's will in the following reasons:

1. **It assures us of eternal life** — *"Not everyone who says to Me, 'Lord, Lord' shall enter the kingdom of heaven, but he who does the will of My father in heaven"* (Matt. 7:21).

2. **It allows us to understand additional truth** — *"If any man will do his will, he shall know of the doctrine"* (John 7:17 KJV).

3. **It guarantees us that God will hear our prayers** — *"But if anyone is a worshiper of God and does His will, He hears him"* (John 9:31).

4. **It secures for us the promises of God** — *". . . after you have done the will of God, you may receive the promise"* (Heb. 10:36).

-6-

THE PRIORITY OF GOD'S WILL

Jesus set the pattern for how the believer should relate to the will of God. In John 5:30 He declares His commitment by saying, *"I do not seek My own will but the will of the Father who sent Me."* In another place He said, *"My food is to do the will of Him who sent Me, and to finish His work"* (John 4:34). Because of this commitment, just before His crucifixion He was able to say, *"I have finished the work which You have given Me to do"* (John 17:4).

Every believer is to have this same level of commitment to doing God's will. We are told to *"seek first the kingdom of God and His righteousness"* (Matt. 6:33). We should live our lives and make our choices according to what God would want for our lives.

-7-

If the will of God is to be a priority in our life, we must be willing to make the following adjustments:

1. **We must sincerely desire to do His will** — *". . . doing the will of God from the heart"* (Eph. 6:6). God looks upon the heart. If our obedience is not from the heart, it is merely religious duty.

2. **We must be willing to change life habits** — *"If anyone desires to come after Me, let him deny himself"* (Matt. 16:24). This may mean changing friends, activities, and commitments.

3. **We must be willing to suffer** — *"Yet if anyone suffers as a Christian, let him not be ashamed"* (I Pet. 4:16). Obedience to God's will can mean difficulties, ridicule, or even persecutions. Jesus faced Calvary with the declaration, *"Nevertheless, not as I will, but as You will"* (Matt. 26:39).

-8-

THE REWARD OF OBEDIENCE

"And behold, I am coming quickly, and MY REWARD IS WITH ME, TO GIVE TO EVERY ONE ACCORDING TO HIS WORK" (Rev. 22:12).

Obedience to the will of God requires that we resist living according to the course of this world. We must conduct our lives in a way that pleases God. **Living a life of righteousness and obedience calls for both discipline and sacrifice.**

Every effort and commitment, though, will be rewarded. The Lord daily blesses those that live in a covenant relationship with Him. God is constantly aware of our behavior and choices. There is even a greater reward awaiting the faithful and obedient when the Lord shall return and give to every person *"according to his work."*

-9-

HOW TO KNOW HIS WILL — TWELVE WAYS

Even after determining to live our life according to the will of God, **we can still be confused about the right choice in a decision we have to make.**

Should I take this job? Should I teach Sunday School? Is the Lord wanting me to move? These are just a few of the many kinds of choices we must face.

In the remainder of this booklet, we will look at the different indicators to consider when searching for God's direction. Finding His will is not always easy. **He may use any one of these following indicators to reveal His will to us.** As a rule, He will use more than one.

◆**Remember, searching for the will of God must be preceded by prayer.** We do not arrive at God's mind through mere thought. Instead, we must cultivate His presence through prayer.

-10-

I. A STRONG SPIRITUAL LIFE

*"And do not be conformed to this world, but **BE TRANSFORMED BY THE RENEWING OF YOUR MIND,** that you may prove what is that good and acceptable and perfect will of God"* (Rom. 12:2).

A strong spiritual life is the best qualification for being able to hear from God. We must reject being conformed to this world, and allow our minds to be renewed daily by the Spirit and the Word of God.

In I Corinthians 2:14, we learn that the things of God are *"spiritually discerned"*. We must develop our spiritual life if we want to be sensitive to the leadings of God. **A life of obedience, commitment, prayer, and Bible study will allow for this development.**

-11-

II. GODLY MOTIVES

*"**KEEP YOUR HEART** with all diligence, for out of it spring the issues of life"* (Prov. 4:23).

The first thing we must do when seeking for the will of God is to check our motives. What motivation is prevailing in my heart? Am I really wanting to please God, or am I acting selfishly? Is my heart free from bad attitudes? Will I be acting in love?

A choice made from a wrong motive will not be God's choice. Our decisions should always be made from a dedication to please the Lord. We are told to live *"not as pleasing men, but God who tests our hearts"* (I Thess. 2:4).

If our hearts are free from bad motives, we are in the right condition to hear from God.

-12-

III. THE WRITTEN WORD

"All Scripture is given by inspiration of God, and is profitable for doctrine, for reproof, for correction, for instruction in righteousness' (II Tim. 3:16).

The Bible is the clear declaration of the mind and will of God. Many of our decisions can be answered through the clear statements of scripture.

For example, Proverbs 29:15 can answer our questions about the value of spanking as a form of child training and discipline. It states, *"The rod and reproof give wisdom, but a child left to himself brings shame to his mother."* **The scriptures are filled with precepts and principles that give us wisdom in our decisions.**

God will never contradict what He has already spoken in the Bible. Failure to obey scripture is failure to do the will of God (James 1:22).

-13-

IV. THE WITNESS OF THE SPIRIT

"The Spirit Himself bears witness with our spirit that we are children of God" (Rom. 8:16).

The Holy Spirit has been given to the believer to guide us into all truth. It is His purpose to receive from the Lord and to show it to us (John 16:14, 15). One of His functions is to provide for us an **inner witness** or indication of the mind and will of God.

As we mature in our relationship to God, we develop a greater capacity to sense the leading of the Holy Spirit. **This spiritual witness is an inner sense of peace and affirmation when our decision is aligned with the will of God.** This witness is lacking when we are moving against God's will.

Again, we must be careful that the peace we sense is not a result of getting to do what we want. To properly receive this witness, we must be totally committed to doing whatever God's will may be, even if it requires sacrifice.

-14-

V. THE RHEMA

*"The word is near you, even in your mouth and your heart (that is, the **word of faith** which we preach"* (Rom. 10:8).

The Greek word "rhema" for "word" means a "specific utterance or saying." It is used to describe the way God may speak to a person in a separate and distinct way. In Mark 1:11 we have such an example when the Father spoke to Christ saying, *"You are My beloved Son, in whom I am well pleased."*

Few people ever hear the audible voice of God. Instead, **we may feel we have heard a "rhema" from God by sensing an inner impression of faith around a thought we are having.** We may also get this "rhema" from a sense of faith in the application of a certain scripture to our situation.

-15-

There are certain **cautions we must exercise** in regards to hearing a "rhema" from God:

1. **God will never contradict what is already written in His Word** — Whatever we hear from God must be in agreement with the scriptures. It must also be in keeping with the nature of God. Revelations 22:18 gives a severe warning to those who *"add to"* His words.

2. **We must look for other confirmations** — There is much potential for personal feelings and desires to creep in to what we hear from God. Because of this, a "rhema" must be confirmed through other indicators.

3. **We must watch for pride** — When we think we have heard from God, there is a tendency for pride to sneak in. *"Pride goes before destruction"* (Prov. 16:18). Be watchful for this tendency.

-16-

VI. GODLY COUNSEL

"The way of a fool is right in his own eyes, but **HE WHO HEEDS COUNSEL IS WISE"** (Prov. 12:15).

One of the most important steps in knowing the will of God is to seek counsel from others. The above scripture reveals that it is the foolish person who ignores the valuable input of good counsel. By ourselves, we may see only a part of the total picture. Others can help enlarge our understanding. Our personal feelings and biases alone may discolor our judgment. Others can offer objective advice from a neutral position. This is why we are told that *"in the multitude of counselors there is safety"* (Prov. 11:14).

We should **choose godly counselors** that have a reputation for wisdom. We must avoid seeking counsel from those who will only tell us what we want to hear.

-17-

Spiritual leaders have been set in the church to help instruct and guide the people of God. **They should have a special counseling role in any major decision which we face.**

The following are some scriptures that show the place of godly overseers in our lives:

*"***Obey those** *who rule over you, and* **be submissive,** *for* **they watch out for your souls,** *as those who must give account. Let them do so with joy and not with grief, for that would be unprofitable for you"* (Heb. 13:17).

"And we urge you, brethren, to **recognize those who labor among you, and are over you in the Lord** *and admonish you, and to* **esteem them very highly in love** *for their work's sake"* (I Thess. 5:12, 13).

Church leaders are usually wise and gifted counselors that we should consult for help in important decisions.

-18-

VII. CIRCUMSTANCES

*"But I will tarry in Ephesus until Pentecost. For a **great and effective door has opened to me,** and there are many adversaries"* (I Cor. 16:8, 9).

We see from the above scriptures that Paul made a decision to remain at Ephesus because existing circumstances indicated that *"a great . . . door"* was opened for the gospel.

Circumstances can often be a strong indication of God's direction for us. A new job offer, an opportunity for advancement, a lack of finances, or other circumstances may indicate the choice we are to make.

However, we must **be careful when making circumstances the only indication of God's will.** Other indicators such as godly counsel or an "inner witness" should also be present.

-19-

There are occasions when **circumstances may warrant us testing the will of God by stepping forward.** In so doing, we hope to get a clearer witness concerning the direction that God would have us take.

We have an example of this with Paul in Acts 16:7: *"After they had come to Mysia, they **tried to go into Bithynia,** but the Spirit did not permit them."*

Before we test the Lord's will by stepping forward, we must be careful to have right motives, good counsel, and a sufficient inner witness to do so.

After stepping forward, we must analyze the circumstances and "inner witness" we receive, and again seek godly counsel for further direction.

-20-

VIII. PROPHECY

*"As they ministered to the Lord and fasted, **the Holy Spirit said,** Now separate to Me Barnabas and Saul for the work to which I have called them"* (Acts 13:2).

The will of God can be revealed through a personal, directive prophecy. There are a number of occasions in the New Testament where this is the case.

There are, however, some cautions to consider regarding personal prophecy. First, prophecies are to be judged (I Cor. 14:29). Personal prophecies should be spoken in the presence of mature leadership ministries so they can be considered and confirmed. **Secondly,** personal prophecy should be received only from those with proven prophetic or leadership ministries. **Thirdly,** the person receiving the prophecy should have a witness in his heart. **If a prophecy is judged and confirmed, it can then be a valid indication of the will of God.**

-21-

IX. VISIONS AND DREAMS

*"And a **vision appeared** to Paul in the night. A man of Macedonia stood and pleaded with him, saying, Come over to Macedonia and help us"* (Acts 16:9). God may speak to us through visions or dreams (see also II Cor. 12:4, Acts 9:10; 10:10; 22:17).

However, it is important to realize some facts about visions and dreams:

1. **They are rare** — Their lack of frequency in scripture, when considering the time periods involved, prove that they are rare.

2. **They were very clear** — Those seen in scripture were both vivid and extraordinary. They could not be a product of imagination or ordinary dreaming.

3. **Their message was obvious and precise** — God always clearly revealed their meaning to the person they affected.

Visions and dreams should not be sought after. If God chooses to communicate to you in this fashion, it will be obvious.

-22-

X. THE FLEECE

*"Then Gideon said to God . . . Look, I shall put a **FLEECE** of wool on the threshing floor; if there is dew on the fleece only . . . then I shall know that You will save Israel by my hand, as You have said"* (Judges 6:36, 37).

This incident recorded in Judges 6 has given rise to a technique of determining God's will called "fleecing the Lord". **It involves setting up a condition that God must meet to prove that He is guiding someone in a particular direction.**

The Lord met Gideon in his request, yet **there are some definite cautions** regarding the idea of "fleecing the Lord". **First,** Gideon's circumstance was unique and extraordinary. **Secondly,** it appears to be a rare technique of determining God's will in scripture. **Finally,** fleecing can be presumptuous. It presumes that we can dictate how God will speak to us. Because of these reasons, "fleecing" can lead to error. Therefore, **we must also require other indicators.**
-23-

XI. NO WITNESS IS GOD'S WITNESS

*"Trust in the Lord with all your heart, and **lean not on your own understanding; in all your ways acknowledge Him, and He shall direct your paths"*** (Prov. 3:5, 6).

It is common when seeking God's will in a decision to not receive any witness at all. In such instances, we may actually be getting a very clear witness. **No witness is often God's way of telling us to continue on in our present direction.** His apparent silence can leave us frustrated and believing that He is not answering our prayer for guidance. Actually, His silence is His way of indicating that there should be no change.

However, we should be careful in accepting a "no witness" as His will too quickly. Further prayer may be required, or it may indicate improper timing. **Such situations should be submitted to church leadership for counsel.**

-24

XII. TWO OR MORE WITNESSES

"*. . . by the mouth of two or three witnesses the matter shall be established*" (Deut. 19:15).

The scriptures give us an important principle in determining the will of God. It is the principle of two or three witnesses. In the Old Testament, it was forbidden to convict a person for a crime on the testimony of only one witness (Deut. 17:6; 19:15). The same principle is found in the New Testament, and requires that an accusation against another be verified by two or three witnesses (see Matt. 18:16; II Cor. 13:1).

This principle can also be applied to establishing the will of God in a matter. **When God is leading you, He will confirm it by two or more witnesses.** For example, a personal prophecy can be confirmed by the witness of leadership. Requiring two or three witnesses in seeking the will of God can prevent us from making a wrong decision.

-25-

◄ CONCLUSION►

God desires that we both know and walk in His will. We have briefly examined the different ways that He can reveal His will to us. **Still, finding the will of God may not always be easy.** Often, He first has to deal with wrong motives or attitudes in our lives, or it may take Him time to arrange the people or circumstances that will eventually bring us the understanding of His will.

However, we do have a promise from God that He will answer. In Jeremiah 29:13, He declares, "*And you will seek Me and find Me, when you search for Me with all your heart.*" If we are conscientious and careful, in due time He will reveal His will to us.

For a brief overview of the main points of this booklet, please re-read the boldly printed words on each page

-26-

Chapter 16

Finding Your Place
In The Body

BY TERRY D. EDWARDS

◀ INTRODUCTION ▶

Forty days after His resurrection, Jesus ascended bodily to be with the Father — but He did not leave! His life and ministry is deposited in all those who join themselves to Him through faith. He continues to orchestrate and administrate His plan of redemption for the human race through the church which is also called His body (Eph. 1:22, 23).

Every believer, at the time of conversion, becomes a member of the body of Christ. Each one of us is a vital member of this divinely structured group of people. We all have a place in the body of Christ and are called to contribute to its growth and ministry. When we discover and accept our place, we receive a fulfillment and peace. **This booklet examines the purposes and ministries of the body of Christ and concludes by giving some helpful tips to finding your place within it.**

-1-

◀ TABLE OF CONTENTS ▶

-2-

WHAT IS THE BODY OF CHRIST?

"And He put all things under His feet, and gave Him to be head over all things to the church, which is His body, the fulness of Him who fills all in all" (Eph. 1:22, 23).

The body of Christ and the church are one and the same. Both terms represent those individuals who have been saved by receiving Jesus Christ as their Lord and Savior. The term "church" is the Greek word "ekklesia" meaning "called out". It refers to those who have been called out of the world into citizenship in the kingdom of God (Col. 1:13). The term "body of Christ" has reference to the organic union between the Lord Jesus and the total company of believers that are joined to Him.

At conversion, every believer is born again by the Holy Spirit who enters our hearts and makes our body the temple of God (Gal. 4:6; I Cor. 6:19). Simultaneously, by the same spirit we are all baptized into the body of Christ (I Cor. 12:13). **Each of us are included as an individual part of the many membered body of Christ of which Jesus is the head.**

-3-

By describing the body of Christ as the *"fulness of Him"* in Ephesians 1:23, the Lord is communicating the inseparable union and complete identification He has with His people. Through the incarnation, Jesus shared in our humanity as the second Adam and forever linked Himself to us in what we might term a spiritually organic realtionship (I Cor. 15:45).

Just as Christ shared in our humanity through actual experience, we, likewise, must commit ourselves to a tangible participation in His body. **We are members of the universal body of Christ, consisting of every believer who has ever lived, but we must also become faithful, contributing members of a local expression of His body through involvement in a church.** It is through the practical commitment of each member to one another, in the will of God, that Christ's purposes with His body will be fulfilled.

-4-

EVERYONE HAS A PLACE

"For as we have many members in one body, but all the members do not have the same function, so we, being many, are one body in Christ" (Rom. 12:4, 5).

Our physical body consists of many parts, from kidneys to fingers and from bone marrow to eyeballs. Every part is absolutely essential in order for our body to function properly. So also is the body of Christ. There are many members, each with his own place and contribution, yet only one body. **We each differ in respective talents, abilities, and areas of ministry, but we are all necessary and important.**

Every Christian has been specifically created, gifted, and graced for a unique place of contribution and service. I Corinthians 12:18 tells us that *"God has set the members, each one of them, in the body just as He pleased."* **Finding our place in the body requires that we acknowledge the fact that we each have a special place and that we should be willing to accept the unique position which God has given us.**

-5-

There are two reactions described in I Corinthians 12 that interfere with the unity and function of the body of Christ:

1. Insecurity — In I Corinthians 12:15 Paul humorously describes the foot, in insecurity, denying its place in the body because it is not the hand. The lesson is obvious: a foot lacks the visibility, creativity, and dignity of the hand and would therefore be the one that tended to insecurity. Many saints who lack distinct gifts or public ministry tend toward the same reaction. We must not allow insecurity or jealous comparison to cause us to depreciate our function or keep us from accepting our place in the body.

2. Pride — In I Corinthians 12:21 Paul pictures the eye proudly rejecting the hand by saying, *"I have no need of you."* We are *"individually members of one another"* (Rom. 12:5), and must acknowledge the value of every person's place. This is especially important for those with a more obvious gift ministry.

-6-

EVERYONE HAS A GIFT

"And to one he gave five talents, to another two, and to another one, to each according to his own ability" (Matt. 25:15).

Jesus related the parable of the talents to **convince each of us that we have gifts, talents, and abilities** that are **to be invested in His work.** This parable also includes these essential points:

1. <u>We All Have Natural Abilities</u> — God created each one of us as a unique person. We were born with certain natural interests and aptitudes. Some are musically inclined, some are mathematically gifted. Some love working with children, while others have carpentry or mechanical skills. Your natural abilities and inclinations are not a coincidence. You were specifically designed for God's purposes: *"we are His workmanship"* (Eph. 2:10.) The Lord equips us for our service and calling according to our *"own ability"* (Matt. 25:15).

-7-

2. **<u>God Graces Our Natural Ability</u>** — In this parable, the talents given by Christ represent God's grace (special endowment for service) being poured upon our natural abilities. These natural abilities, energized by the Spirit of God, then become gifts to the body of Christ. We are told in Romans 12:6 *"Having then gifts differing according to the grace that is given to us, let us use them."* Without the special edowment of God's grace on our natural abilities, we will not profit His purposes. Jesus describes this relationship in John 15:5: *"He who abides in Me, and I in him, bears much fruit; for without Me you can do nothing."*

3. **<u>We Must Be Faithful</u>** — The major point of the talents is that God requires us to be faithful with our gifts and callings: *"Moreover it is required in stewards, that a man be found faithful"* (I Cor. 4:2, K.J.V.). Those that wisely invested their talents were commended with *"Well done, good and faithful servant"* (Matt. 25:21). The one who hid his talents was rebuked and his talent was given to another. God desires our fruitfulness through faithfulness.

-8-

OUR GIFTS ARE MEASURED

"But to each one of us grace was given according to the measure of Christ's gift" (Eph. 4:7).

The Holy Spirit was given without measure to Jesus *"For in Him dwells all the fulness of the Godhead bodily"* (Col. 2:9). He is the head of the body and *"of His fulness we have all received"* (Jn. 1:16). The body of Christ consists of many members, each with gifts and talents that have been measured to them. As we find our place, invest our gifts, and receive each others' ministry, we grow to *"a perfect man, to the measure of the stature of the fulness of Christ"* (Eph. 4:13).

The measure of our gift is seen in the quality, scope, and effectiveness of it in relationship to God's purposes. The following are four considerations concerning the measure of our gift:

1. Relate To Your Gift Realistically — We need a realistic appraisal of our gifts and abilities. Romans 12:3 teaches a man *"not to think of himself more highly than he ought to think, but to think soberly, as God has dealt to each one -9- a measure of faith."*

2. *The Measure of Your Gift Can Increase* — The present measure of our gift can increase in quality, scope, and effectiveness in time. God rewards faithfulness and diligence. In the parable of the pounds, those who invested theirs received more in proportion to their initiative even though each was initially given only one talent (Lk. 19:11-26).

3. Don't Step Beyond Your Measure — Paul said, *"We, however, will not boast beyond measure, but within the limits of the sphere which God appointed us"* (II Cor. 10:13). Our participation and service should always be aligned with God's grace and calling. Do not step into areas of ministry where the gift is either lacking, insufficient, or non-existent.

4. Do Not Measure Yourself by Yourself — Those using only themselves or a select group of close peers for their standard of measurement are not wise (II Cor. 10:12). A more valid estimation of our gifts and abilities can be derived through a broader comparison of other ministries and functions in the larger body of Christ. A healthy contact, interaction, and exposure to other ministries helps give us balance and definition. It also positively provokes us and stimulates refinement in our progress and development in ministry.

-10-

OUR GIFTS ARE FOR SERVING

"For who is greater, he who sits at the table, or he who serves? Is it not he who sits at the table? Yet I am among you as the One who serves" (Lk. 22:27).

Jesus was nearing the time of His crucifixion. He had demonstrated the power and character of the kingdom of God to His disciples for over three years. Yet at the last supper a dispute arose among them as to who would be the greatest after He left. The above words spoken by Jesus were meant as both a rebuke and a teaching. It was essential that the disciples recognize that those who represent Jesus do so with the motive to serve.

Jesus is among His body as one who serves. **Our gifts and callings are for the purposes of serving others and building up the body of Christ.** We naturally receive a sense of usefulness and fulfillment whenever our gifts provide a contribution to others. The scriptures remind us of the source of our abilities: *"What do you have that you did not receive?"* (I Cor. 4:7). We must become servants and do what we do for the glory of God.

-11-

INTRODUCING THE GIFTS

There are many functions and ministries necessary for the proper growth and expression of the body of Christ. The New Testament provides a listing of twenty-one of these. On the following pages we will briefly describe each of these since they provide a foundation for the majority of body ministry. Other vital ministries that are not included in these include such areas as singing, worship leading, intercession, the playing of instruments, etc.

The gifts we will define are a part of the following three categories:

1. The Gifts of Function (Romans 12:6-8) — These seven gifts provide the motivation and outworking for most of the body ministries.

2. The Gifts of the Spirit (I Cor. 12:8-10) — These nine gifts are manifestations of the Holy Spirit and provide a supernatural dimension to the body of Christ.

3. The Five-Fold Ministry (Eph. 4:11) — These five gifts are offices given to equip and edify the body of Christ.

-12-

THE GIFTS OF FUNCTION

1. The Gift of Prophecy — The gift of prophecy involves speaking under the direct unction of the Holy Spirit. It is primarily "forthtelling" under the influence of the Holy Spirit to declare with a heightened sense of inspiration and quickening the mind of God. It can include foretelling as well, though this predictive element functions more fully in the office of the prophet.

The forthtelling aspect of this gift includes speaking unto *"edification and exhortation and comfort"* (I Cor. 14:3). It differs from the prophecy gift of I Corinthians 12 only by degree. The prophecy of I Corinthians 12 is a manifestation of the Spirit and may not necessarily imply a consistent, abiding, personal gift as does that of Romans 12 (Example: read Acts 21:9).

2. The Gift of Ministry (Service) — The gift of service involves the motivation to serve in practical, necessary ways in order to meet a current need. Individuals with this ministry are usually responsible, willing helpers that experience a great sense of fulfillment in getting the job done. They can be a special blessing to the leadership by their responsive volunteer labor.

-13-

This gift is the incentive for the ministry of helps as seen in I Corinthians 12:28, and should be resident in those functioning as deacons (Example: read Acts 6:2, 3).

3. The Gift of Teaching — The gift of teaching involves the motivation and ability to search out and expound to others the truths contained within the Word of God. The Greek word for teaching found in Romans 12 is the word "didaskalia" and means "instruction". Many can teach the Word of God, but the gift of teaching is apparent in an individual's drive for truth and in his motivation and ability to convey it. Those with this gift can be a valuable asset in Sunday School catechism courses, home meetings, etc. Depending upon the degree of gift, with proper training and supervision some of these individuals may develop into the five-fold office ministry of a teacher (Example: read Acts 18:24).

-14-

4. The Gift of Exhortation — In the New Testament, exhortation means an appeal, an entreaty, encouragement, consolation, and comfort. To exhort is to admonish or urge someone to follow some course of action. We are all called to *"exhort one another daily"* (Heb. 3:13). However, a person with the gift of exhortation will be a concerned individual with an eye to see the area of need and the ability to communicate the proper advice, encouragement, warning, or direction to others. If the gift is there, the burden to assist others in this way will be consistent and bear fruit (Example: read Acts 2:40).

5. The Gift of Giving — A person with a gift of giving is one who enjoys giving financially to contribute to the advancement of the kingdom of God. This person usually has the ability to make money and in turn, gives it generously. The gift of giving is seen in its consistency and in the increase and blessing of God on the one with the gift (Example: read Acts 4:36, 37).

-15-

6. The Gift of Leadership — The person with this gift has the ability and motivation to lead others in accomplishing God's purposes. These individuals clearly grasp the vision of the kingdom of God and have the capacity to both inspire and guide others in establishing different areas of ministry. The gift of leadership is necessary for the function of *"administrations"* spoken of in I Corinthians 12:28. It must be present in the eldership of a local church. It is important for the pastoral ministry, and is essential for the office of an apostle (Example: read Acts 2:14).

7. The Gift of Mercy — Those with the gift of mercy naturally identify with and feel strong empathy for those who suffer misfortune or are experiencing some type of hurt. Their sympathy leads them to acts of kindness, help, and comfort towards those in need. God is the source of all mercy (Ps. 103:8), and He requires all of His children to be merciful (Lk. 6:36). However, this attribute is especially manifest in those with a gift of mercy (Example: read Acts 9:36).

-16-

THE GIFTS OF THE SPIRIT

1. The Word of Wisdom — This involves the quickening, illumination, or impartation of divine inspiration to see, understand, and respond to life situations from God's frame of reference. It is a specific impartation given by the Spirit of God granting divine insight and understanding as to how to proceed in a given circumstance or situation (Example: read Matt. 22:17-22).

2. Word of Knowledge — This is the supernatural revelation to men of some detail of the knowledge of God. It is the impartation of facts, information, and details which are humanly impossible to know. The manifestation of the word of knowledge is a direct impartation or quickening to the recipient mind of a portion of the all-knowing mind of God (Example: read John 4:18).

3. Faith — This gift is the God-given ability to believe Him for the impossible in a situation beyond the normal faith potential. It is the faith to accomplish specific tasks, face potentially overwhelming circumstances, or to perservere in the face of dangerous situations (Example: read Acts 27:21-25).

-17-

4. Gifts of Healing — The gift of healing is the supernatural ability to minister physical healing to those who are sick or infirm. The plural "healings" in I Corinthians 12:9 may imply the idea of spiritual, emotional, mental, or psychological healing (Example: read Acts 3:6, 7).

5. The Working of Miracles — A miracle is a phenomenon that is supernatural — an act which is contrary to the physical laws of nature. Miracles defy reason and transcend natural laws. This gift requires God working through individuals to perform the impossible (Example: read Acts 13:11).

6. Prophecy — Prophecy is speaking under the direct unction of the Holy Spirit. It is primarily "forthtelling" and speaking forth with a heightened sense of inspiration and quickening of the mind of God. It can include a quality of foretelling as well, though this predictive element functions more fully in the office of a prophet. Every saint is encouraged in this manifestation (I Cor. 14:1 - Example: read Acts 21:9).

-18-

7. Discerning of Spirits — This gift involves the divine ability to perceive the spiritual source behind a word, motive, attitude, mood, or action in an individual or group. The spiritual source being discerned may be either heavenly, human, or demonic. This gift is manifested in the lives of all Spirit-filled believers at various times (Example: read Acts 8:20).

8. Tongues — The gift of different kinds of tongues is the supernatural linguistic ability to communicate in a language or languages that you are unfamiliar with. It may involve the languages of men, or the supernatural languages of angels. This gift is available to all believers (I Cor. 14:5), and is important for our spiritual edification (I Cor. 14:4 - Example: read Acts 10:45, 46).

9. Interpretation of Tongues — The gift of interpretation is the supernatural, spontaneous ability to interpret an utterance given in tongues into the language understood by the people present. This gift has nothing to do with a natural knowledge of languages but rather comes directly from God (Example: read I Cor. 14:13).

-19-

THE FIVE-FOLD MINISTRY

"And He Himself gave some to be apostles, some prophets, some evangelists, and some pastors and teachers" (Eph. 4:11).

The Apostle — The ministry of the apostle has continued throughout church history. It must be distinguished from that of the first apostles in that they were uniquely used to lay the foundation of the church and to establish the doctrines and teachings of the New Testament. Apostles were *"wise master builders"* (I Cor. 3:10), able to lay a healthy spiritual and doctrinal foundation in a local church. They are usually pioneers with a vision for the "church at large". Church movements with a world vision often arise out of their ministry.

Apostles must be spiritual, self-sacrificing men whose ministries are witnessed by both fruit and signs (II Cor. 12:12). They must work well with the other five-fold ministries since theirs is an administrative and co-ordinative position.

-20-

189

The Prophet — The New Testament prophet must have the gift of prophecy along with the "forthtelling" dimension. They speak forth the mind and will of God in a predictive, directive, and oftentimes corrective message. Those recognized in this office must be mature, seasoned men, strong in the Word of God and of excellent character.

The New Testament prophet differs from that of the Old Testament in that their prophecies rest on a finished revelation. Besides this, their prophecies are to be examined and judged (I Cor. 14:29).

The Evangelist — The ministry of the evangelist is to preach the good news of Jesus Christ. Evangelists have a special burden for the lost. Besides people being saved, their ministry can be accompanied by signs and wonders (Acts 8:6, 7). Evangelists should be committed members of a local church. Their ministry to the church includes inspiring the saints in a burden for the lost and equipping them in evangelism.

-21-

The Pastor — The title "pastor" literally means "a shepherd". The pastor is called to tend and care for the flock of God. The nature of his calling demands a broad area of ministry. He must be able to feed the flock with proper teaching from the Word of God. His character example must be above reproach. The demands of the flock also require that he raise up other shepherds to assist him.

The Teacher — The ministry of the teacher is vital to the growth and health of the church. This ministry is foundational in establishing the saints in sound doctrine as well as inspiring them to search out the precious truths contained in scripture.

The five-fold ministry teacher must have a well developed and anointed gift of teaching. His life must also be a teaching by example.

-22-

FINDING YOUR PLACE

Many Christians have a real struggle finding their "ministry". They live anxiously and confused, waiting for God to say, *"This is the way, walk in it"* (Isa. 30:21). Remember, God has not called you to be something you are not. He wants us to be released for service in what we are. **God has made you perfectly suited for the particular ministry He has called you to.** Following are some additional tips for finding your place in the body:

1. <u>Submit Yourself to God's Calling</u> — Jesus Christ is the head of the body. We must be willing to accept whatever place or function He has for us. Every ministry and area of service is important. You will find personal contentment when you accept the place God has for you. Remember, what God calls you to, He equips you for. It is also essential not to negatively or competitively compare your place with that of others (II Cor. 10:12). Envy and covetousness destroy our spiritual life.

-23-

2. <u>Give God Time</u> — Many Christians get ahead of God in their expectation of their place of service. In the earlier part of our Christian development, the Lord wants us to learn to know Him and His Word. He would rather we be like Mary sitting at His feet learning His Word rather than like Martha scurrying about in over-busyness (Lk. 10:40-42).

3. <u>Get Involved</u> — Once a basic foundation is laid in our life, we should get involved. There are many areas of service that all saints are called to such as prayer, witnessing, church work days, other helps, etc. We are called to general involvement. Often our experience in these activities will help reveal our interests and callings.

4. <u>Consider Your Abilities and Desires</u> — We should evaluate our talents and abilities to realistically determine what we are qualified for. A person who is tone deaf is certainly not called to songleading. God's grace energizes our natural abilities. Strong and consistent interest or desire may also indicate a calling to an area of ministry.

-24-

5. The Evaluation of Others — The comments and opinions of others can give us insight into our own abilities and areas of effectiveness. Leaders can be a special help in this way as God usually gives them a sensitivity to the gifts and callings of members of the church. Personal prophecy may occasionally confirm an area of calling.

6. Further Training and Preparation — Once we discover our place of function and calling, we must be diligent to further prepare ourselves. We should employ those disciplines that will enhance our ability to be effective in our area of ministry. We should seek the advice of those with an established "like ministry" in our local chruch.

7. Be Willing to Sacrifice — There is a cost involved with every calling in the kingdom of God. The Lord tests our commitment and motives by our willingness to sacrifically apply ourselves. Through testings and sacrifices, our character is strengthened and God blesses with a greater anointing and effectiveness.

-25-

◄ CONCLUSION ►

The Spirit of God is currently at work in the church to bring a new and deeper revelation of the body of Christ. Those sections of scripture dealing with the body have received increased interest and attention in the last few years. People have been earnestly seeking out their place of service and function. Because of this, the church is in a time of growth and fruitfulness. Along with this there has been a breaking down of man-made barriers that separate Christians from one another. We must pray that the move of God continues. The results will be a greater revelation of Jesus Christ to the world.

For further study on this area we recommend reading:

Finding Your Place in the Body of Christ, by Dick Benjamin
2626 Abbott Road
Anchorage, Alaska 99507

For a brief overview of the main points of this booklet, please re-read the boldly printed words on each page.

-26-

Chapter 17

Overcoming Offense

By William R. Kimball

◀ INTRODUCTION ▶

We've all experienced offenses. Each of us have been responsible for offending others, as well as having been offended ourselves.

Often, offenses are little more than minor injustices and misunderstandings. At other times, they are severe and long lasting. Sometimes offenses are unintentional; at other times they are deliberate and malicious. **Regardless of the nature of the offense, the Bible teaches us to respond to this problem in a righteous manner.**

In this booklet, we will examine this subject and review the steps to overcoming the offenses in our life.

-1-

◀ TABLE OF CONTENTS ▶

-2-

HOW CAN WE DEFINE OFFENSE?

An offense can be defined as **"a feeling of being insulted, slighted, or wronged."** It is an emotional response to an injustice or indignity.

When we are offended we often experience hurt feelings, resentment, anger, contempt, and personal outrage. Offenses are usually the result of being unfairly treated, or feeling that our rights have been violated.

The word "offense" is found in the scriptures. It originally meant a trap or snare. It simply means a "stumbling block". Offenses are anything which becomes a hinderance or obstacle to ourself or to another.

-3-

HOW COMMON ARE OFFENSES?

Life is filled with potential offenses. Offenses are inevitable. Jesus confirmed this when He stated: *"IT IS IMPOSSIBLE THAT NO OFFENSES SHOULD COME"* (Luke 17:1).

Not only do we repeatedly experience them, but we are all guilty of causing offenses in the lives of others. James proved this when he wrote, *"For in many things we offend all"* (James 3:2, KJV).

Many things can cause an offense. They can range from a thoughtless word, to a failure to greet someone. They can arise from a slanderous tongue, to something as simple as a passing glance. On the next few pages, we will consider some of the most predominant causes of offense.

-4-

COMMON CAUSES OF OFFENSE

I. THE TONGUE

The most common source of offense is the tongue: *"If any man offend not in word, the same is a perfect man"* (James 3:2, KJV).

Since none of us have reached perfection, we all tend to offend with our mouths. Occasionally, **we have all failed to avoid words which have caused others to be offended.**

The tongue can be used creatively or destructively: *"Death and life are in the power of the tongue"* (Prov. 18:21). It is an unruly member which can inflict injury upon others: *"It is an unruly evil, full of deadly poison. With it we bless our God . . . and with it we curse men"* (James 3:8, 9).

-5-

II. AN UNFORGIVING SPIRIT

When we fail to exercise a forgiving spirit, offenses often result. The tendency to hold a grudge, nurse a grievance, or keep a record of wrongs is a common cause of offense. For this reason, Jesus admonished us to forgive: *". . . if you have anything against anyone, forgive him . . ."* (Mark 11:25).

In fact, **Jesus told Peter that we were responsible to forgive our brother for as many as 490 offenses in one day!** (Matthew 18:22).

One of the greatest safeguards against possible offense is the willingness to **forgive and forget quickly**. This is at the very heart of Christian love: *"And be kind to one another, tenderhearted, FORGIVING ONE ANOTHER, just as God in Christ also forgave you"* (Ephesians 4:32).

-6-

III. OVERLY SENSITIVE

Some people are just too quick to be offended, even for the slightest reason. The Bible refers to some who are easily offended: *"Immediately they are offended"* (Mark 4:17, KJV).

Some offenses are blatant and deliberate, and people are offended for obvious reasons. But too often, offenses are not justifiable. Some people are prone toward offense. **They are overly touchy and sensitive.** They tend to view every infraction as a grounds for offense. They wear their feelings on their sleeves, just waiting for the slightest brush.

It is good to be sensitive, but not so sensitive that we are overly suspicious, critical, or tempermental. Undue sensitivity is an imbalance which needs to be corrected. A failure to do so is a common cause of needless offense.

-7-

IV. INSENSITIVITY TO OTHERS

The opposite of sensitivity is insensitivity. **Some people are insensitive to the feelings of others.** They have not learned to avoid wrong actions, attitudes, or words which contribute to offending others. They tend to be rude, pushy, and indifferent to the sensitivities of others. They often lack tact and courtesy.

This callous and sometimes belligerent attitude is contrary to the Spirit of Christ and the character of God's love. **The Bible teaches us that the love of God *"does not behave rudely"*** (I Cor. 13:5).

God's love is not ill-mannered, discourteous, or rude. It is respectful and considerate of the proper time and place for its actions. **The love of Christ compels us to care for the feelings of others rather than carelessly and mindlessly trampling upon them.**

-8-

V. A FAILURE TO YIELD OUR RIGHTS

When we demand our rights at any cost, we set the stage for offense. **If we have not yielded our rights to God, we may be offended if they are violated or ignored.**

When we go through life expecting everything to go our way and for everyone to respect our rights, we are bound for offense. **The opposite of an unyielded spirit is a meek spirit.** It is a quality of humility and yieldedness of our personal rights which is more concerned with another's welfare.

Paul captured this thought when he stated, *"Let no one seek his own, but each one the other's well-being"* (I Cor. 10:24). The love of Christ *"does not seek its own"* (I Cor. 13:5). God's love, embodied in meekness, is primarily concerned with others, not in demanding our own rights and way. **If we embrace this same spirit of meekness towards other, we soon discover that *"YIELDING PACIFIETH GREAT OFFENCES"*** (Eccles. 10:4, KJV).

-9-

VI. A BITTER SPIRIT

A root of bitterness can often contribute to the rise of further offense. Bitterness is a common source of continuing offense in a person's life.

The Bible tells us that a *"root of bitterness"* defiles many (Heb. 12:15). **If we harbor unresolved resentment in our hearts, it negatively effects every area of our life and pollutes our relationships and attitudes towards others.**

Past bitterness which has not been confessed and cleared up is like an open sore. It is a touchy area which causes a person to be overly sensitive and respond quickly to further offenses, especially when it is similar to the unhealed offenses from our past. Bitterness is a deadly and destructive condition which is an underlying cause of much of the offenses we experience.

-10-

WHAT ARE THE RESULTS OF OFFENSES?

Offenses can have many undesirable consequences. They can produce many detrimental side effects:

1. They generate **resentments** and deepen a root of **bitterness.**

2. They contribute to an atmosphere of **hatred, hostility,** and **tension** within the church.

3. They reinforce a spirit of **distrust, suspicion,** and **misunderstanding** among the brethren.

4. They develop an **unforgiving spirit** which is quick to see the faults in others, and equally as quick to condemn.

5. **They grieve the Holy Spirit** and quench the *"fruit of the Spirit"* in our lives.

-11-

6. They generate **slander, backbiting,** and **gossip** which further contribute to the cycle of offense by involving others in the offense.

7. They build a **critical, judgmental attitude** towards those who have wronged us.

8. **They tend to harden our hearts** against others and God, and produce a **callous spirit** which rejects conviction.

9. They instill a **sense of guilt** and **nagging condemnation** in our hearts because of the unresolved sin.

10. **They create physical, mental, and emotional problems** as a result of the **inner stress** from unresolved offense.

As we can see, offenses can lead to many destructive consequences in our relationship with God and others.

-12-

WHY SHOULD WE STRIVE AGAINST OFFENSE?

★Because offenses are so destructuve.**They damage our relationships with others, grieve the Holy Spirit, and mar the testimony of the kingdom of God.** The Bible teaches us that the kingdom of God is " . . . *righteousness and peace and joy in the Holy Spirit*" (Rom. 14:17).

An important ingredient in kingdom living is right relationships with others. Offenses hinder this. They are a breech in the Spirit, and a source of discord and disharmony. One of the guarantees for maintaining right relationships in the kingdom is to diligently guard ourselves from being a cause of offense and injury to others, and in committing ourselves to healing offenses promptly when they occur.

-13-

THE IMPORTANCE OF NOT OFFENDING

This goal was extremely important to **Paul. He constantly strove to keep his life clear of offenses:** *"This being so, I myself always strive to have a conscience without offense toward God and men"* (Acts 24:16). He also stated that **he endeavored to give " . . . no offense in anything"** (II Cor. 6:3).

Paul's desire should also be reflected in our life, attitude, and testimony. It was his desire that we each fellowship this objective. This was his prayer for the church:

" . . . *that you may be sincere and without offense till the day of Christ"* (Phil. 1:10).

If we also embrace this desire, we will do a lot towards preventing potential offenses.

-14-

HOW SHOULD WE RESPOND?

In order to solve the problem of offense, we must not ignore it. We must respond to offenses in God's prescribed manner.

Even though offenses are a familiar experience, **we find it very convenient to disregard them** or deal with them superficially. This is because it is so uncomfortable to face up to them.

One of the greatest problems associated with offense is our reluctance and failure to face up to them and handle them in a godly manner. We often treat the problem like the proverbial ostrich who buries his head in the sand and simply hopes that it will go away.

-15-

WHAT DOES THE BIBLE SAY?

Overcoming offenses can be a difficult challenge: *"A brother offended is harder to win than a strong city"* (Proverbs 18:19).

The only way to heal offenses is to follow God's directions and willingly submit ourselves to His counsel. God's Word provides clear guidelines for healing offenses. Matthew 18:15 holds one of the most important keys: *"Moreover if **your brother sins against you, go and tell him his fault between you and him alone. If he hears you, you have gained your brother.***"

We will examine the five steps to overcoming offenses on the following pages.

-16-

STEP ONE

"Moreover IF your brother sins against you . . . " (Matthew 18:15).

The first step in handling possible offenses is to **determine whether or not an offense has actually occured.** As we have seen, some people are too sensitive. They tend to be too easily offended for the slightest reason. Often, minor offenses are completely innocent and unintentional.

In these instances, it is best to examine our own attitudes which may need to be challenged, and allow the longsuffering and love of Christ to prevail, realizing that *"love will cover a muiltitude of sins"* (I Peter 4:8).

-17-

STEP TWO

"Go and tell him his fault between you and him ALONE" (Matt. 18:15). **If a real offense has occured, commit yourself to approach your brother alone.**

One of the greatest errors in handling offenses is the tendency to involve others. This only complicates the problem and magnifies the offense. **When others are needlessly involved, people take sides and further fan the flames of discord and misunderstanding.**

We must approach our brother privately and deal with the offense in a considerate and Christ-like manner between ourselves and *"him alone".* **This is as strong safeguard against a wider sphere of offense.**

-18-

STEP THREE

*"If he hears you, you have **GAINED** your brother"* (Matt. 18:15).

Our primary objective should be to win our brother. We must earnestly desire reconciliation, simply because we are dealing with a brother in Christ and not an enemy.

We must not go in a harsh, unforgiving, or judgmental spirit, but in a sincere spirit of meekness and love. We should earnestly seek the ultimate restoration of the offender. **We must go with an attitude which is quick to forgive and ready to restore.**

Therefore, we must carefully **examine our hearts and motives before we attempt to handle an offense.**

-19-

STEP FOUR

*"If you . . . remember that your brother has something AGAINST you . . . **GO YOUR WAY . . . BE RECONCILED TO YOUR BROTHER"*** (Matthew 5:23,24).

It may be that we have not been offended, but that we have offended others, or each party has been responsible for offending each other.

If this is the case, **we bear the personal responsibility, according to the Word of God, to take the initiative to go to those we have offended and seek reconciliation and forgiveness.** This requires a confession of our faults and a sincere clearing of any sin which has caused offense to another. A failure to do this will only result in a continuing offense.

-20-

STEP FIVE

In dealing with offenses, **the real goal is not just in treating offenses when they occur, but endeavoring to walk in a way which does not cause offenses in the first place.**

Our goals should be the same as Paul who stated: *"**GIVE NO OFFENSE,** either to the Jews or to the Greeks or to the church of God"* (I Cor. 10:32). **We should strive to avoid any action, attitude, or word which would needlessly cause an offense to another.**

To do this, we must covenant in our hearts to guard against all possible offenses before they occur. We must join with Job in our hearts and sincerely confess that, *"I will offend no more"* (Job 34:31).

-21-

◀ CONCLUSION ▶

We have reviewed the basic steps for overcoming offenses. We have seen the importance of dealing with this problem promptly, and in the right spirit. If we follow God's prescription for this problem, we can successfully heal offenses whenever they occur.

◀ ASSIGNMENT ▶

If you are aware of any existing offense, you should commit yourself to go to the person, or persons involved and seek forgiveness. This will require a repentant attitude on your part, and a sincere desire to seek reconciliation and healing.

For a brief overview of the main points in this booklet, please re-read the boldly printed words on each page.

-22-

Chapter 18

Overcoming
Bitterness

By William R. Kimball

◀ INTRODUCTION ▶

Bitterness affects everyone. Each of us have wrestled with our personal bouts of bitterness. Usually it is a minor irritation, while at other times it can become a deep-seated sickness which affects every area of our life. Usually, it is a temporary problem which is soon resolved. At other times, it becomes a long-standing condition which lingers for a lifetime.

The world is filled with bitter, resentful people who have never come to grips with bitterness or learned to adequately deal with it.

This counseling booklet confronts the problem of bitterness in a concise yet comprehensive manner. It is designed to help Christians overcome this problem by examining the scriptural guidelines offered by God.

-1-

◀ TABLE OF CONTENTS ▶

-2-

WHAT IS BITTERNESS?

Bitterness can be defined as "an intense, deep-seated feeling of resentment, indignation, and ill-will against someone or something which we feel has committed an insult, injustice, or offense against us." It is an emotional response which results from failing to properly deal with feelings of personal outrage, anger, unforgiveness, and contempt.

It is a condition which can arise when we fail to adequately resolve feelings of personal injury such as being humiliated, offended, unfairly treated, slighted, misunderstood, misused, misinterpreted, wronged in some way, or having our rights violated or ignored.

-3-

HOW COMMON IS BITTERNESS?

The Bible warns us to be *"looking diligently lest anyone fall short of the grace of God; **lest any root of bitterness springing up cause trouble, AND BY THIS MANY BECOME DEFILED"*** (Heb. 12:15).

Feelings of bitterness and resentment are universal. They are so common and widespread that they affect everyone at some point in their life. No one is exempt or totally immune. It strikes young and old, male and female, rich and poor, learned and unlearned, healthy and unhealthy, believers and unbelievers.

Whether bitterness is severe or mild, isolated or widespread, a short term problem or one which lingers for a lifetime, everyone has had to struggle with this area.

-4-

WHAT ARE THE EFFECTS OF BITTERNESS?

Bitterness breeds a wide variety of destructive conditions. **It adversely affects every area of our mental, emotional, physical, social, and spiritual well-being.**

Bitterness contaminates us with feelings of hostility, animosity, resentment, antagonism, hatred, suspicion, jealousy, and vindictiveness. It can quench our joy and enthusiasm for life, undermine our interest for the things of God, harden our hearts, pervert our spiritual judgment, distort our image of God, and ruin relationships.

Bitterness generates irritability, frustration, discontent, anger, apathy, stress, and feelings of rejection and condemnation. It can cause nervous tension, insomnia, physical and emotional fatigue, headaches, high blood pressure, loss of appetite, and ulcers.

-5-

HOW SERIOUS IS BITTERNESS?

Bitterness is like a festering sore. **It is a cancerous condition which can consume us** with ill-will, negativity, slander, fault-finding, cynicism, criticism, complaining, and an argumentative spirit.

The Bible compares bitterness to a *"root"* and declares that many have been *"defiled"* by it (Heb. 12:15).

The scriptures speak of a *"root of bitterness"* because its potential effect upon our life can be as widespread and deeply embedded as the action of spreading roots which take hold and entangle our life. When bitterness is allowed to take root, it becomes an increasingly deadly and destructive problem which chokes every area of our existence. **If left unchecked, it will completely contaminate us and eventually undermine our relationship with God, spell spiritual shipwreck, and seriously damage our relationships with even our closest loved ones and friends.**

-6-

COMMON CAUSES OF BITTERNESS

I. UNFULFILLED EXPECTATIONS

The seeds of bitterness often take root when we fail to achieve our goals, fulfill our dreams, and realize our expectations in the timing and manner in which we had hoped.

Many feel that life has somehow cheated them. Some individuals harbor deep resentments that life has dealt them a raw deal. They may feel that God or other people have been cruel, unjust, and unfair by shortchanging them or giving them a rough break. Bitterness may stem from feeling neglected, left out, bypassed, or overlooked.

Often, it seems that the course of our lives is beyond our control. When we feel that we have no say concerning the events which befall us, we may feel trapped, frustrated, and a helpless victim of circumstances. This condition provides the fertile soil for a root of bitterness to take hold.

-7-

II. UNRESOLVED OFFENSES

Conflicts with others are a common source of lingering bitterness and resentment. Arguments and quarrels can produce longstanding rifts and feelings of bitterness even between the closest loved ones and friends.

Disagreements, contentions, and strife often create offenses in our hearts. Offenses arise when we feel that an injustice has been committed against us. This can be in the form of feeling insulted, maligned, slighted, mistreated, misinterpreted, misunderstood, abused, or wronged by another party.

When interpersonal feuds, conflicts, disputes, controversies, grudges, antagonisms, jealousies, and competitiveness towards others are not resolved, our failure to reconcile them will result in increasing feelings of bitterness which poison and pollute our entire system.

-8-

III. UNRESOLVED ANGER

Bitterness and anger are closely related. **Bitterness is often the by-product of an angry spirit.** When we fail to deal with the sin of unrighteous anger, the consequence is often an embittered spirit.

Some individuals are infected with hostility and anger. They are consumed with an angry and antagonistic spirit. The focus of their anger can be a person, circumstance, or thing. It can even be directed against God.

Some people express their anger outwardly, while others bottle it up and secretly conceal their inner rage and frustration. Those who quietly repress their hostility generally end up with a great deal of pent-up animosity and hatred which eats away at them in the form of deep resentment and bitterness.

-9-

IV. A FAILURE TO FORGIVE

An unwillingness to forgive others is usually at the very heart of bitterness. When we stubbornly refuse to forgive an offending party, we begin to lay the groundwork for longlasting bitterness.

The tendency to hold a grudge, nurse a grievance, dwell upon past offenses, or keep a record of wrongs is a common cause of continuing bitterness. One of the great contributing factors in a deepening root of bitterness is a person's persistent refusal to forgive.

Many people suffer from a bitter spirit simply because of their reluctance to forgive. This failure to forgive can actually cause a person to spend a lifetime brooding over the offenses of yesterday and reinforcing their feelings of animosity, vengefulness, and resentment towards other people.

-10-

V. A FAILURE TO YIELD OUR RIGHTS

Individuals who have not genuinely submitted their lives to the Lordship of Christ or yielded their personal rights to God are particularly prone to offenses and feelings of resentment.

People who go through life demanding their own way, expecting everything to be in their favor, and for everyone to respect their rights are especially susceptible to feelings of resentment. They become bitter towards God and others when their feelings are overlooked, their freedoms violated, their plans disrupted, or their rights aren't honored.

The failure to exercise a yielded spirit or meekly surrender our rights unto God often results in resentment. This is a common reaction in those who secretly harbor the selfish, self-centered attitude that the world revolves around them. Consequentty, mounting feelings of animosity and a preoccupation with bitterness arise when they discover the sobering reality that this is not the case.

-11-

VI. FELLOWSHIPPING BITTERNESS

Sometimes a person will unconsciously acquire the bitterness and offenses of another. **Bitterness is like a contagious disease which can be caught through our fellowship and contact with a bitter person.**

QUARANTINE!
BITTERNESS ~ HIGHLY CONTAGIOUS

Often an innocent person is exposed to the bitterness of another. If the relationship is close and a person fails to guard his heart or exercise godly cautions, he (or she) may subtlely fall prey to the same feelings of resentment and ill-will contained in the heart of the bitter party.

Not only can an innocent person acquire the seeds of bitterness from another, but if bitterness already exists, those feelings may be reinforced. Bitter people often gravitate towards each other for sympathy and mutual self-justification. This common tendency often results in a deeper root of bitterness forming.

-12-

A COMMON TENDENCY

Bitter people often make excuses for their bitterness by blaming God and others. Instead of accepting responsibility for their sin, they attempt to justify their resentment by shifting the blame. They often emphasize the faults of others and rationalize their feelings of offense in order to minimize their guilt, justify their bitterness, and defend their unwillingness to deal with the problem.

However, **before we can successfully overcome this problem, we must confront any unwillingness or reluctance to accept personal responsibility for our bitter feelings.** Rather than pointing the finger at others, we must commit ourselves to deal with our sin in a sincere, willing, and godly manner. A refusal to do so will only result in a continuation of the problem. As long as we persist in making excuses or shifting the blame, the root of bitterness will continue to strengthen its deadly stranglehold upon our life.

-13-

HOW SHOULD WE RESPOND?

Though there are no simple, quick-fix solutions to bitterness, there are several essential steps for successfully overcoming this problem:

I. TAKE IMMEDIATE ACTION

We must recognize that we have a serious problem. We must endeavor to take prompt and decisive action against it. Bitterness is not a condition which we can afford to procrastinate about, take lightly, or allow to remain unchecked in our life. If we fail to act, it will have a devastating and far-reaching impact upon our spiritual, mental, emotional, and physical well-being.

If we allow bitterness to remain unchallenged by justifying it, minimizing its seriousness, or by ignoring the inevitable consequences, the problem will only intensify and reinforce its destructive effects upon our life.
-14-

II. WE MUST SINCERELY REPENT

"If we confess our sins, He is faithful and just to forgive us our sins and to cleanse us from all unrighteousness" (I John 1:9). Repenting is a fundamental step towards overcoming bitterness.

We must go to the root of the problem by recognizing that bitterness is a serious sin which must be sincerely repented of or it will contaminate and corrupt every area of our life.

A refusal to co-operate with the convicting power of the Holy Spirit will only prolong our bitterness. We must come to a place of heartfelt brokenness and repentance before God. We must confess the sin of bitterness and ask for God's cleansing power and forgiveness. This must also include a repentance of any additional feelings of anger, hatred, animosity, vindictivenss, or lack of forgiveness. This is an essential step towards achieving a lasting victory.

-15-

III. WE MUST BE WILLING TO FORGIVE

We must recognize that unforgiveness is a sin which generates grievances, resentment, vindictiveness, and offenses. If a failure to forgive someone is a contributing factor in our bitterness, we must commit ourselves to genuinely forgive those who have offended us.

The Bible appeals to us to *"Let all bitterness, wrath, anger . . . be put away from you, with all malice. And be kind to one another, tenderhearted, forgiving one another, just as God in Christ also forgave you"* (Eph. 4:31, 32).

We must confront any tendency on our part to hold a grudge, nurse a grievance, or dwell upon past injustices. **Forgiveness is not only a preventative safeguard against potential offenses and resentment, but it is also an essential prescription for healing existing bitterness.** If we will commit ourselves to forgive and permit the love of God to prevail, we will eliminate a major obstacle in the pathway to overcoming bitterness.

-16-

IV. WE MUST RECONCILE OFFENSES

If existing offenses between yourself and another are a cause of bitterness, you must take the initiative to heal the offense and reconcile the relationship according to the guidelines provided by God's Word.

No matter how inconvenient or awkward this may be, we must strive for forgiveness and reconciliation. **As long as offenses continue to exist, our feelings of bitterness will continue to thrive and sink their roots deeper into our hearts.** It's not sufficient just to ask God to forgive us for the sin of bitterness if others are involved. We must give more than lip service to the problem. We must accept our personal responsibility to heal any existing offenses, ill-will, and misunderstandings towards those against whom we are harboring bitterness.

We recommend that you read the C.E.I. counseling booklet entitled, "OVERCOMING OFFENSE" for the scriptural steps for accomplishing reconciliation.

-17-

V. WE MUST EMBRACE A GODLY PERSPECTIVE OF LIFE

"And we know that all things work together for good to those who love God, to those who are the called according to His purpose" (Romans 8:28).

Feelings of bitterness and resentment will continue to dominate us as long as we fail to view our life from a godly perspective.

The Bible doesn't say that all things are good, but that *"ALL THINGS WORK TOGETHER"* for our good. This includes ALL of our trials, hardships, disappointments, setbacks, delays, frustrations, circumstances, handicaps, and limitations.

We must recognize that the circumstances of life which we may resent are actually a tool for God to perfect and produce His virtues, character, and good pleasure in us. We must, therefore, stand on this scriptural reality rather than allow ourselves to succumb to feelings of bitterness against either God or our life situation.

-18-

VI. WE MUST APPROPRIATE GOD'S POWER

If we attempt to overcome bitterness in our own strength and determination, we are doomed to failure and disappointment. We must appropriate the power and resources of the Holy Spirit through prayer.

After identifying this problem, we should begin to aggressively attack it through fervent, persistent prayer, knowing that *"The effective, fervent prayer of a righteous man avails much"* (James 5:16).

After we have committed ourselves to following whatever steps are necessary for achieving a victory over our bitterness, we must not ignore or neglect our need for prayer. We must follow through with consistent prayer until this problem is completely eliminated. If we will bring the power of God to bear through prayer, He will impart the necessary grace, strength, and guidance to wage successful warfare and totally eradicate this problem.

-19-

VII. WE MUST NOT FELLOWSHIP BITTERNESS

"Make no friendship with an angry man, and with a furious man do not go, lest you learn his ways and set a snare for your soul" (Prov. 22:24, 25).

When fellowshipping with others, we must cautiously avoid fellowshipping with their bitterness lest we run the risk of acquiring their ways. Bitter people generate bitter feelings which can infect others. Their bitterness subtlely flavors their attitudes, speech, and judgments. Just as people can pick-up on the offenses in others, people can also be gradually influenced and contaminated by the bitter undercurrents in bitter people.

The scriptures warn us of the potentially destructive power through wrong relationships: *"Be not misled: Bad company corrupts good character"* (I Cor. 15:33, N.I.V.). Therefore, we must diligently avoid fellowshipping or sympathizing with the bitterness in others lest we either inherit their resentment or reinforce any existing, unresolved bitterness in our own heart.

-20-

VIII. WE MUST EXERCISE
PREVENTATIVE MAINTENANCE

Because bitterness is such a potentially devastating condition, we must always exercise godly cautions and restraints lest we fall prey to this sin or fall back under its corrosive influence after we have recovered from it.

The scriptures exhort us to *"Keep your heart with all diligence, for out of it spring the issues of life"* (Prov. 4:23). We must be careful not to allow offenses, misunderstandings, anger, disappointments, sensitivities, trials, delays, setbacks, or any other factor to plant the destructive seeds of bitterness in our hearts.

The scriptures further admonish us to be *"looking diligently lest . . . any root of bitterness springing up cause trouble"* (Heb. 12:15). We must be alert, therefore, diligently guarding our attitudes, reactions, motives, confessions, and thought life. We must regularly examine each of these areas and cleanse any tendency on our part to cultivate the seeds of bitterness.

-21-

◄ CONCLUSION ►

We have carefully examined the causes and cures for bitterness. We should review the scriptural responses which apply to our personal situation and make a determined commitment to follow them:

1. **We must take immediate action.**
2. **We must sincerely repent.**
3. **We must be willing to forgive.**
4. **We must reconcile offenses.**
5. **We must embrace a godly perspective of life.**
6. **We must appropriate God's power.**
7. **We must not fellowship bitterness in others.**
8. **We must exercise preventative maintenance.**

Because bitterness is often associated with other problem areas, we strongly recommend that you read the C.E.I. counseling booklets on ANGER, AFFLICTION, and OFFENSE. **For a brief overview of the main points in this booklet, please re-read the boldly printed words on each page.**

-22-

Chapter 19

Overcoming
Worry

By William R. Kimball

◀ INTRODUCTION ▶

Worry is one of the most common dilemmas confronting modern man. We have all experienced repeated bouts with worry. Occasionally, our worry is minor and short-lived, while at other times it is severe and longlasting.

Though we have all experienced some degree of anxiety, some individuals are more prone to worry. They have established a habitual pattern of worry which lasts for a lifetime and progressively dominates every area of their lives.

It may be easy to understand why unbelievers suffer from worry, but it is sometimes difficult to comprehend why Christians suffer from its torturous effects, especially when they have the support of God and his Word on their side.

This counseling booklet is designed to help Christians overcome worry. It offers a comprehensive yet concise examination of this disturbing subject, and presents the liberating insights and scriptural solutions for obtaining a worry-free life.

-1-

◀ TABLE OF CONTENTS ▶

-2-

WHAT IS WORRY?

Though each of us are familiar with the sensation of worry, many of us would have difficulty defining it. Simply stated, **worry can be defined as "a state of mental and emotional agitation and distress resulting from undue concern over something impending or anticipated."** Worry involves an uneasiness of mind or a brooding anxiety about a real or imagined situation or possibility. It is an unresolved feeling of fretful apprehension and mental unrest which is a close companion of fear, anxiety, stress, insecurity, and tension.

In the Bible, the word which characterizes worry is translated "anxiety or care". For example, the scriptures declare, *"Do not be anxious* (worried) *about anything"* (Phil. 4:6, N.I.V.). It is taken from a Greek word which literally means, "to divide, rip, or tear apart". It aptly describes the torturous effects of worry which tears at our heart, mind, and emotions.

-3-

WHO SUFFERS FROM WORRY?

Everyone! Feelings of worry are so prevalent and widespread in today's society that they have reached epidemic proportions. **Worry is one of the greatest problems affecting mankind.**

Everyone experiences worry in some degree of intensity and duration during their life. No one is exempt or totally immune. Worry afflicts both young and old, children and adults, men and women, rich and poor, educated and uneducated, healthy and unhealthy, godly and ungodly. It is a universal problem which cuts across every conceivable social, ethnic, and racial barrier.

Worry is such a commonplace problem that it has been referred to as the "official emotion of our age", and "the most pervasive psychological phenomenon of our time". It stands out as one of the greatest sources of human suffering and distress.

-4-

WHAT ARE THE EFFECTS OF WORRY?

Worry can produce a wide variety of destructive symptoms which can aggravate our mental, emotional, physical, and spiritual well-being. These can include the following:

- mental and emotional fatigue
- drug and alcohol dependance
- loss of appetite
- lack of concentration
- stomach problems

- ulcers
- frequent headaches
- backaches
- insomnia
- skin rashes

- high blood pressure
- migrains
- hyper-tension
- heart problems
- nervousness

Worry can paralyze us with fear, confusion, and insecurity. It can cripple our faith and undermine our joy, peace of mind, and our sense of contentment. Worry can destroy our physical, mental, and spiritual enthusiasm, motivation, and energy. It can cause us to withdraw from life, become antisocial, and sink into depression. It can stifle our creativity, dull our personality, and distort our judgment. As we can see, worry breeds a whole host of harmful consequences which can hinder our well-being if not handled properly.

-5-

COMMON CAUSES OF WORRY
I. UNCERTAINTY ABOUT THE FUTURE

An anxious anticipation about future uncertainties is a major cause of worry. Jesus indicated this fact when He cautioned, *". . . do not worry about tomorrow"* (Matt. 6:34).

We live in a world of constant change, unrest, and instability. The current climate of international tension generates a constant undercurrent of apprehension. This tends to reinforce an atmosphere of worry, insecurity, and uncertainty concerning the possibilities of tomorrow. The arms race, the threat of nuclear holocaust, the growing crime rate, the ever-changing economic scene, political upheaval, and the "doomsday" forecasts both within and without Christendom create a mental environment conducive for breeding worry and apprehension.

Whether our worry involves the minor consequences of life or major life changing possibilities, our ability to pay a bill or our chances of surviving a nuclear holocaust, **the uncertainty about the conditions of tomorrow stands out as the greatest, single source of worry.**

-6-

II. THE CARES OF THIS WORLD

Christ cautioned us about being overly concerned with the cares of this life (Lk. 21:34). **The carnal concerns of this present life often intensify the potential for spiritual unrest, anxiety, and worry.**

This is especially true in our materialistic age. We live in a world of carnal value systems, demands, and expectations. Christians are constantly harassed and bombarded by secular enticements and influences which promote carnal cares and encourage us to measure up to the standards of success and security which the world embraces.

Some Christians succumb to unnecessary worry because they are overly anxious and agitated about the affairs of this present life. Instead of confidently trusting God as their provider and establishing a priority of seeking *"first the kingdom of God and His righteousness"* (Matt. 6:33), they are overwhelmed with worry about making a living, acquiring possessions, saving for the future, achieving material expectations, or "keeping up with the Joneses".

-7-

III. THE PRESSURES OF LIFE

The pressures of life are a close companion to the cares of this world. **The challenges, concerns, and complexities of modern life exert tremendous pressures upon us which can overwhelm us with worry and anxiety.**

The unrelenting demands of our pressure cooker world, the constant crush of responsibilities, and the never ending strain of meeting deadlines, achieving goals, or fulfilling expectations can often create a state of stress and worry concerning our ability to meet the obligations of life.

The Bible gives a clear example of the worry which can arise when we fail to handle the pressures of life in a scriptural manner. This can include even the pressures of ministry and service to Christ. In the story of Martha and Mary (Lk. 10:39-42), Jesus gently reproved Martha for her agitation and anxiety. He challenged the worry which had gotten out of control in her rush to fulfill the responsibilities and meet the deadlines confronting her.

-8-

IV. PAST INFLUENCES AND EXPERIENCES

A person's present worries are often the result of past conditioning. Many are victimized by repeated episodes of worry due to the contributing factors from their past. **Yesterday's worries often lay the groundwork for today's anxieties. Previous fears, insecurities, disappointments, traumas, and problems can create a sensitivity in certain areas of our life which manifests itself in the future through recurrent bouts of worry.**

Children can subtly acquire a specific pattern of reoccurrent worry due to repeated exposure to their parents' influence. For example, if their parents suffered from financial distress and upheaval, a child may grow up with a tendency to nurse financial insecurity and worry. If the parents were overly anxious about health problems, a child may grow up with exaggerated anxieties and hypochondria in this area also.

Whatever the cause or source of past worries, our failure to specifically resolve them can result in a prolonged pattern of repetitious worry which can linger for a lifetime and end up reinforcing itself as the years pass.

-9-

V. SELF-DEPENDENCE

When we focus our attention upon ourselves and our own natural abilities to cope with the challenges and responsibilities of life, we begin to prepare the groundwork for worry.
Worry is often the direct result of failing to trust in Christ and depend upon the power of God to confront life's problems. When we assume that we possess the capabilities to solve our problems or manage the challenges and decisions of life, we quickly fall prey to mounting feelings of worry. **When we try to shoulder the burdens of responsibility for our life, we are left to our limited resources and the inevitable consequences of frustration and worry set in.**

Worry is often the result of self-dependence and self-sufficiency. This is a common pitfall which many fall into. Leaning upon our own understanding is hopelessly inadequate. When we fail to surrender our cares to Christ, our burdens grow heavier and our worries gradually intensify.

-10-

VI. SATANIC ATTACK

Satan is often the indirect source of our worry. He recognizes that worry is an extremely effective weapon for undermining our spiritual well-being and bringing us into mental bondage. He is the great instigator behind much of our anxiety. Satan is only too willing to agitate our thinking and encourage us to worry. He knows that if he can direct our attention away from Christ's sufficiency and provision, he can stifle our confidence and faith. He endeavors to focus our attention upon our problems, ourselves, and our natural understanding rather than upon God's counsel, answers, and assistance.

He often paints grim pictures of foreboding possibilities and embellishes our worries with additional suggestions, insights, considerations, and fears in order to further fan the flames of insecurity and worry. Those whose character and temperament are prone to worry are especially susceptable to his attacks.

-11-

THREE REVEALING FACTS ABOUT WORRY

1. <u>**Most of our worries are based upon groundless, imaginary, unsubstantiated fears.**</u> The overwhelming majority of our worries are based on "what ifs" rather than reality.

2. <u>**Worry accomplishes nothing beneficial.**</u> **It is not constructive but destructive. It is not a help but a hindrance. It is not part of the solution but part of the problem.** One of the greatest arguments justifying worry is the deceitful lie that worry can help us solve our problems. Worry solves nothing. It only complicates and intensifies our dilemmas. Even Jesus challenged the uselessness of worry when He stated, *"And which of you by worrying can add one cubit to his stature?"* (Lk. 12:25).

3. <u>**Worry breeds worry.**</u> The more we dwell upon our worries, the more worries we have to dwell upon. **When we preoccupy ourselves with our worries, they become bigger than life and eventually consume us.** The more we focus upon our insecurities, fears, and anxieties, the more distorted and exaggerated they become until God fades from the picture and they completely dwarf the scriptural solutions for our problems.

-12-

IS THERE HOPE?

Absolutely! **God did not intend for worry to be a normal part of the Christian experience.** For this reason the Word of God exhorts us, *"Do not be anxious about anything"* (Phil. 4:6, N.I.V.).

Whether we seldom worry about anything or are chronic worry warts who spend most of our waking hours looking for something to worry about, it is not God's will that we worry. Whether our motto is "Don't sweat it" or "Come worry with me", we can take comfort in the awareness that God's Word provides scriptural solutions for the problem of worry.

The Bible offers a number of liberating guidelines for achieving a permanent victory over anxiety and maintaining a worry-free lifestyle. On the following pages we will carefully consider the scriptural steps which lead us to freedom from worry and anxiety.

-13-

I. REPENTANCE

It may come as a shock to some but worry is actually a sin. Worry is a spiritual problem involving distrust and a lack of faith in Christ. The Bible reveals that *"whatsoever is not of faith is sin"* (Rom. 14:23, K.J.V.).

Before a Christian can overcome worry, he must recognize that it is a sin. Repentance is a crucial first step in successfully waging warfare against our worry. We must not attempt to apply superficial, cosmetic remedies to our worry until we have first dealt with the root problem.

Instead of ignoring or bypassing this underlying problem, we must take prompt, decisive action. We must sincerely ask God to forgive us and cleanse us from our doubt and spiritual unbelief. When we have laid this proper foundation, we can move on to the other essential steps for victory contained in God's Word.

-14-

II. WE MUST PRAY

"BE ANXIOUS FOR NOTHING, but in everything by prayer and supplication, with thanksgiving, let your requests be made known to God; and the peace of God, which surpasses all understanding, will guard your hearts and minds through Christ Jesus" (Phil. 4:6,7).

Prayer is one of the most effective antidotes against worry. It is also one of the greatest safeguards against recurring worry. Prayer represents God's scriptural alternative for anxiety and worry. Prayer is God's channel of release, relief, and resolution.

A great deal of our worry is the result of shouldering the burdens of life without turning to the Lord in prayer. We have instant access to *"the peace of God"* when we release our burdens to the Lord. For this reason, the scriptures exhort us about *"casting all your care upon Him, for He cares for you"* (I Pet. 5:7). When we fail to focus upon Christ through prayer, we begin to experience increasing amounts of anxiety. Prayer is the answer to much of our worry.

-15-

III. WE MUST DISCIPLINE OUR THINKING

One of the greatest contributing factors in our worry is our thought life. **Many individuals slip in to habitual worry ruts because of their unrestrained thoughts.** They tend to magnify, distort, and perpetuate their worries through a failure to control their thoughts.

In order to overcome our mental anxieties we must discipline our thinking. If we focus our minds upon godly realities and truth, we will reinforce faith and security. However, if we dwell upon our fears, yield to our insecurities, or indulge in our worries, we will blow them out of proportion and undermine our spiritual well-being. We must not allow our minds to drift into anxious meditation.

Though the scriptures admonish us to pray instead of worry, they also exhort us to rivet our minds upon those things which are true, honest, just, pure, lovely, and of a good report (Phil. 4:8). **Mental discipline and restraint, working in cooperation with prayer, is an important safeguard for securing the peace of God and maintaining it.**

-16-

IV. TRUST IN GOD'S WORD

We must confront our worries with God's Word. We must discipline our anxious thoughts with the absolutes of scriptural reality instead of dwelling upon our worries, fears, and insecurities.

The truth of God's Word counteracts the faith-defeating effects of unrestrained worry. The Bible not only supplies solutions, but it also instills faith: *"faith comes by hearing, and hearing by the word of God"* (Rom. 10:17).

The promises and assurances of God's Word provide a powerful antidote for the specific areas of worry we are experiencing. If we will search the scriptures for scriptural solutions and then confront our problems, uncertainties, and dilemmas with them, we will effectively overcome a great deal of the anxieties we encounter. When we firmly fix our confidence, reliance, and faith upon God's answers to life's problems, we achieve a victory over our worries.
-17-

V. WE MUST EXERCISE FAITH

The ultimate answer to worry is faith: *"without faith it is impossible to please God"* (Heb. 11:6). Without faith we will never achieve a decisive victory over our worries. For this reason the Bible declares: *"And this is the victory that has overcome the world – our faith"* (I Jn. 5:4). Faith is often the missing ingredient for victory.

Faith does not have to involve feelings. It is an act of our will in obedience to God's Word, whether we feel good or not. The power of faith does not reside in ourselves or in faith itself, but in God. The power of faith is in focusing upon God's power, ability, and desire to meet our needs rather than upon our self-defeating doubts, insecurities, and fears.

Faith involves a reliance in the absolute reality of God's Word. We must stand upon the truth instead of our worries. If God says *"I will never leave you nor forsake you"* (Heb. 13:5), we must believe it. If God says He will *"supply all your need according to His riches in glory by Christ Jesus"* (Phil. 4:19), He means it. Therefore, we must confront our fears with that quality of confident faith which trusts in God and rests in His Word.

-18-

VI. RENEW A PROPER PERSPECTIVE

An important key for overcoming our worry is to renew a godly perspective of our life situation. If we fail to perceive our life situations, at any point, as God perceives them, then we become susceptible to worry.

Worry is a common by-product of unbelief. Unbelief is a failure to see God as a loving, compassionate, all-powerful being who is in absolute control of the universe. Faith arises when we see that God is still in control of our lives and that everything we experience has a divine purpose.

One of the greatest truths a Christian can embrace is the scriptural revelation that *"ALL THINGS WORK TOGETHER FOR GOOD TO THOSE WHO LOVE GOD"* (Rom. 8:28). **This liberating truth can free us from much of the self-imposed worry, insecurity, and fear we experience.** Why fall prey to worry when God is in control of our life and working everything together for good? If we will embrace this fact, we will lay hold of a dynamic faith-builder which will undermine much of the worry we experience.

-19-

VII. SEEK A SPIRITUAL REFRESHING

"REJOICE IN THE LORD ALWAYS. Again I will say, Rejoice! . . . Be anxious for nothing, **but in everything by prayer and supplication, WITH THANKSGIVING,** *let your requests be made known to God"* (Phil. 4:4, 6).

A great deal of our worries can be alleviated when we obtain a spiritual refreshing. **Spiritual refreshing comes as a result of spending quality time with God in worship, praise, and rejoicing.** When we touch God's Spirit through worship, we often discover a powerful release from the self-imposed bondage of mental anxiety and agitation, for *"where the Spirit of the Lord is, there is liberty"* (II Cor. 3:17).

Instead of dwelling upon our self-reinforcing worries, we should separate ourselves unto a time of spiritual communion. This will cause us to rise above our worries and will usher us into a conscious state of anointed confidence, victory, and freedom from our worries.

-20-

VIII. CHRISTIAN FELLOWSHIP

An often overlooked solution to much of the worry we encounter is found through Christian fellowship and involvement with others. Fellowship often provides a healthy means of release from our anxieties and worry fixations.

Contact with others sometimes serves as an effective distraction which diverts our attention away from our self-focusing worries. Fellowship and involvement with Christian friends provides access to a wealth of godly insight, encouragement, counsel, positive exhortation, and comfort which helps relieve the pressures of worry.

The scriptures declare, *"As iron sharpens iron, so a man sharpens the countenance of his friend"* (Prov. 27:17). Fellowship with Christian friends is often the missing ingredient needed to relieve the dulling effects of anxiety and sharpen our spiritual focus, perspective, and discernment concerning God's answers to our worries.

-21-

◄ CONCLUSION ►

We have carefully examined the subject of worry. The scriptures reveal that it is not God's will that we suffer from anxiety and worry. Not only does the Bible admonish us to *"Be anxious for nothing"* (Phil. 4:6), but it also provides the practical insights needed to achieve a worry-free life. If we will apply the following steps, we will overcome our present worries and effectively prevent future recurrences.

1. Repentance
2. Prayer
3. Discipline our thinking
4. Trust in God's Word
5. Exercise faith
6. Renew a proper perspective
7. Seek spiritual refreshing
8. Christian fellowship

For a brief overview of the main points in this booklet, please re-read the boldly printed words on each page. We also recommend that you read the C.E.I. booklets entitled, "Victory in Affliction" and "Fighting Fear".

-22-

Chapter 20

Fighting
Fear

BY TERRY D. EDWARDS

◀ INTRODUCTION ▶

We live in an unpredictable world. Everyday brings new reports of things which people fear most, actually happening. Besides the experiences of others, there are those events that have already taken place in our own lives to remind us of how vulnerable we are.

The Bible has much to teach us about this area of fear. II Timothy 1:7 states, *"For **God has not given us a spirit of fear, but of power and of love and of a sound mind.**"* We are to be free from a life dominated by fear.

In this booklet, we will see what God has to say about fear and how we can have a victory over it.

-1-

◀ TABLE OF CONTENTS ▶

-2-

UNDERSTANDING FEAR

Fear is a God-given emotion that every person experiences. **It is a feeling aroused in us when we perceive something as a threat or a danger to our lives.** We can feel fear in physical, emotional, financial, social, and spiritual areas.

Whether our fear is justifiable or not depends upon our response to these two questions:

Q. Is there a real threat or danger?   _____Yes _____No

Q. Is our fear in balance with the threat or danger?   _____Yes _____No

-3-

Fear is a positive emotion when there is a real danger, and the level of fear is in balance with that danger. Such fear is realistic and under control.

But there is a problem! **Most of us have fears that are not based upon a real danger,** or our feelings are out of proportion to the threat. We are overcome by the *"spirit of fear"* whenever we consider certain possibilities or have to confront specific situations. Some fears even develop into phobias (something you dread) such as fear of crowds, bridges, or the dark. All such fears plague our lives and rob us of the peace we are promised in Christ.

Our discussion of fear in this booklet will center on these unrealistic fears.

-4-

THE CAUSES OF FEAR

Unrealistic fear is fear that is not based on a real danger or is out of proportion to the danger involved. What might be a realistic fear to the unbeliever could often be unrealistic to the Christian, considering our relationship to a loving and sovereign God. For instance, it would be realistic for a non-Christian to fear death, while such a fear is unrealistic for a believer. Other unrealistic fears would be: financial fears, the fear of man, fear of the future, etc.

Here are some of the major causes of fear:

1. **Parental Influence** - Some of our fears have been learned from the fears of our parents.

-5-

2. **Past Association** - A bad experience from the past can cause a fear in some area of our life. The memory of what happened causes a fear to persist in that same area.

3. **Guilt** - Proverbs 28:1 states, *"The wicked flee when no one pursues."* Many difficulties with fear come from a guilty conscience. **Unresolved guilt can produce fear** in different areas of a person's life. **Only honesty and repentance can correct the problem.**

4. **Attention-Getting** - Some fears begin with an attempt to get attention. At a young age, a person may develop a fear of the dark, mice, insects, etc. He exaggerates his fear so much it becomes even stronger.

-6-

THE EFFECTS OF FEAR

I John 4:18 puts it well when it says that *"fear involves torment."* It affects our entire life.

We become preoccupied with ourselves and our problem. We become anxious, tense, and irritable. Our mind is gripped by thoughts about the fear. Our spiritual life is drained by our self-preoccupation.

Even our physical well-being can deteriorate through headaches, increased pulse rate, high blood pressure, ulcers, etc.

Our social relationships with other people can also be seriously affected.

-7-

SOME FACTS ABOUT FEAR

There was a time you did not have the unrealistic fear that now plagues you. This fear grew as you carried your bad experience from the past into the present. Here are some facts about fear:

1. Your **fear is real**, even if it is **not realistic.**
2. Because it is not realistic (the danger is not genuinely there), **you are the one who is feeding the fear.**
3. Your **fear is more related to "what if's"**, than it is to certainties.
4. **The more you look at it, the more it grows.**
5. You become **preoccupied with the fear** and, consequently, with yourself.
6. The power of God and the truth about the situation become **less meaningful** than the fear.

-8-

THE FEAR CYCLE

Once we are gripped with a **fear**, it **begins to perpetuate itself.** The fear grows through a self-producing cycle. Because of our preoccupation with the fear, we **end up creating the thing we feared.** Here is a description of the "fear cycle":

1. We have a **bad experience** that **causes hurt** or pain.

2. We begin to **fear it will happen again.**

3. Our **fear preoccupies our attention,** disabling us from reacting properly to the situation.

4. **We have another bad experience.**

-9-

5. **Our fear is** encouraged and **enlarged.**

6. **We become unable to separate the fear from the facts** of the situation.

7. **We try to avoid the situation** so that we will not repeat the bad experience.

8. **We begin to fear the "fear experience"** as much as the idea of what could happen.

9. If we can't avoid the situation, our increased fear and **self-preoccupation causes the cycle to repeat itself.**

The fear cycle ususally takes a period of time to develop to a place of intensity. At its peak, it can be a debilitating experience, crippling our ability to relate normally to life's situations.

-10-

FEAR CAN BE OVERCOME

*"But thanks be to **God, who gives us the victory through our Lord Jesus Christ"** (I Cor. 15:57).*

Yes, you can have the victory over your fear! You may have lost many battles until now. You may have gone into retreat and isolated yourself from whatever you fear. You may have lived in the "fear cycle" for a long time. It does not matter.

What matters is that you now want the victory. God also wants you to have the victory. He has made it possible through Jesus Christ. **If you are willing to face the enemy again and enter the arena God's way, you can triumph.**

-11-

Fear does not give up easily, but light always dispels darkness. We must remember that unrealistic fear is not based upon reality. We are the ones who produce such fear. Therefore, **the keys to seeing it overcome lie in your relationship to God and the fear.**

Until now, your attention has been on the fear. This has produced a self-preoccupation in this area. Sin always prevails when our attention is on ourselves.

You must now turn your attention to God. Your confidence should be *"I can do all things through Christ who strengthens me"* (Phil. 4:13).

There are **four areas of response** that work together to give us victory over fear. We will look at these on the following pages.

-12-

I. TRUTH OVERCOMES FEAR

*"If you abide in My word . . . you shall know the truth, and **THE TRUTH SHALL MAKE YOU FREE"** (John 8:31, 32).*

It is very important to bring truth into our area of fear. First we need to understand the cycle of fear that goes on inside of us. We must see also that we are facing a fear and not a fact.

We should identify the facts and hold fast to them. **We should find either a promise from the scriptures or a spiritual fact that we can use to counteract the fear.** Whenever we begin to dwell upon our fear, we must immediately turn our mind to the truth.

-13-

A SCRIPTURAL EXAMPLE

David and Goliath - In I Samuel 17 we read the amazing story of young David's triumph over Goliath. David would have been overwhelmed by fear if his attention had merely been on the natural facts. Instead, **he saw the situation through the eyes of God. Next to God, Goliath looked small.**

His truth was based on the fact of God's favor toward Israel. In verse 45 he cries, *"I come to you in the name of the Lord of hosts, the God of the armies of Israel, whom you have defied."*

God has claims on our lives that the Goliath of fear has no right to challenge.

-14-

II. LOVE OVERCOMES FEAR

"There is no fear in love; but perfect LOVE CASTS OUT FEAR" (I John 4:18).

Love is more powerful than fear. Fear is centered in ourselves. Love is centered in God and others. We must turn our concern from the fear, to seeking to do that which pleases God and helps others.

Fear acts selfishly. We must commit ourselves to act responsibly, in love, even if we must encounter another fear experience in doing so.

We must direct our mind to think in terms of love, rather than of fear. Instead of trying to stop fear thoughts, we need to turn our attention to thoughts of truth and love concerning the matter.

-15-

JESUS CHRIST - A SCRIPTURAL EXAMPLE

The most powerful example of love prevailing over fear is seen in Christ facing the agonies of the crucifixion. Along with the physical suffering, He would also have to bear the sin of the entire human race.

So how did He triumph over such fears? He triumphed through love for God and others! In Matthew 26:39 He cries, *"O My Father, if it is possible, let this cup pass from Me; nevertheless, not as I will, but as You will."* He resolved to please God first. In Hebrews 12:2 we are told that Jesus, *"for the joy that was set before Him endured the cross."*

Fear could not prevail over His desire to please God and to bless others. We must follow His example.

-16-

III. FAITH OVERCOMES FEAR

*"But without faith it is impossible to please Him, for he who comes to God must believe that He is, and that **He is a rewarder of those who diligently seek Him.**"* (Heb. 11:6)

Faith reasons from God and His Word. Fear reasons from self and circumstances. Our fears can seem very reasonable. They have proven to be very powerful in our lives.

But now we must see that God has made us new creations. We belong to Him. We are being conformed to the image of His Son. I Thessalonians 5:24 claims, *"He who calls you is faithful, who also will do it."*

Take hold of the truth. Make your prime motive to please God and bless others, then faith will work by this love (Gal. 5:6).

-17-

A SCRIPTURAL EXAMPLE

•**Sarah** - We are told in Hebrews 6:12 that we *"through faith and patience inherit the promises."* Whatever God has for us is ours if we will move forward in faith and continue in patience.

Sarah conceived a child when she was long past age because *"she judged Him faithful who had promised"* (Hebrews 11:11).

Our victory will probably not be instantaneous. But as we are patient, looking to God, moving forward in faith, and doing what God's Word says to do, we will see our fears steadily fade away.

-18-

IV. COURAGE TO ACT OVERCOMES FEAR

"BE STRONG AND OF GOOD COURAGE; DO NOT BE AFRAID, NOR BE DISMAYED, for the Lord your God is with you wherever you go" (Joshua 1:9).

We can know all of the facts and still be afraid to act. Until we step forward in faith, with the right motive, armed with the truth, we will not see victory.

David *"ran toward the army* to meet the Philistine" (I Sam. 17:48). We must be willing to **step into the situation** associated with our fear. **The real enemy is fear, not the situation.**

As we step forth, our focus should be on God being glorified. As we act courageously, **He will give us the strength** and assistance we need.

-19-

A SCRIPTURAL EXAMPLE

•**Queen Esther** - In the book of Esther, the Jewish people of the Persian Empire were facing annihilation through a decree of the king.

Queen Esther had kept her Jewish identity a secret. Because of the crisis with her people, she was forced to act. She had to approach the king, even if it meant her death. In Esther 4:16, she says *"And so **I will go to the king,** which is against the law; **and if I perish, I perish!"**

She committed her fate into God's hands and faced her fear. This act of courage brought the salvation of the Jewish people.

-20-

WHAT IF I FAIL?

TRUE failure is allowing the fear to prevail over your life. Victory always involves a campaign against the enemy. We must not accept the tyranny of fear any longer. The road to victory may involve some defeats. If so, we must regroup, re-affirm the truth, and go forward.

The fear of failure is part of the problem. Put it aside. It will only cripple you from making an effort. Remember, temporary failure is no worse than what you already have. God will even use your failures to show you the right direction to go in in order to achieve ultimate victory.

-21-

◀ CONCLUSION ▶

Full victory over your fear may take some time. You should **re-read this booklet in order to fully understand this area.** It is essential to become familiar with the steps to victory.

As a final reminder, **your attention must move** from seeing fear defeated, **to seeing God glorified - whatever gets your attention, gets you.**

If you need additional help, we suggest that you contact your pastor.

For a brief examination of the main points in this booklet, please re-read the boldly printed words on each page.

-22-

Chapter 21

Defeating
Anger

BY TERRY D. EDWARDS

◀ INTRODUCTION ▶

You are reading this booklet because **you have a problem with your temper.**It has probably been there for a long time. You can look back on your life and remember many incidents where anger has caused you to say and do things you later regretted.

For many people, **anger seems to be an emotion that is out of control.** They don't like that part of their personality, but lack the power to do anything about it. Their best attempts have ended in failure. Some, in frustration, may eventually accept the idea that "That's just the way I am!"

God has some good news! **We can have victory over anger!** In this booklet, we will see what the Bible teaches about anger, and how that victory can be ours.

-1-

◀ TABLE OF CONTENTS ▶

-2-

WHAT IS ANGER?

Anger is **a feeling of irritation or offense** that arises when we don't like something that is taking place. It occurs in different degrees of intensity — from mild irritation, to violent rage. Sometimes we can hold it, and other times we just let it go. It may last only a short time, or it may continue on as a deep-seated bitterness and resentment.

Anger, itself, is not necessarily bad. It can be either destructive or constructive, depending on how it is used. However, all too often we see it expressed destructively.

The Bible reveals that **anger is also a part of God's nature.** Since He is perfect, we need to see how He uses anger. We can then establish this as a goal toward which we can work.

-3-

GOD'S ANGER

The Bible justifies the anger of God, yet warns against human anger. There is a good reason for this. God is perfect and holy, and therefore **His anger is just and constructive.** Let's examine the nature of God's anger:

1. **He has perfect understanding** — *"Oh, the depth of the riches both of the wisdom and knowledge of God!"* (Rom. 11:33).

2. **His anger is directed at sin** — *"God is angry with the wicked every day"* (Psalms 7:11).

3. **His justice is fair** — *"But we know that the judgment of God is according to truth"* (Rom. 2:2).

4. **His anger is patient and controlled** — God is *"slow to anger, abounding in love and faithfulness"* (Psalms 86:15, NIV).

5. **He wants the transgressor restored** — *"He is patient with you, not wanting anyone to perish, but everyone to come to repentance"* (II Pet. 3:9, NIV).

-4-

WHERE WE FAIL

Man's anger is usually different from God's anger. James 1:20 states, *"for the wrath of man does not produce the righteousness of God."* Our anger is often dangerous and destructive because of a failure in the following areas:

1. **We have limited understanding** — Much of the time we only see a part of the picture. We don't consider the reasons for the other's behavior. Our own frustration clouds our understanding.

2. **Our anger is directed at a wrong done to us** — Our reaction is from personal threat or hurt, rather than a concern for righteousness and truth.

-5-

3. **Our sense of justice is wrong** — Whenever anger is in the judgment seat, what we think is the right way to react will be wrong. We can only judge correctly when we consider all of the facts in the right frame of mind.

4. **We quickly lose control** — Our anger seeks immediate vengeance. We act from emotion rather than reason. We strike out at the person who has offended us.

5. **We seek to hurt rather than restore** — Because of our imperfect love, we want revenge instead of restoration. Our main desire is to get the best of our opponent.

-6-

WHEN ANGER IS DESTRUCTIVE

If our anger does not contribute to love, truth, and righteousness, then it is sin. It is destructive to both our life and the lives of others. **Anger leads to sin when it results in any of the following:**

1. **Seeking vengeance for yourself** — *"Do not take revenge, my friends, but leave room for God's wrath"* (Rom. 12:19, NIV).

2. **Verbal abuse of another** — *"Reckless words pierce like a sword, but the tongue of the wise brings healing"* (Prov. 12:18, NIV).

3. **Concealing ill will** — *"Faithful are the wounds of a friend, but the kisses of an enemy are deceitful"* (Prov. 27:6).

4. **Repressing anger** — *"Whoever hides hatred has lying lips, and whoever spreads slander is a fool"* (Prov. 10:18).

-7-

ANGER CAN BE CONSTRUCTIVE

Many injustices have small consequences and can be passed over. I Peter 4:8 states that *"love will cover a multitude of sins."* Others are more serious and should be confronted. Anger can be constructive if we follow these principles:

1. **Do not avenge yourself** — Do not act out of personal hurt. God has promised to defend those who are treated unfairly (Rom. 12:19).

2. **Direct our anger toward the sin** — Solutions come when we focus on the problem rather than the people involved.

3. **Desire to see the offender restored** — When a person commits a wrong, we should approach them with a spirit of meekness, and a desire to restore (Gal. 6:1).

4. **Discipline must be according to scripture** — Some offenses require discipline. It must always be according to scripture (Matt. 18:15; 16; Rom. 16:17, etc.).

-8-

THE RESULT OF UNCONTROLLED ANGER

We are warned in Ephesians 4:26, *"IN YOUR OWN ANGER DO NOT SIN"* (NIV). Uncontrolled anger can have devastating affects in a number of areas:

1. **It ruins our Christian witness** — Uncontrolled anger destroys our testimony and reputation (James 3:9).

2. **It destroys the peace of the church** — It results in strife and division among the brethren (Eph. 4:31).

3. **It hurts our loved ones** — Our homes become a place of tension and fear instead of peace and love (Eph. 6:4).

4. **Our attitudes are passed on to our children** — Many attitudes and responses are learned behavior (Prov. 22:24,25).

5. **We suffer physical consequences** — Anger, bitterness, and resentment produce tension, headaches, colitus, ulcers, etc. (Eccles. 7:9).

-9-

YOU CAN CONTROL YOUR ANGER

This may surprise you, but **God makes it clear that you have the power to control your anger.** In Colossians 3:8 we are commanded: *"But now you must also put off all these: ANGER, wrath, malice, blasphemy, filthy language out of your mouth."* These and many other scriptures reveal that God holds us responsible for our anger.

You may have accepted the idea that you just have a bad temper, that it runs in your family, or that it is out of your control. You must **get rid of these false notions and accept responsibility for your behavior.**

Let's examine some of the conditions that will give us control over our anger.

-10-

CONDITIONS FOR CONTROL

1. **You must desire a victory** — We must see our uncontrolled anger as an enemy. Our attention must be focused more on this area of sin in our behavior than on the faults of others. **We must be willing to repeatedly humble ourselves** if we are to see anger defeated.

2. **Ask God for help** — We must confess a genuine need for God's help. Our own willpower is not enough. When we approach Him in this condition, He will assist us. *"WHATEVER YOU ASK IN PRAYER, BELIEVING, YOU WILL RECEIVE"* (Matt. 21:22).

-11-

3. **Identify the problem areas** — There are many possible reasons for a consistent anger problem. **Bitterness** from a situation in our life can cause an "angry spirit" to prevail. **Pride** can produce impatience. **Insecurity** and **fear** may cause us to use anger as a protection. We must examine ourselves to see what the root of the problem may be.

4. **Bring God into the situation** — We must allow God into the situations that cause anger in our life. We need an overall trust that *"ALL THINGS WORK TOGETHER FOR GOOD TO THOSE WHO LOVE GOD"* (Rom. 8:28). **God can use every situation for His glory and our good** if we will relate to it in a proper way.

-12-

SPECIFIC STEPS TO VICTORY

The real test of our new commitment to bring anger under control happens when we begin to get irritated. In these moments, we become like gladiators pitted against our enemy. **Whether we or anger will triumph depends on how we respond to the feelings of irritation.** The first few seconds are the most critical.

During this time, our temptation will be to point the finger at the faults of others or center our attention on the external cause of our irritation.

Instead, **we must stop ourself and apply the following steps** that can lead us to victory.

-13-

I. CONFESS ANGRY THOUGHTS IMMEDIATELY

"IF WE CONFESS OUR SINS, He is faithful and just to forgive us our sins and to cleanse us from all unrighteousness" (I John 1:9).

Most angry thoughts are sin. They are filled with destructive potential. **When you begin to get angry, immediately confess your thoughts to God.** We must identify our anger as the potential enemy rather than the external causes that provoked it. Through identifying the true enemy (anger) and turning to God, we will sense a new control.

When we are free from the grip of our temper, we are then able to properly judge and react to the circumstances we are in. **Remember — you must make this confession immediately since anger builds quickly.**

-14-

II. CONTROL YOUR RESPONSE

*"He who is **SLOW TO ANGER** is better than the mighty, and he who rules his spirit than he who takes a city"* (Prov. 16:32).

What we say and how we say it will determine the direction of a conversation. Words are especially important when tensions begin to grow. Proverbs 15:1 tells us, **"a soft answer turns away wrath, but a harsh word stirs up anger."** It is very important that we **consider our words and our spirit before answering** whenever things are tense. We are commanded in Romans 14:19 to *"pursue the things which make for peace and the things by which one may edify another."* If we really desire peace and understanding, it is in the power of our tongue to produce it.

-15-

III. FORGIVE THE OFFENDER

*"And be kind to one another, tenderhearted, **FORGIVING ONE ANOTHER,** just as God in Christ also forgave you"* (Eph. 4:32).

We get angry when we feel we have been offended or an injustice has been done. We must remember that **we are all susceptible to error.** We have all offended others and committed injustices. When we admit our own susceptibility to error, it becomes easier to forgive others.

Usually when there is conflict, there is fault on both sides. Ours may be less, but we are not without sin. Therefore, we must ask God to forgive us. We must likewise forgive others. **It is wrong to be condemning of others when God is forgiving of us.**

-16-

IV. ACT IN LOVE

"But I say to you, LOVE YOUR ENEMIES, bless those who curse you, do good to those who hate you, and pray for those who spitefully use you and persecute you" (Matt. 5:44).

Conflicts are over issues, not people. Avoid centering in on the person and concentrate upon the problem. Avoid personal assaults. **Our goal should be to correct the problem and restore the person.** This must be done in a very sensitive way. We are warned in Galatians 6:1 to *"restore such a one in a spirit of gentleness, considering yourself lest you also be tempted."* If we show the other that love and fairness are behind our efforts, they will usually respond.

-17-

V. BE PATIENT WITH YOURSELF

"But You, O Lord, are a God full of compassion, and gracious, longsuffering and abundant in mercy and truth" (Psalms 86:15).

Uncontrolled anger is a deadly enemy. We must have an absolute commitment to see it contained. Yet on our way to victory, it is inevitable that we will experience some failures. When this happens, **we must not give up.** We must ask forgiveness from both God and those whom we offend. Then we must renew our commitment and continue on. Though we are making constant gains, full victory over anger may take months or years.

As we continue to apply the truths contained in this booklet, **we will experience victory over anger.**

For a brief summary of the main points in this booklet, re-read the words in bold print on each page.

-18-

Chapter 22

Restoring The Backslider

By William R. Kimball

◀ INTRODUCTION ▶

Backsliding is a serious condition which undermines the spiritual welfare and jeopardizes the eternal destiny of the individual seized in its deadly grip.

Some have had to wrestle with a temporary bout of backsliding, while others have found themselves the victims of a perpetual pattern of backsliding from which there appears to be no lasting escape.

The issue of backsliding is a controversial and confusing subject to many. But **it is not a problem which can't be solved by the power of God.** Backsliding need not be an irreversible condition. It is a problem which can be corrected if a person is willing to sincerely respond to the scriptural solutions offered by God.

This booklet is designed to assist the backslider in achieving a permanent victory over this problem by directing him to the road to recovery and restoration in the Lord.

-1-

◀ TABLE OF CONTENTS ▶

-2-

WHAT IS A BACKSLIDER?

There are no gentle ways to define the word backslider. Simply stated, **the word backslider means "someone who has turned away or drawn back from his faith in Christ"**. It is a blunt, biblical expression which characterizes a person who has turned his back on Christ and has willfully reversed the direction of his or her spiritual walk. The word depicts an individual who has abandoned his loyalty, dedication, and enthusiasm for Christianity. It is a sobering term which describes someone who has turned away in heart and deed from faithfully serving God, and has retreated to the beggarly affections and pursuits of this world.

Another biblical term applied to backsliding is the word apostasy. It also characterizes someone who has deviated from the faith and is no longer abiding in a vital relationship with Christ and His Word.

-3-

THE DANGER OF BACKSLIDING

No one should take backsliding lightly, minimize the consequences, or doctrinally dismiss its seriousness. We should each have a godly fear concerning the awesome results of unrepented backsliding. The Bible clearly warns us not to be misled or deceived about the consequences of unrighteousness and unresolved backsliding:

"Do you not know that the unrighteous will not inherit the kingdom of God? Do not be deceived" (I Cor. 6:9).

"But if a righteous man turns from his righteousness and commits sin and does the same detestable things the wicked man does, will he live? None of the righteous things he has done will be remembered. Because of the unfaithfulness he is guilty of and because of the sins he has committed, he will die . . . If a righteous man turns from his righteousness and commits sin, he will die for it; because of the sin he has committed he will die" (Eze. 18:24, 26, N.I.V.).

-4-

GOD'S WARNINGS AGAINST BACKSLIDING

The Bible contains strong cautions about the seriousness of backsliding:

- *"Beware, brethren, lest there be in any of you an evil heart of unbelief in departing from the living God; but exhort one another daily, while it is called Today, lest any of you be hardened through the deceitfulness of sin"* (Heb. 3:12, 13).

- *"This charge I commit to you . . . having faith and a good conscience, which some having rejected, concerning the faith have suffered shipwreck"* (I Tim. 1:18, 19).

- *"You therefore, beloved, since you know these things beforehand, beware lest you also fall from your own steadfastness, being led away with the error of the wicked"* (II Pet. 3:17).

- *"Looking diligently lest anyone fall short of the grace of God"* (Heb. 12:15).

-5-

THE SYMPTOMS OF BACKSLIDING

Backsliding is not a problem which develops overnight. It is generally a gradually worsening condition which progressively weakens our spiritual health like the deadly effects of an accumulative poisoning. Though backsliding is usually a subtle condition of the heart which does not immediately manifest itself in outright acts of defection from the faith, it does produce some common telltale symptoms.

These can include such typical telltale tendencies as a growing attitude of spiritual apathy, an increasing disinterest in spiritual disciplines such as prayer, worship, and the reading of God's Word, and a lack of commitment to church activities and ministerial responsibilities. Backsliding is often accompanied by a deepening spirit of distrust, rebellion, suspicion, fault-finding, and murmuring. It also manifests itself in an increasing pattern of worldly involvements and carnal flirtations.

-6-

THE RESULTS OF BACKSLIDING

The consequences of unrepented backsliding are serious and progressively worsening. The devastating results of spiritual apostasy affect every area of our spiritual, emotional, mental, and physical well-being.

1. _**Our Condition Grows Worse Than in the Beginning**_ — *"For if, after they have escaped the pollutions of the world through the knowledge of the . . . Savior Jesus Christ, they are again entangled in them and overcome, the latter end is worse for them than the beginning. For it would have been better for them not to have known the way of righteousness, than having known it, to turn from the holy commandment delivered to them. But it has happened to them according to the true proverb: 'A dog returns to his own vomit' and 'the sow, having washed, to her wallowing in the mire' "* (II Pet. 2:20-22; Prov. 26:11).

-7-

2. _**Bondage and Oppression**_ — *"But now after you have known God . . . how is it that you turn again to the weak and beggarly elements, to which you desire again to be in bondage?"* (Gal. 4:9; see also Jer. 5:19).

3. _**Cursing, Disappointment, Frustration, and Emptiness**_ — (Read Deut. 28:15-68).

4. _**Shame and Dishonor**_ — *"All who forsake You shall be ashamed"* (Jer. 17:13).

5. _**Spiritual Worthlessness**_ — *"No one, having put his hand to the plow, and looking back, is fit for the kingdom of God"* (Lk. 9:62).

6. _**Self-Contempt**_ — *". . . they will loathe themselves for the evils which they committed in all their abominations"* (Eze. 6:9).

7. _**God's Wrath, Judgment, and Displeasure**_ — *"His power and His wrath are against all those who forsake Him"* (Ezra 8:22).

8. _**Separation and Rejection by God**_ — *"If you seek Him, He will be found by you; but if you forsake Him, He will forsake you"* (II Chron. 15:2).

-8-

COMMON CAUSES OF BACKSLIDING

Many factors are commonly associated with backsliding. We will briefly examine some of the more predominant ones as follows:

1. ___A Lack of Sufficient Grounding___ — An absence of adequate Christian grounding is a frequent factor in backsliding. For this reason, the scriptures urge the absolute necessity of being *"rooted and built up in Him and established in the faith"*, and continuing to be *"grounded and steadfast"* in the faith (Col. 2:7; 1:23). **A tumbleweed spirit which fails to establish and maintain a strong commitment to a healthy, local church and take root in vital Christian fellowship and involvement inevitably leads to spiritual shipwreck.**

Often, a person's reluctance and refusal to identify with a church is the direct result of a maverick, lone ranger mentality and an unsubmitted spirit. Salvation was meant to birth us into an intimate union with a spiritual church family for instruction, nuturing, and care. A failure to embrace this pattern is equivalent to placing a new born baby in an open field and expecting him to survive by fending for himself.

-9-

2. ___Love of the World___—The Bible speaks about the seed which was choked out by *"the cares of this world, the deceitfulness of riches, and the desires for other things"* (Mk. 4:19). **Some return to the world because they have never made a clean break with it.** An attraction and lingering affection for the pleasures, pastimes, and pursuits of the world often undermine the faith of many. This factor can influence new and old saints alike. Paul demonstrated this when he referred to Demas who abandoned him, *"having loved this present world"* (II Tim. 4:10), after serving with him faithfully for many years.

3. ___Temptation___—The Bible refers to those *"who believe for a while and in time of temptation fall away"* (Luke 8:13). The worldly enticements to sin are many. Often the carnal allurements of this world exert a tremendous influence upon the hearts of Christians to return to the sinful pleasures of this age. **A failure to overcome the magnetic pull of temptation results in a gradual defection from the faith and a return to the beggarly passions of the carnal lifestyle.**

-10-

4. *Satanic Deception*—Satanic deception is often an ingredient in apostasy from the faith. Paul indicated this when he wrote, *"lest by some means the tempter had tempted you, and our labor...be in vain"* (I Thess. 3:5). **Satan uses such devices as deceit, doctrinal error, doubt, and temptation to sidetrack and mislead the believer, and to detour his life from serving God.**

5. *Persecution and Affliction*—**The pressures, adversity, and difficulties encountered in the course of following Christ can lead to disillusionment, disappointments, and defection from the faith.** The scriptures speak of those who *"endure only for a time"* but eventually stumble when tribulation and persecution arise (Mk. 4:17). When new converts realize that Christianity is more than a spiritual joyride and is a life of discipleship and commitment involving suffering and hardship as well as victory and blessing, they sometimes fall away.

-11-

6. *Offenses*—**The world is filled with individuals who attribute their backslidden condition to wounds, offenses, and hurts acquired while they were an active member of a church.** Jesus revealed that offenses were inevitable (Matt. 18:7). But a failure on the part of Christians to scripturally respond to the personal injuries and misunderstandings of life can lead to disillusionment and defection from the faith.

7. *A Breakdown in Spiritual Disciplines*—**A failure and inconsistency to faithfully exercise the spiritual disciplines of prayer, worship, fellowship, church involvement, and the study of God's Word can result in a spiritual disinterest, weakness, and anemia which often leads to a backslidden condition of the heart.**

8. *A False Conversion*—Just because a backslider demonstrated a semblance of interest, enthusiasm, and commitment to Christ does not mean that they ever had a genuine conversion and born-again experience. This is an important consideration when confronting the backslider. **Every backslider should carefully examine his heart to see whether there had been a real repentance in the first place.**

-12-

BIBLICAL EXAMPLES OF BACKSLIDING

The Bible contains many examples of backsliding:
- **Israel** had a chronic problem with backsliding (see Ex. 32:1; Judges 2:17; 10:13; I Sam. 8:8; I Kings 11:33; Neh. 9:26; Isa. 1:4; Jer. 2:3).
- **Sampson** manifested a repetitious pattern of spiritual compromise and backsliding (Judges 16).
- **King David** experienced a season of deep backsliding involving his adulterous relationship with Bathsheba and the murder of Uriah (II Sam. 11,12).
- **Solomon** started well spiritually, but eventually turned away his heart from God to serve idols (I Kings 11:1-11).
- **Peter** temporarily backslid when he denied the Lord (Matt. 26:69-75).
- **The disciples**—At one point in Christ's public ministry, many of His disciples *"went back and walked with Him no more"* (John 6:66).
- **Demas** was one of Paul's closest advisors and co-laborers but defected from the faith *"having loved this present world"* (II Tim. 4:10).

-13-

IS THERE HOPE FOR THE BACKSLIDER?

YES, providing there is a genuine repentance and willingness to change. A backslidden person is not beyond the realm of recovery and restoration as long as he sincerely desires to be restored.

Some have pointed to Hebrews 6:4,6 as proof that there are no second chances for the backslider: *"For it is impossible for those who were once enlightened . . .if they fall away, to renew them again to repentance, since they crucify again . . .the Son of God, and put Him to an open shame"* (see also Heb. 10:26-29).

However, this sobering verse is referring to those who stubbornly reject God's mercy and so persistently harden their hearts against the loving conviction of God that they blaspheme the Holy Spirit. In this extreme case, an individual has passed the point of no return and is beyond the ability to be convicted of sin and repent. But as long as the fear of the Lord is present and there is a strong desire to be reconciled to God, the backslider has not committed the unpardonable sin.

We will examine the specific steps to restoration on the following pages.

-14-

I. GODLY REPENTANCE

"If we confess our sins, He is faithful and just to forgive us our sins and to cleanse us from all unrighteousness" (I Jn. 1:9). **Restoration is dependent upon a sincere repentance and willingness to change direction.**

A failure to take prompt, decisive action will only complicate the backslidden condition by reinforcing the hardness of heart against the convicting power of the Holy Spirit. **The backslider must not persist in procrastination or make feeble attempts to justify his sin, rationalize his lifestyle, blame others, or make convenient excuses for his condition.** He must cooperate with the convicting power of the Holy Spirit.

There must be an open recognition of the seriousness of his condition and the eternal consequences which will result if there is a refusal to repent and surrender his life wholeheartedly to the Lordship of Christ.

-15-

II. STRIVE FOR GODLY CHANGE

*"He who covers his sins will not prosper, **but whoever CONFESSES AND FORSAKES them will have mercy"*** (Prov. 28:13).

The backslider can take comfort in the assurance that mercy and forgiveness are available. However, without corresponding action, his sorrow and repentance is in vain. Many backsliders are burdened by a nagging sense of sorrow for their sins, but have never taken aggressive steps to correct their condition.

Repentance is an insufficient response by itself. The backslider must follow through by taking decisive action to commit himself to godly change. **Repentance requires much more than a confession of sin. It demands a genuine change of heart, a permanent change of direction, a rededication of our entire life to Christ, and a determination to forsake the sin of backsliding.** The mercy and healing of God comes as a result of repentance and a genuine endeavor to abandon the pattern of backsliding.

-16-

III. WE MUST TERMINATE WORLDLY INVOLVEMENTS

"And have no fellowship with the unfruitful works of darkness" (Eph. 5:11).

"Do not be unequally yoked together with unbelievers. For what fellowship has righteousness with lawlessness? And what communion has light with darkness?" (II Cor. 6:14).

"Do not be misled: Bad company corrupts good character" (I Cor. 15:33, N.I.V.).

One of the greatest potential pitfalls for the repentant backslider is the snare of carnal relationships, activities, and influences. They often exert a tremendous influence and entice him to return to his worldly affections rather than Christ. For this reason, the repentant backslider must make a clean break with the bonds of worldly attachments, associations, and involvements. He must avoid any friendships, individuals, locations, or situations which could cause him to compromise his rededication to Christ, reinforce his sin, and repeat the cycle of backsliding.

-17-

IV. ESTABLISH GODLY RELATIONSHIPS

We must not only terminate those carnal associations and activities which can hinder our Christian commitment, but **we must also surround ourselves with healthy relationships, activities, and influences which strengthen our commitment and reinforce godliness.**

A determination to sever destructive influences which can undermine our spiritual walk is only half of the solution. We must also establish a godly alternative and lifestyle. **The repentant backslider needs to saturate his life with Christian fellowship and involvements** in order to immunize his life from carnal influences and insulate himself from the temptations that previously ensnared him. **This necessitates an active, consistent commitment to a healthy, local church and close, ongoing fellowship with strong Christians who can provide the vital support, counsel, and encouragement which is needed during the transition phase of his recommitment.**

-18-

V. RE-ESTABLISH GODLY DISCIPLINES

An essential step in achieving a lasting victory over backsliding is the urgent need to re-establish the personal disciplines of prayer, worship, reading God's Word, and Bible study.

A diligence and consistency in these disciplines provides edification, encouragement, direction, and strength, and promotes healthy spiritual growth.

1. **_The Word_**—The repentant backslider should saturate himself with the Word of God and partake regularly of the spiritual nourishment which is available to him through the Bible.

2. **_Prayer_**—Prayer brings us closer to God and reinforces our relationship and intimate communion with Jesus Christ.

3. **_Worship_**—Worship ushers us into a heightened dimension of anointing and contact with the presence of God. It is also a source of spiritual refreshing, liberty, and vitality.

-19-

VI. ACCEPT GOD'S FORGIVENESS

A potential danger to the repentant backslider is the failure to accept the assurance that, *"If we confess our sins, He is faithful and just to forgive us our sins and to cleanse us from all unrighteousness"* (I John 1:9).

Many repentant backsliders never secure a permanent foothold in the kingdom because their recommitment is undermined by an inability to forget their error, forgive themselves, or accept God's **forgiveness.** They consequently fall prey to self-condemnation which reinforces their sense of failure and futility. Many are overcome with a sense of spiritual inferiority and a nagging feeling of being an outsider or a second class citizen because of their past failures, sins, and inconsistencies.

For this reason, the repentant backslider must stand upon the absolute reality of God's forgiveness, acceptance, and approval.

-20-

VII. WE MUST CHALLENGE CONDEMNATION

Those who have returned to Christ from a pattern of backsliding often fall prey to an overwhelming sense of dispair and condemnation because of their previous sins and rebellion against Christ.

For this reason, **the repentant backslider must carefully guard his heart and mind against the potentially devastating consequences of condemnation.** He must stand on the reality that *"There is therefore NOW NO CONDEMNA-TION to those who are in Christ Jesus, who do not walk according to the flesh, but according to the Spirit"* (Rom. 8:1; see also Rom. 8:33,34).

Not only must he guard his own heart from self-condemnation, but he must guard against satanic assault. Satan is called the *"accuser of our brethren"* (Rev. 12:10, K.J.V.). He constantly badgers Christians with accusation, criticism, and condemnation in order to discourage them. He knows that repentant backsliders are especially prone to condemnation so he viciously attacks them in order to defeat and dislodge them from their recommitment to Christ.

-21-

VIII. DON'T GIVE UP!

"A JUST MAN FALLETH SEVEN TIMES, AND RISETH UP AGAIN" (Prov. 24:16, K.J.V.). In the process of striving for victory, we will occasionally fall short; however, we must rise up and continue to press on.

A lasting victory over backsliding requires perseverance and patience. **Difficulties, testings, temptations, and adjustments will inevitably confront the repentant backslider, but he must press forward in the confidence that we "CAN DO ALL THINGS THROUGH CHRIST who strengthens"** us (Phil. 4:13).

We must not give up or entertain a spirit of quitting, futility, or defeat. We must hang in there even if we encounter slip-ups or setbacks. We must not allow our failures to discourage, frustrate, or disillusion us. We must recognize that it takes time to re-establish a strong commitment.

-22-

GOD'S ATTITUDE AND RESPONSE

Though God hates the sin of backsliding, He still loves the backslider and yearns for his restoration. He takes no delight in seeing the unrepentant backslider come to judgment.

"Do I take any pleasure in the death of the wicked? declares the Sovereign Lord. Rather, am I not pleased when they turn from their wicked ways and live?" (Eze. 18:23, N.I.V.).

God's attitude towards the repentant backslider is one of open acceptance and forgiveness. He does not subject him to everlasting disgrace, contempt, or condemnation. He does not expect him to grovel in perpetual pennance or assume a second class status in the kingdom. He does not manifest rejection or reserve His love but embraces the repentant backslider with the same degree of love and forgiveness as the father in the parable of the "prodigal son" who openly restored his son to blessing and dignity (Lk. 15:20-24).

-23-

GOD'S PROMISE TO THE REPENTANT BACKSLIDER

1. *He Takes Pleasure in Their Repentance*—"Am I not pleased when they turn from their wicked ways and live?" (Eze. 18:23, N.I.V.).
2. *Love, Healing and Forgiveness*—"I will heal their backsliding, I will love them freely, for My anger has turned away from him" (Hos. 14:4).
3. *Care, Instruction, and Guidance*—"Return, O backsliding children, says the Lord . . . I will take you . . . and I will . . . feed you with knowledge and understanding" (Jer. 3:14, 15).
4. *Salvation*—"Brethren, if anyone among you wanders from the truth, and someone turns him back, let him know that he who turns a sinner from the error of his way will save a soul from death and cover a multitude of sins" (James 5:19,20).
5. *Spiritual Preservation*—"Again, when a wicked man turns away from the wickedness which he committed, and does what is lawful and right, he preserves himself alive . . . he shall surely live; he shall not die" (Eze. 18:27,28).

-24-

THE CHRISTIAN RESPONSE

The church has a responsibility not only to set a high standard of holiness and to scripturally challenge the sin of spiritual compromise and backsliding, but it also bears the responsibility of seeking the total restoration of the backslider. **The church must provide an atmosphere conducive to recovery.** The church must welcome the backslider home.

This requires a spirit of love, acceptance, and forgiveness. Christians must be aware of the awkwardness, alienation, and embarrassment which often confronts the repentant backslider, and the difficulties often encountered when endeavoring to make a permanent recommitment to Christ. The church must be careful not to manifest a harsh, judgmental spirit of rejection and disapproval which can breed defeat, discouragement, and disillusionment. We must not withhold love, acceptance, or forgiveness. For this reason, when dealing with the return of a repentant backslider, Paul cautioned the Corinthians, *"so that, on the contrary, you ought rather to forgive and comfort him, lest perhaps such a one be swallowed up with too much sorrow. Therefore I urge you to reaffirm your love to him"* (II Cor. 2:7,8).

-25-

◄ CONCLUSION ►

We have carefully examined the subject of backsliding and have seen that it is an extremely serious condition which requires a complete repentance and change in direction.

The backslider can take confidence in the scriptural assurance that abundant pardon and mercy awaits him if he will forsake his sin and return to the Lord. However, on a more sobering note, he must also recognize the eternal consequences of hardening his heart, resisting the convicting power of the Holy Spirit, and persisting in his rebellion and sin. The choice is with the backslider.

For a quick review of this booklet, we recommend that you re-read the bodly printed words on each page. We also recommend that you read the C.E.I. booklets on "The Church Family", "Overcoming Temptation", "Conquering Condemnation", "Breaking Bad Habits", "Building Your Prayer Life", and "Your Bible and You".

-26-

Chapter 23

The Christian Marriage

By Terry D. Edwards

◄ INTRODUCTION ►

Marriage is the basic unit of society. When marriages break down, the devastating effects are far-reaching. Both husbands and wives suffer deep emotional and psychological repercussions. Very often their spiritual lives will go into a tailspin. The children, though seeming to cope well enough on the surface, usually harbor deep-seated confusion, fears, and insecurities that may manifest themselves later in life. There are other detrimental consequences which affect family, friends, and even the health of the church.

Satan has come to *"steal, and to kill, and to destroy"* (Jn. 10:10), aiming some of his most poisonous darts at the marriage relationship. Christ has come to give us an abundant life. Building our marriage according to His plan and purpose will ensure us victory.

This booklet is designed to give you an understanding of that plan, and to provide the key principles for building a strong Christian marriage.

-1-

◄ TABLE OF CONTENTS ►

-2-

WHAT IS MARRIAGE?

This is a good question! The answer is not as simple as it may seem. You may say, "Well, it's two people in love, taking vows to live together as husband and wife." Yes, this is a part of it — but marriage involves much more than this!

The failure to truly understand marriage and the principles for its success is the primary cause of ruin in so many of today's relationships. The vast majority of married people are "marriage ignorant". They know more about the T.V. Guide than what makes for a successful husband-wife relationship. They approach marriage with high expectations but inadequate knowledge, insight, and preparation. Too many rely on the Hollywood formula: fall in love and live happily ever after. Many who trust in this model are gravely disappointed.

-3-

Too often they find their relationship following this pattern: love — marriage — trials — disillusionment — unhappy endurance or divorce.

But it doesn't have to be this way! God intended marriage to be a successful and fulfilling experience, one that would grow in both depth and commitment through time, and be able to stand strong in the midst of the trials and the adjustments of life. Marriage is a glorious institution created by God to perpetuate the human race, to provide for a proper and fulfilling relationship between a man and woman, and to be the basis of a society.

God has given us the pattern and principles for building a successful marriage relationship in His Word. **Every marriage can realize God's intended plan and purpose.**

On the following pages we will examine the foundational facts and practical principles that are necessary for building a godly marriage relationship.

-4-

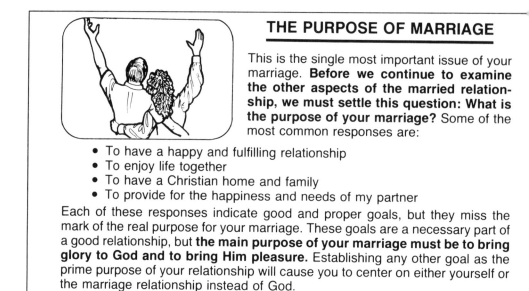

THE PURPOSE OF MARRIAGE

This is the single most important issue of your marriage. **Before we continue to examine the other aspects of the married relationship, we must settle this question: What is the purpose of your marriage?** Some of the most common responses are:

- To have a happy and fulfilling relationship
- To enjoy life together
- To have a Christian home and family
- To provide for the happiness and needs of my partner

Each of these responses indicate good and proper goals, but they miss the mark of the real purpose for your marriage. These goals are a necessary part of a good relationship, but **the main purpose of your marriage must be to bring glory to God and to bring Him pleasure.** Establishing any other goal as the prime purpose of your relationship will cause you to center on either yourself or the marriage relationship instead of God.

-5-

Revelation 4:11 teaches us that all things were created for God's pleasure (K.J.V.). Likewise, in Ephesians 1:12 Paul states *"that we who first trusted in Christ should be to the praise of His glory."* We are also told in Colossians 1:17 that *"He is before all things, and in Him all things consist."*

Our marriage, like every aspect of our life, must exist to bring glory to God and to give Him pleasure. **Firmly establishing our relationship on this purpose will free us from humanistic and self-centered goals that cloud our perspective and judgment.**

Putting God's pleasure and will at the center of our concern will allow every facet of our relationship to be shaped by His Spirit so that we *"may grow up in all things into Him who is the head – Christ"* (Eph. 4:15).

-6-

THE MODEL FOR MARRIAGE

"For this reason a man shall leave his father and mother and be joined to his wife, and the two shall become one flesh. This is a great mystery, but I speak concerning Christ and the church" (Eph. 5:31, 32).

God has given us the perfect model for the relationship between husband and wife in the relationship between Christ and the church. In the above scriptures, Paul reveals that the institution of marriage is a foreshadowing and an earthly type of that beautiful union that Christ will consummate with His church. All those that will respond to His proposal of love initiated at Calvary will become a part of the bride of Christ.

As Ephesians 5:32 declares, this is a great mystery now revealed to every believer and it contains the principles and insights for a successful marriage relationship.

-7-

Most of the points of this booklet are directly based upon the understanding gained from using this model. In the remainder of this section, we will examine two qualities of marriage revealed in Ephesians 5:31.

1. **Marriage Is "Leaving"** — Marriage is a special and primary relationship that requires putting your mate before everyone except God. We are to subordinate even our closest family and friendship ties to the relationship with our marriage partner. Our marriage to Christ is both heavenly and eternal, and supersedes all earthly relationships when it comes to priority end responsibility.

2. **Marriage Is "Joining To"** — Marriage is two people joined in a covenant union, working together to realize God's ideal for their relationship. Both husband and wife must subordinate their own rights and demands to the requirements of building a marriage that truly reflects their oneness.

-8-

THE FOUNDATION OF MARRIAGE

"Therefore shall a man leave his father and his mother, and shall cleave unto his wife" (Gen. 2:24, K.J.V.).

When God produced the original blueprint for marriage, He designed it to work. He established its foundation upon the highest expression of genuine love — **COMMITMENT!** A vivid picture of this level of intense commitment is seen in the word "cleave". A man is to "cleave" to his wife. The word cleave comes from the Hebrew word "dabaq" and means "to cling to, to adhere, or to stick together." It conveys the idea of taking ahold of something with a refusal to let go. **Both husband and wife are to take hold of their marriage with a dedicated commitment to its development and success.** Jesus Christ displays this degree of commitment by pledging to His earthly bride, *"I will never leave you nor forsake you"* (Heb. 13:5).

This same type of vital foundational commitment is defined in the vows taken between a man and a woman at the time of their marriage.

-9-

The following is a sample vow containing the conditions of commitment to which a man and woman pledge themselves when they are married:

"I, _____, take thee, _____to be my wedded husband/wife, to have and to hold from this day forth, for better or for worse, for richer or for poorer, in health and sickness, to love and to cherish, until death do us part, according to the commandment of God, and to this I do promise you my faithfulness."

The wedding day is characterized by love, romance, and high future expectations. The pledge is made before the real tests of life together begin. The years ahead will bring both joy and sorrow, good times and tough times, unforseen circumstances, adjustments, and adaptations. All of these situations can be victoriously met if the marriage partners remain steadfast in their commitment to one another.

Marriage is love realized through commitment. The demands and trials of life will work to perfect and strengthen the love of those whose marriage is based on commitment.

-10-

THE POWER OF MARRIAGE

"Husbands, love your wives, just as Christ also loved the church and gave Himself for it" (Eph. 5:25).

Love is the source of power behind a successful and fulfilling relationship. It is like the water pouring over a hydroelectric dam providing the energy and dynamic to propel the relationship forward to its appointed ideal.

But what exactly is love? It is such a commonly used and frequently misunderstood term. We most often describe it by feelings of deep or warm emotions that we have for another person. But is this really love? Maybe, and maybe not! Feelings are a part of love, but feelings alone do not necessarily indicate real love. **Genuine love is based upon a desire to please God and a commitment to your mate to behave in a way that demonstrates your regard for his or her best.**

-11-

Love is more a condition of the will than the emotions. Love is based more upon intentions and actions, than the whims of feelings. Emotions will always follow our acts of love. Love based upon commitment will bring consistency. On the other hand, if our love is only feeling-oriented, our marriage will be a real roller coaster ride — up today, down tomorrow!

God's pattern of love is revealed through a close look at Calvary. We are to love as Christ *"loved the church and gave Himself for it"* (Eph. 5:25). The important elements of this kind of love are seen in I Corinthians 13:4-8: *"Love suffers long and is kind; love does not envy; love does not parade itself, is not puffed up; does not behave rudely, does not seek its own, is not provoked, thinks no evil; does not rejoice in iniquity, but rejoices in the truth; bears all things, believes all things, hopes all things, endures all things. Love never fails."*

Realizing this kind of love in your marriage requires the inner workings of the cross. There must be a denial of self, along with an embracing of self-giving love where the needs of your partner become the priority. This allows for a release of God's love within us and through it, a new power in our relationship.

-12-

THE NEED OF MARRIAGE

"And the Lord God said, It is not good that man should be alone; I will make him a helper comparable to him" (Gen. 2:18).

There are a number of reasons people give for marrying. There is the desire for love, the goal of raising a family, the fulfillment of sexual needs, and even the pressure of being "socially normal". But the prevailing need for marriage was seen by God immediately after creating Adam: *"It is not good that man should be alone."* **The very nature of our humanity demands a need for COMPANIONSHIP. God designed the marriage relationship to meet this need of companionship in the most complete way possible.**

Companionship is more than just being together. **It is to involve an intimate interaction with our mate on the total level of our humanity: spiritually, emotionally, socially, and physically.** Only a Christian marriage can offer this.

-13-

Those that are joined to the Lord are said to be *"one spirit with Him"* (I Cor. 6:17). The Christian marriage offers a spiritual companionship through mutual fellowship with Christ. We choose our mates through mental, emotional, spiritual, and physical attraction. During marriage, this personality affinity provides the joy of personal companionship. The Bible describes the sexual relationship as "knowing your mate" (Gen. 4:1). Sexual union in marriage produces a deep intimacy of companionship.

Marriage partners must work toward the goal of fulfilling this companionship ideal on every level of their life. An ever present danger is to slip into "role ruts" where each concentrates on being a good wife or husband, while ignoring the goal of genuine companionship.

Companionship is helped through developing good habits of communication. A husband and wife must oppose the drift of "marriage erosion" where he has his life and she has hers, and there is little mutual sharing. Cultivate an interest in the interests of your mate. Set apart days and times to be alone. Work to build your lives together in the midst of diverse responsibilities and activities.

-14-

THE ORDER OF MARRIAGE

"But I want you to know that the head of every man is Christ, the head of woman is man, and the head of Christ is God" (I Cor. 11:3).

Everything in existence is designed to fit into a God-ordained order. The relationships within the family are no exception. God sustains His order in the universe by a hierarchy of authority and headship. In Romans 13:1 Paul reminds us that all authority is of God and therefore demands our respect and submission. **The family has been given the headship structure of Christ over the man, the wife in submission to her husband, and the children in obedience to both parents.**

Because of misconceptions and abuses, there must be a clarity on this issue of male headship. **First of all, headship implies responsibility and covering and not superiority.** Neither does male leadership signify greater intelligence,

-15-

gift, or status in God. Male and female are created equal before the Lord, and are to relate as *"being heirs together of the grace of life"* (I Pet. 3:7).

God established this order based upon the unique nature of the male and female. The woman was created with a more sensitive and vulnerable emotional and psychological nature than the man. Because of this, she is more subject to emotional pressures and the tendency to be deceived (I Tim. 2:14).

Biblical submission requires the wife to yield to and be supportive of her husband's leadership as he in turn yields to and obeys the headship of Christ. Under his covering, she is free to be a creative counterpart, expressing her unique individuality and cooperating with him in establishing the direction of the home and family.

The husband must endeavor to secure his wife's respect by being a good example of spiritual headship. Good headship requires a good example. Paul was able to say to others, *"Be ye followers of me, even as I also am of Christ"* (I Cor. 11:1, K.J.V.). The man should measure the effectiveness and quality of his leadership by his obedience and submission to Jesus Christ. He should use his headship to both establish his home in a godly order, and to cultivate his wife's potential as his helpmate.

-16-

EIGHT KEYS OF A SUCCESSFUL MARRIAGE

1. CHRIST AS THE CENTER

"All things were created through Him and for Him. And He is before all things, and in Him all things consist" (Col. 1:16,17).

Setting Jesus on the center stage of your marriage is the first and greatest key for a fruitful relationship. He is the great architect of marriage and holds the blueprint for its success. In Colossians 1:17 we are given the insight that *"in Him all things consist"*. This word consist means "to be constituted of". Christ alone can give the essential consistency to our marriage.

How do we put Him in the center? First, by making Him the center of our individual lives. This is only accomplished by regular and consistent prayer and study of the Bible. **Secondly,** we must build a spiritual communication with our mate. We should pray together, share spiritual insights and experiences, and become comfortable together with Jesus. **Thirdly,** we should establish the goals and direction of our marriage upon the Word of God.

-17-

2. MUTUAL EDIFICATION

"Let all bitterness, wrath, anger, clamor, and evil speaking be put away from you, with all malice. And be kind to one another, tenderhearted" (Eph. 4:31, 32).

The marriage relationship offers tremendous opportunity to create or destroy human potential, and with it, a person's happiness, sense of growth, and self-worth. Proverbs 18:21 tells us that *"Death and life are in the power of the tongue."* Our words and actions toward our mate day after day have an accumulated effect of either building them up or tearing them down.

God has entrusted us with a stewardship over our marriage partner. His goal is to help conform that person into the image of Christ (Rom. 8:29). How well are you cooperating with His efforts in accomplishing this?

Once the initial euphoria and newness is over, we often allow destructive patterns of criticism, anger, and frustration to dominate our communication. Prince Charming now becomes the frog!

Our goal should be mutual support and encouragement, relating to the other out of kindness and a tender heart, and acknowledging his or her positive qualities and virtues (Phil. 4:8).

-18-

3. ACCEPTING YOUR COMPLEMENT

"And Adam said: This is now bone of my bones and flesh of my flesh" (Gen. 2:23).

In the unfallen state, Adam had an immediate revelation of his oneness with Eve. In the pattern of this first divine union, God has ordained marriage to produce that same consciousness of oneness. **Husband and wife are to relate to life together as one, in self-giving love, fully embracing the other as part of themselves.** Oneness does not imply likeness. In fact, the usual rule is for opposites to attract. The secret of marital oneness is realizing that your mate is a complementary opposite to yourself.

By God's divine design, your partner is different in personality, temperament, and tendencies than yourself. It is usually these opposite qualities that inspire our initial attraction for each other. The Lord uses the opposite characteristics in our mates to complement, shape, and enlarge the other person. **A key to building oneness is to fully accept your marriage partner as your complement, created as a unique expression of the image of God.**

19

4. WILLINGNESS TO CHANGE

"Therefore let us pursue the things which make for peace and the things by which one may edify another" (Rom. 14:19).

The balance in accepting your compliment is the willingness to change. Both partners should maintain a loving acceptance of each other's basic personality and temperament, but each must also be willing to make adjustments in those attitudes and habits that offend or hurt the other. Just because your mother picked up your dirty socks does not mean that your wife should have to. Just because your father washed the car every Saturday doesn't mean your husband will.

A relationship growing in its expression of oneness requires change in both outward habits and in the ways we relate to each other. There is no "change list" that will fit for every couple. The simple rule is that each partner should maintain a willingness to change and be flexible wherever it is reasonable and will help build the relationship. The key principle is found in Romans 14:19 where we are taught to *"pursue the things which make for peace and the things by which one may edify another."*

-20-

5. MAINTAINING GOOD COMMUNICATION

Young lovers never seem to have a communication problem, but somehow this area is often threatened after marriage. **Good communication is one of the most important elements of marriage since it is so necessary for close companionship.** Many people settle for second rate marriages because they fail to maintain good communication.

The following are some areas that create barriers in communication:

1. **Exploding** — Reactions of anger and frustration destroy communication.
2. **Tears** — The tendency, especially among women, to react quickly to hurt and withdraw can hinder communication.
3. **The Silent Act** — Resorting to silent warfare is a destructive pattern.
4. **Lack of Interest** — A failure to share and maintain common interests will reduce the number of topics for communication.

The best defense is a good offense. **Commit yourself to building interests and communication with each other.** Identify and discuss those areas that hurt communication. Work toward a life of enjoyable companionship.

-21-

6. CREATING ROMANCE

"Let the husband render to his wife the affection due her, and likewise also the wife to her husband" (I Cor. 7:3).

Like communication, romance seems to come automatically during the time of courtship. Unimaginative men become veritable Don Juans, bringing flowers, whispering sweet nothings, and suggesting romantic things to do together. Too often, after the vows, this kind of behavior quickly evaporates!

Romance must be kept alive! Women especially need this element in the relationship. Their view of marriage is colored with visions of romance. **If the man will inject romance into the relationship, the woman will quickly respond.** She needs the times of warmth and affection, the tender touch, the sense of being desired. One writer put it like this: "Men, what it takes to get her, it takes to keep her."

Both partners must work at cultivating romance. Speak sweetly to each other. Remember special occasions with flowers. Get away alone together often. Frequently reaffirm your love for each other. Romance in a marriage is like the icing on a cake, adding a dimension of sweetness and attraction to the relationship.

-22-

7. SEXUAL INTIMACY

"Marriage is honorable among all, and the bed undefiled" (Heb. 13:4).

God created sex for two basic purposes: procreation and intimacy. In Genesis 1:28 the mandate was given to *"Be fruitful and multiply"*. Marriage is to provide for the care and nurturing of offspring. But sex in marriage is to accomplish much more than this. Through the sexual relationship, a husband and wife can enjoy an intimacy, a "knowing of each other", impossible through any other kind of communication.

Both partners must work to make this vital element of their marriage enjoyable and mutually fulfilling. A long term satisfying sexual relationship is built upon love and emotional closeness. This is best cultivated by being sensitive to your partner's physical and emotional needs and by an attitude of preferring the other.

It should be "How can I give?", not "What can I get?" If both partners have this concern, matters of techique, timing, and frequency can be resolved, and a mutually satisfying relationship will result.

-23-

8. GUIDELINES FOR "CONSTRUCTIVE DISAGREEMENTS"

Disagreements can be constructive or destructive depending on how they are conducted. The following are some helpful guidelines:

1. **Stop and Pray** — When a matter of disagreement arises, center your hearts in God, ask for patience, deference, and understanding (I Cor. 13:4).
2. **Don't Raise Your Voice** — *"A soft answer turns away wrath"* (Prov. 15:1).
3. **Identify the Issue** — Stick to it and don't be sidetracked to other points of irritation (Matt. 18:15).
4. **Don't "Dig Up Old Bones"** — Bringing up old wounds always creates a destructive pattern (II Cor. 5:17).
5. **No Name Calling** — This is character assassination and creates deep wounds (Eph. 4:29).
6. **Avoid Generalizations** — "You always do this", or "You never do that" are destructive exaggerations (Eph. 4:15).
7. **Finish the Discussion** — Don't burst into tears, stomp out of the house, or turn over and go to sleep (Eph. 4:26).
8. **Reaffirm Your Love to Each Other** — Finish your disagreement with tenderness and forgiveness (Eph. 4:31, 32).

-24-

TIPS FOR HUSBANDS

"Likewise you husbands, dwell with them with understanding, giving honor to the wife, as to the weaker vessel" (I Pet. 3:7).

As the head of the relationship, the man is in a more critical position to determine the course and atmosphere of the home. It is essential that he relate wisely and with understanding to the mate God has given him. **The following are some areas he must understand about his wife:**

1. **A More Emotional Nature** — A woman has been given a more emotional and sensitive nature than the man. She sees and feels things differently than her husband. This gives her the advantage of greater compassion and sensitivity, and the disadvantage of being more easily affected, influenced, and hurt. Don't treat her like one of the boys but rather respect this part of her God-given nature.

2. **A Need For Love** — If marital counsel to husbands could be summed up in four words it would be, *"Husbands, love your wives"* (Eph. 5:25). When a

-25-

woman feels truly loved by her husband, she enjoys a deep, inner security and peace. This love must be demonstrated daily in acts of kindness, preference, and expressions of affection.

3. **A Need for Self-Esteem** — Many women struggle with low self-esteem, feelings of inadequacy, feelings of inferiority, and a lack of self-worth. Many also feel ugly, unattractive, unintelligent, and lacking in real virtues. Husbands, compliment and encourage your wives! Build her sense of value and self-worth. As her head, she looks to you for much of her definition of herself.

4. **A Need For Security** — The man is to be the prime provider for his family. God has given him the charge of headship, and the main responsibility for financial support. By your ambition, work habits, and diligence, demonstrate to your wife that she can be secure with you as provider.

5. **A Biological Difference** — The reproductive cycle of a woman affects her moods and feelings. During menstruation and the pre-menstruation period, her estrogen and progesterone levels are at their lowest and this affects her emotional condition. Employ extra patience, understanding, and sensitivity during this time.

-26-

TIPS FOR WIVES

"Who can find a virtuous wife? For her worth is far above rubies. The heart of her husband safely trusts her; so he will have no lack of gain. She does him good and not evil all the days of her life" (Prov. 31:10-12).

This scripture reveals something a husband greatly desires from his wife: a person he can fully trust. **He needs to know that his wife is loyal, faithful, supportive, and protective toward him — someone who will not talk critically of him to others.** He needs a true helpmate who will carry the yoke of life with him, doing him *"good and not evil"*. The following are some important areas a wife must understand concerning her husband:

1. **Respect and Honor** — *"And let the wife see that she respects her husband"* (Eph. 5:33). A man needs to know that his wife enjoys a reverence for him as a person and as her head. This should be communicated by actions and words. Compliment him on the positive qualities of his character and leadership.

-27-

2. **A Man's Productivity** — God made man's identity to be linked to productivity. Your husband needs to feel that you appreciate his work and other areas of productivity, i.e., around the home, hobbies, spiritual labor, etc. Much of his self-respect and sense of self-worth comes through his feelings of productivity.

3. **His Home — His Castle** — The desire to provide for his family is at the base of a man's willingness to punch the time clock day after day. His home is his castle and needs to be a place where he can relax and be refreshed. Wives, be good homemakers. Make your home comfortable and attractive. Cook good meals. Do extra things to communicate your love and appreciation for your husband.

4. **Male Sexuality** —
The sexual responsiveness of a man's wife can do much to affect his male identity. Frequent turn-off and coldness at bedtime can be devastating to this area of male identity and need. A wife must understand this need in her husband and, through her response, communicate her love and desire for him.
-28-

DANGERS TO AVOID

There has been much advice already given on the building blocks for a successful marital relationship. Ignoring any of the points previously made will have a detrimental effect on your marriage. There are, though, several additional dangers that have not been mentioned that deserve watchful avoidance:

1. **Overextended Lives** — Overextended lives produce fatigue and depression and drain the energy and time required to build a good relationship. Your marriage must be a priority if it is to grow. You must realize that other areas are less important.

2. **Unrealistic Expectations** — This booklet has set forth the ideals of marriage. Work toward them, but do not expect instant perfection. Realistically, you will be working toward these goals, making gradual headway, the rest of your married life.

3. **Comparing With Others** — Don't compare your marriage or your mate with others. Each of you, as well as your marriage, is unique. God created you this way. Continue to apply the principles and rejoice in your progress.

-29-

◄ CONCLUSION ►

This booklet is designed as a brief and simplified coverage of those principles and practical keys that make for a fulfilling Christian marriage. At best, it is a "Reader's Digest" version of the subject. It provides for a quick overview and outline of the necessary elements of a good marriage.

There are many excellent marriage books written that give more extensive coverage to the topics contained in this booklet. The reader is encouraged to read these. A list of some of the more popular ones are given below:

- **How To Be Happy Though Married,** by Dr. Tim LaHaye
- **What Wives Wish Their Husbands Knew About Women,** by Dr. James Dobson
- **The Christian Family,** by Larry Christenson
- **Intended for Pleasure,** by Ed and Gaye Wheat

Those readers with marriages experiencing serious conflict should contact their pastor for help.

For a brief overview of the main points of this booklet, please re-read the boldly printed words on each page.

-30-

Chapter 24

Raising Christian Children

By Terry D. Edwards

◄ INTRODUCTION ►

A child is a gift of God, a little package of human potential placed in the hands of parents to be nurtured and shaped according to the plan and purpose of God. **A child raised in an atmosphere of love, under biblical training and discipline, will grow up to be a responsible and productive adult, bringing great joy to the diligent parents.** On the other hand, the scriptures warn that *"a child left to himself brings shame to his mother"* (Prov. 29:15).

A pastor rightly made the observation, "There are no problem children, only problem parents." The happiness, stability, and destiny of a child's life rests in the philosophy employed in his upbringing. Too many parents have failed in this regard, resorting to liberal and humanistic approaches to raising their children. The kids are the losers, later suffering the manifold consequences of sin and selfishness.

The Christian parent has access to the keys for successful parenting in the scriptures. In this booklet we will examine the biblical principles for raising Christian children.

-1-

◄ TABLE OF CONTENTS ►

-2-

THE BLESSING OF CHILDREN

"Behold, children are a heritage from the Lord, the fruit of the womb is His reward. Like arrows in the hand of a warrior, so are the children of one's youth. Happy is the man who has his quiver full of them" (Ps. 127:3-5).

Children are a blessing from God meant to bring joy, reward, and fulfillment to the parents. In our offspring, we are able to be co-creative with God, reproducing life that, in essence, is a combination of ourself and our mate. Though children require constant care and attention, their presence sets in motion that responsible, self-sacrificing love that is depictive of the nature of God. This kind of love is to be at the heart of the family and, likewise, becomes the basis of a society.

Christian parents must be responsible to the purposes of God with their children. Although we call them "ours", they actually belong to God. They have been entrusted to our care for a short season, but their nurturing and training is to prepare them for eternity.

-3-

God's great concern for children is seen in a number of places in the Bible. Jesus challenged His disciples' intolerant attitude toward children by saying, *"Let the little children come to Me . . . for of such is the kingdom of heaven"* (Matt. 19:14). Previous to this, He had revealed that children have angels that stand in the presence of God constantly watching over them.

All human life is created in the image of God (Gen. 1:26). The prime responsibility of parenting is to help develop and shape the child into this image. This is a tremendous responsibility considering the enemies that work against us (i.e., the world, the flesh, and the devil). Our faith, though, rests in the divine guidelines given to us in the Word of God, along with the encouragement that *"He who is in you is greater than he who is in the world"* (I Jn. 4:4).

Children who are raised in the *"training and admonition of the Lord"* (Eph. 6:4) will be a source of blessing to their parents. **The time and energy spent laying a foundation of faith and righteousness in their lives will later pay large dividends as they develop into responsible men and women of God.**

-4-

GOD'S PATTERN FOR CHILD REARING

God's pattern for child rearing can be summarized under three basic commands: 1.) love, 2.) discipline, and 3.) teach. These three areas of parental responsibility are patterned after God's own method of fatherhood. God is the perfect father, employing the right blend of these three areas in fashioning His children into His likeness.

In the following pages of this booklet we will examine these three essential areas of parenting. God's approach to child rearing is best understood by appreciating the interaction between the love of God and the nature of man.

THE NATURE OF MAN

The philosophy of humanism, with its various schools of psychology, has greatly erred in assuming the inherent goodness of man. The Bible rightly defines man as a sinner. It is our nature to sin. Because of his transgression, Adam received a fallen nature which he passed on to the entire human race (Rom. 5:12). David understood this and declared, *"I was brought forth in iniquity, and in sin my mother conceived me"* (Ps. 51:5).

-5-

The major characteristics of the Adamic nature are sin, selfishness, independence, and rebellion. Unless given proper love, training, and discipline, a child will develop and mature with these qualities dominating his or her life.

THE LOVE OF GOD

The Bible teaches that *"God is love"* (I Jn. 4:8). His love is characterized by perfect affection and benevolence. He wills the best for all of His creation and acts accordingly. His methods of love, training, and discipline in child rearing emerge from His perfect love and wisdom relating to the fallen nature of man.

Our response to this should be, *"Shall we not much more readily be in subjection to the Father of spirits and live?"* (Heb. 12:9). As parents, we must readily submit to God's method of raising our children so that they too might *"live"* and bring glory to God. **We must diligently instruct, train, and discipline our offspring, bringing them into subjection to the ways and principles of God.**

-6-

INDIVIDUALITY

Just as every snowflake has a different structure and design, so God has created every person as a unique individual. **Every child has his or her own God-given temperament and personality.** These inherent traits give a child his own disposition and nature.

A child's temperament is that combination of character traits, tendencies, gifts, and abilities that are unique to him. A child can be extrovert or introvert, active or passive, strong-willed or flexible, mathematically inclined or more artistic. These are just some of the general differences.

Though God's principles for child rearing are consistent and universally applicable, parents must tailor their approach to their child's individuality. There must be no compromise with proper training and discipline, but there must also be a consideration of the child's temperament and personality. God shapes us individually into unique expressions of Himself. Parents have the same assignment with their children.

-7-

I. TEACH YOUR CHILDREN

"Train up a child in the way he should go, and when he is old he will not depart from it" (Prov. 22:6).

God has an intended direction in which each child should go. First, each individual is to pursue a way of life reflecting righteousness and faith (I Tim. 6:4). Secondly, every person has a unique destiny in life, a place of service and contribution designed by God for him.

Parents have the primary responsibility to see that their children receive the instruction and training that will prepare them to fulfill these two goals.

The two most important methods of teaching children are instruction and example. A child must be instructed in proper behavior, morals, work habits, attitudes, respect for rules, etc. Parents must assume a teacher's role through the duration of a child's formulative life.

A picture is worth a thousand words. Parents must set a good example in their own lives of what they want to impart to their kids. On the following pages we will present some of the necessary areas to include in teaching your children.

-8-

1. MANNERS, MORALS, ATTITUDES

Teaching manners, morals, and right attitudes should begin at a very early age. Small children should be taught to wash their hands before meals, how to behave at the table, and how to say "Thank you". They should be taught to share their toys, and how to respectfully relate to adults.

Parents should use every opportunity to structure and teach right attitudes. Children should be taught to control their anger and fits of emotion. Learning self-control at an early age will spare them a lot of trouble later on. They should also be taught to forgive those who hurt them, however petty the offense may seem to us.

Children must be taught truthfulness, morals, and modesty. Television programs must be carefully screened by parents for their moral content. We should observe the impact of friends and playmates upon them and teach them to stand upon their own principles. They should be taught modesty of dress and behavior.

-9-

2. RESPECT FOR RULES

By training children to respect rules, we indirectly teach them respect for authority and order. God would have all things be done *"decently and in order"* (I Cor. 14:40). Rules set necessary boundaries for children and create a sense of order and structure in their lives. They help them to accomodate themselves to the laws of society and the commandments of God.

There are essentially two dangers involved with rules. One is failing to establish firmly set rules. The other is legalistically establishing and enforcing too many petty rules and regulations.

Children are, by nature, undisciplined and feeling-orientated. Their nature drives them to resist order and to test the strength of those rules that have been established. **Parents must be ready to punish infractions against established rules. However, we should avoid giving our homes the atmosphere of a military camp.** An older Christian lady once wisely made the observation, "It's hard to put a big head on those little shoulders", referring to the need for kids to be allowed to be kids.

-10-

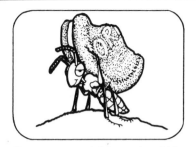

3. BUILDING WORK HABITS

One of the most loving things parents can do for their children is to teach them how to work. We are exhorted in Proverbs 6:6 to *"Go to the ant ... Consider her ways and be wise."* Why? Because the ant knows how to work and prepare for the future. A child's future success depends upon the development of good work habits at an early age.

Even young children should be required to participate in household chores such as emptying wastebaskets or helping mom set the table. As they grow, they can clean the living room or help dad wash the car.

Parents should take time to teach them how to do a job correctly, patiently remembering that you didn't do it right the first time either. Children should be required to see a job through to the end.

Building the habit of productivity through schoolwork, household chores, odd jobs, music lessons, etc. will harness a child's potential and insure a responsible adulthood.

-11-

4. BUILDING SPIRITUAL DISCIPLINE

Children can learn good manners, morals, attitudes, proper respect for rules, and good work habits and still be failures if they do not grow up to serve God. **Our first priority must be to bring up our children *"in the training and admonition of the Lord"*** (Eph. 6:4).

Our kids must be trained in spiritual disciplines: reading the Bible, prayer, worship, and church attendance. In this case, our example is not enough. They must be guided and trained. Especially with a child, the spirit may be willing, *"but the flesh is weak"* (Matt. 26:41).

Family devotions are important in providing set times for prayer, worship, and Bible study. Our homes, though, should be saturated with a Christian atmosphere where there is frequent prayer and discussion of the Word of God. Children should be required to attend church and taught how to worship. Parents should endeavor to bring God into their children's world by praying about their concerns.

If spiritual disciplines are instilled in children while they're young, they will more easily bring them into adulthood.

-12-

II. DISCIPLINE YOUR CHILDREN

Discipline is a divine method of child rearing. The scripture teaches *"For whom the Lord loves He chastens, and scourges every son whom He receives"* (Heb. 12:6). Through discipline, we are exercised toward righteousness and holiness (Heb. 12:10).

God's mandate to parents is that they should love the Lord God with all their heart, soul, and might, and that they should diligently teach their children to obey His Word (Deut. 6:5-7). **The goal of all instruction and discipline is that our children would love and honor the Lord and obey His commandments.**

Discipline must be used in conjuction with instruction. If our teaching and instruction is not met with obedience, we must respond with discipline. **Discipline has a two-fold purpose: to punish, and to correct.** Through punishment, our child learns the vital lesson that if we disobey rules or instruction, we must suffer for it. A little physical pain now prevents much more severe consequences later.

-13-

The other aim of discipline is to produce a correction in the child's attitude or behavior (Heb. 12:11). It is to restore him to a place of humility and obedience.

The nature of children demands correction. Left to themselves, they gravitate toward sin, selfishness, and rebellion. **Discipline checks the expression of the sin nature, stucuring the child's development around righteousness, obedience, and morality.**

Discipline is not optional, it is required. All parents are under God's delegated authority and commandments to raise their children according to His principles. Children are commanded to obey and honor their parents (Eph. 6.1, 2). They must be disciplined whenever there is a deliberate disobedience, an unacceptable carelessness, or a display of rebellion.

In the majority of cases, discipline should be in the form of a spanking. This, of course, may exclude older teenagers who should be punished in other forms such as grounding, loss of privileges, etc. If, in certain cases of lesser offense, another form of punishment is used with children, it must work the intended goal of punishment that produces correction.

-14-

GUIDELINES FOR DISCIPLINE

On the following five pages we will briefly consider some of the questions and considerations in the disciplining of our children.

1. _Parental Agreement_ - _"Can two walk together, unless they are agreed?"_ (Amos 3:3). **Parental agreement is essential in the disciplining of children.** Both parents must agree to the biblical approach to discipline. If a child senses or observes disagreement, he or she will attempt to pit one parent against the other. If the discipline is carried out, the child may retain the idea that the one who did it was unfair.

2. _Support One Another_ - Often only one of the parents observed the disobedient conduct and determines what punishment is warranted. Sometimes there is a tendency for the other to want to be more lenient. The parent involved should be deferred to and supported.

3. _Be Realistic in Your Expectations_ - The Bible teaches us that God _"pities His children . . . for He knows our frame"_ (Ps. 103:13, 14). God's behavior toward us is based on understanding. **We, likewise, must not expect more of**

-15-

our children than they can realistically give. Our expectations should be based on their physical and mental abilities. Is their failure to perform a chore correctly due to irresponsibility or inability? Is their grouchy mood based on disrespect or the fact that they are sick or did not get enough sleep?

4. _The Role of Reproof_ -_"He who regards reproof will be honored"_ (Prov. 13:18). Some foolish or careless behavior may not reflect disobedience or warrant a spanking. In such cases, reproof is a more effective and realistic form of correction.

5. _Make Discipline Proportionate_ - _"A just weight is His delight"_ (Prov. 11:1). **Our reaction to a child's unacceptable behavior must be in proportion to the transgression involved.** Over correcting may _"provoke . . . your children to anger"_ or produce discouragement (Col. 3:21, K.J.V.). Some infractions require reproof; others a spanking; still others a spanking and a loss of privileges.

-16-

GUIDELINES (Cont.)

6. _Don't Discipline in Anger_ - _"The wrath of man does not produce the righteousness of God"_ (James 1:20). When we discipline, we represent the delegated authority of God. We administer discipline to punish disobedience and bring correction. Discipline properly given leaves a child with the sense that justice has been done. Our anger will obscure this and often cause us to ignore the proper procedure of correction. **Parents should bring their anger under control before disciplining.**

7. _Discipline Disobedience Immediately_ - **The Bible teaches that prolonging the punishment of a transgression produces habits of rebellion and disobedience** (Ecc. 8:11). Once a child is clear on what's right and wrong, his disobedience must be punished immediately. Many parents err by resorting to several warnings or threats of spankings. This establishes the pattern of resistance and testings in the child. If a child does not obey the command the first time it is spoken, he should be punished.

-17-

8. _Begin While They're Small_ - **Discipline should begin when the child is a baby.** An infant soon learns whether he or she can manipulate their parents. Their independent nature runs head on into parental efforts of training and socialization. When it is obvious that a child is demanding his own way and resisting your authority, your displeasure should be communicated. For example, if a child continues to throw food on the floor after being reprimanded, his hand should be spanked. The object is to imprint the principle of obedience at the earliest possible age.

9. _Punishment Must Hurt_ - _"Let not thy soul spare for his crying"_ (Prov. 19:18, K.J.V.). **Punishment must not be physically abusive, but it must cross the pain threshold to be effective.** Pain soon passes, but the lesson remains. A spanking should always cause a child to cry, thereby producing an emotional release, a break in his resistance, and a humility that leads to obedience. Parents should avoid letting natural compassion restrain them from carrying out proper discipline.

-18-

GUIDELINES (Cont.)

10. _Who Disciplines - Mom or Dad?_ - Both parents should discipline the children. Children are to _"Honor . . . father and mother"_ (Eph. 6:2). As the head of the house, the father should discipline when he is home. When he is away, the mother should assume this responsibility.

11. _Be Consistent_ - Our disciplinary habits and procedures must be consistent. What is punished today, must be punished tomorrow. The promise that chastening _"yields the peaceable fruit of righteousness"_ (Heb. 12:11) is to those who are consistent and enduring. Life styles and behavioral patterns are formed through years of training.

12. _What About Teenagers?_ - If proper discipline is begun young enough, there will be far less of a necessity for it as kids hit the teens. Younger teenagers that are disobedient can still be spanked. Grounding and loss of privileges are also acceptable, but must be watched as to whether they reinforce bad attitudes or further rebellion. Parental discretion based on wisdom should be used with teenagers.

-19-

WHAT ABOUT THE ROD?

"He who spares his rod hates his son, but he who loves him disciplines him promptly" (Prov. 13:24).

The Bible promotes spanking as the most effective means of discipline. It awakens and sharpens the awareness that there is a moral power over us and that laws cannot be broken without suffering. The Bible also promotes the rod.

A rod is an instrument or tool used to help us administer firm discipline. It can be a switch, ping-pong paddle, or a wooden spoon. Its advantage over the hand is that it produces the necessary pain without requiring a jarring force against the child's body. Another advantage is that the rod, rather than the hand, becomes the symbol of retribution.

All spankings should be given on the bare rear so as to be keenly felt without involving too much force. On occasions where the rod is unavailable, it is better to use our hand than to neglect warranted discipline.

-20-

THE STEPS OF DISCIPLINE

The following steps outline the procedure to follow in administering a spanking. These steps reveal the pattern God uses to chasten us and bring us to full reconciliation.

1. _Disobedience_ - Once an act of disobedience, rebellion, or stubbornness has occurred, the child must be disciplined. He or she should be taken to a private location for the discipline. Public spankings bring embarrassment for the child as well as other adults.

2. _Explanation_ - The child should be given a clear explanation for what he did wrong and brought to a place where he acknowledges his transgression (I Jn. 1:9).

3. _Spanking_ - The child should be told to lower their pants and to bend over your knees or a chair. The rod should be applied with enough force to make him cry. However, care should be taken not to produce welts or bruises.

-21-

4. _Prayer for Forgiveness_ - After the spanking, the parent should have the child pray and ask God for forgiveness for the offense that was committed. The parent should then pray for the child, thanking God for His grace and forgiveness over our lives.

5. _Re-Affirm Your Love_ - The parent should then warmly embrace the child and re-affirm his love. The child should be reassured that you think highly of him and that you consider him to be a good child.

6. _Reconciliation With Others_ - After reconciliation with God and yourself, there must be reconciliation with others. The child must go and apologize to any others who have been offended. This not only will bring restoration to the situation, but will further promote humility. The incident must then be forgotten.

-22-

III. LOVE YOUR CHILDREN

"And he will turn the hearts of the fathers to the children, and the hearts of the children to their fathers" (Mal. 4:6).

The successful Christian home is characterized by an atmosphere of love. In our quest to be responsible parents, we must take care that our home does not reflect the atmosphere of a classroom, penal colony, or a court-house. The home and family should be the center of a child's happiness. It is so easy to fall into the role of a policeman with our kids, projecting an overly rigid world around them. **We fail if we are faithful only to teach and to discipline, while neglecting to cultivate a relationship of love.** The following are some ways a parent may demonstrate love to their children:

1. _Touch_ - Just as punishment demands physical expression, so does love. The sense of touch can convey care like nothing else. Children thrive on affection. Parents should continue the "cuddling habit" begun with babies through the

-23-

earlier years. Even as kids approach the teens, frequent hugs and affection are important. **Families should never cease to demonstrate love through physical expression.**

2. _Time_ - There is no adequate substitute for time together with our children. Christian families should establish set times when they are alone together on "family nights" and "family days". Kids need a sense of the family unit. **Spending time with your kids produces genuine relationships and conveys your love for them.**

3. _Fun_ - **Parents should be able to have fun with their children.** They should promote recreation in the form of games, biking, going to the beach, etc. A sense of humor is also an invaluable part of a happy family life. Parents should attempt to share in some of the humor and fun of their children. We should also be willing to laugh at ourselves when we are caught in blunders.

-24-

LOVE YOUR CHILDREN (Cont.)

4. _Listening_ - Parents need to cultivate the art of listening to their children. Too often, kids receive the impression that we are not interested in their world or that we know what they want to say before they say it. By listening, we can build a genuine understanding of them, as well as communicate our interest.

5. _Encouragement_ - Children receive their basic self-image from our reactions to them. We must be as careful to identify the good and the positive qualities in their lives as we are to point out the negative. **Parents must assure their children of their value and self-worth.**

6. _Courtesy_ - Children are little human beings created in the image of God. **While exercising our parental responsibilities and rights, we must remember to treat them with dignity and courtesy.** This is especially important when they are with their friends. Avoid harsh correction or discipline of your children in front of their playmates.

-25-

◀ CONCLUSION ▶

Reading material on raising Christian children provides the necessary insights and guidelines for proper parenting, but expertise is only developed in the day-to-day experience of relating to our kids. Being a parent, especially today, is filled with tremendous challenges and frequent frustrations. We can easily conclude that our best efforts are not good enough. Christian parents have this consolation: God is also raising your children. We must do our best and trust Him to fill in the holes. We must include daily prayer for our children as one of our primary methods of child rearing. The following books are recommended for further study:

Withold Not Correction, by Bruce A. Ray
The Christian Family, by Larry Christiansen

For a brief overview of the main points of this booklet, please re-read the boldly printed words on each page.

-26-